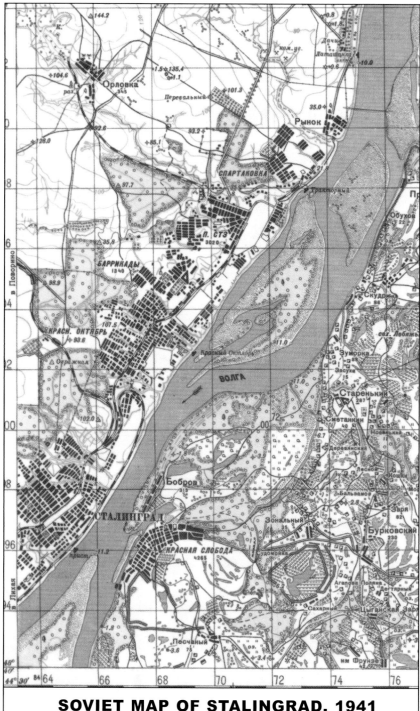

SOVIET MAP OF STALINGRAD, 1941

Reading Vassili Zaitsev's memoir of his nightmarish experiences as a sniper at Stalingrad is both a frightening and fascinating experience. Despite doubts concerning some of the details of the fighting, and its initial appearance under communist auspices, as a literary work, *Notes of A Sniper* is comparable to E.B Sledge's *With the Old Breed,* and as a memoir of courage reminiscent of Xenophon's *Anabasis*. Zaitsev's account of the carnage in the hellish war between Hitler's shock troops and Stalin's desperate defenders is right out of Dante's Inferno, and should be read by every student of World War II--and anyone else interested in the human condition.

Victor Davis Hanson
Author: *Carnage and Culture* and
       The Soul of Battle

Vassili Zaitsev's account of
the Battle of Stalingrad

Edited by Neil Okrent

Translated by David Givens,
Peter Kornakov, and Konstantin Kornakov.

2826 Press, Inc.
Los Angeles, California, and
Las Vegas, Nevada

www.notesofasniper.com

NOTES OF A SNIPER, by Vassili Zaitsev
Copyright ©2003, 2826 Press, Inc.

Published by 2826 Press Incorporated,
Los Angeles, California and Las Vegas, Nevada

1st printing   10   9 8 7 6 5 4 3 2 1

Library of Congress Control Number: 2002109736
Library of Congress Cataloging-In-Publication Data
Zaitsev, Vassili.
Notes of a Sniper: For Us There Was No Land Beyond the Volga/
[editor Neil Okrent] [translators David Givens, Konstantin Kornakov,
Peter Kornakov]
1. Stalingrad 2. Vassili Zaitsev 3. Russian Snipers
4. World War II 5. Eastern Front

First Publication in English 2003
First Publication in Russian 1956

ISBN number 0-615-12148-9

Disclaimer: The translation has been edited for readability.
All efforts have been made to conform to the original
Russian language text.

PRINTED IN THE REPUBLIC OF SOUTH KOREA

C R E D I T S

Notes of a Sniper translation by David Givens. Additional translation by Peter Kornakov and Konstantin Kornakov.

Sniper Story (Vassili Zaitsev's short book from 1943) translation by Elena Leonidovna Yakovleva.

Front Cover Illustration and Cover Lettering by Anthony Cacioppo and Ed Coutts.

Map of Stalingrad courtesy of librarian Jennie Dienes, the University of Kansas Map Library.

Translation of the Stalin 'No Retreat' order, courtesy of Valeriy Potapov of the Russian Battlefield web site, translator Bair Irinchev. http://www.battlefield.ru/index.html

Layout Design by Sonia Gunawan Fiore.

Rear cover photo of Vassili Zaitsev, collection of the editor.

Inside front cover photo of Vassili Zaitsev, collection of the editor.

All interior photos, collection of the editor.

NOTES OF A SNIPER - FOREWORD
by Max Hardberger

Vassili Zaitsev's story is now famous as a result of the Jean Jacques Annaud movie, *Enemy at the Gates*. However, the real Vassili Zaitsev was a much different and more complex person than the character played by Jude Law.

An expert hunter from the *taiga*[1] of the Ural Mountains, 27-year old Vassili Zaitsev was an accountant and payroll clerk in the Soviet Pacific fleet. He volunteered to fight at Stalingrad, along with a detachment of fellow sailors and marines. His superiors in the embattled city soon recognized Vassili's shooting ability and made him a sniper.

Vassili adapted his hunting and trapping skills to the wilderness of Stalingrad, and the tactics and ruses that he developed among the ruins of factories and on the scarred slopes of Mamayev Hill are still being studied in war colleges to this day.

Vassili quickly became famous as his exploits circulated throughout the Soviet Union. During the battle Zaitsev was wounded by shrapnel. After his hospitalization he was awarded the country's highest honor, the gold star of the Hero of the Soviet Union.

Those who have seen *Enemy at the Gates*, a virulently anti-Communist film, may have been persuaded that Vassili himself was merely a creation and tool of the Communist propaganda machine, but nothing could be further from the truth. Vassili was a member of the Young Communist League and a Communist Party member. *Notes of a Sniper* is filled with references to his passionate allegiance to the Soviet state.

We note that several incidents in the movie *Enemy at the Gates* do not exist in Zaitsev's book. We note specifically that one of the film's most horrifying scenes, depicting NKVD troops machine-gunning Soviet soldiers retreating from a disastrous

[1] *taiga*: forest

charge, was never documented in Zaitsev's book. Although there were penal companies fighting in Stalingrad, Zaitsev himself was a volunteer – not a convict. We believe Zaitsev would have been appalled by this fiction, and disgusted that his name has been associated with it.

The film also incorrectly depicts Vassili as an unschooled peasant. In fact, he had strong elementary schooling—thanks to the Soviet system Annaud so despises—and after the war, Vassili continued his education and became a professor of engineering at the University of Kiev.

Although Vassili was not trained as a writer, *Notes of a Sniper* bursts with energy and ready wit, and stands as a classic of war literature. In a ruined city on the bank of the Volga River, at a turning-point in his country's history, Vassili Zaitsev's courage, intelligence, and patriotism gave his country hope in her darkest hour. It is for this he would wish to be remembered.

Max Hardberger is the author of *Freighter Captain*

Vassili Zaitsev-
For Us there Was No Land Beyond The Volga –
Notes Of A Sniper

For the honor and glory of the motherland.

C O N T E N T S

What soldier from the battle of Stalingrad does not know the name of Vassili Zaitsev? His glorious deeds served as an example of courage and military skill for all of our soldiers, for both the men who fought at Stalingrad, and for those who fought on other fronts. The enemy certainly was aware of his exploits. During the German advance toward the Volga at Stalingrad, Vassili Zaitsev did away with over three hundred Nazi officers and soldiers. A superior marksman and a wise tactician, it is no wonder that Zaitsev's activities alarmed the Nazis. Major Konings, a "super-sniper" and the head of the Nazi's Berlin sniper school, was flown to Stalingrad with the special task of eliminating the unstoppable Russian sharpshooter. But a bullet from Zaitsev's rifle found the veteran Nazi wolf first.

I had occasion to meet the renowned snipers of Stalingrad. Vassili Zaitsev, Anatoly Chekhov and Viktor Medvedev, were the best known. From their appearance, it would be impossible to distinguish any of them from average soldiers.

But upon first meeting Vassili Zaitsev, I was struck by several things: his modesty, the slow grace of his movements, his exceptionally calm character, and his attentive gaze. His handshake was firm, and he pressed your palm with a pincer-like grip.

At my first encounter with Zaitsev, during the most difficult days of the city's defense, he said, "We've got nowhere to run. For us there is no land beyond the Volga." This would become the catch phrase of the hour, with every soldier of the 62nd army repeating it.

Because he had great organizational talent, Vassili Grigorievich headed up the army's sniper group. He had several students, and all became first-rate shooters. Fascists fell by the hundreds and even thousands at the hands of Zaitsev's gang and

Medvedev's pack[1] (as a joke, Zaitsev's students were often referred to as "Zaitsev's litter," and Medvedev's students, as "Medvedev's bear cubs").

Nearly a quarter century has passed since then, and it is a pleasant surprise that today, on the pages of this book, Vassili Grigorievich Zaitsev tells the readers about the school of military expertise, and discusses the secrets behind the sniper's art. I think Zaitsev's reflections will add to the moral defenses of our youth; and I recommend to my young friends – members of the armed forces, college and university students, *Komsomol*[2] activists at workplaces, on *kolhozes*[3] and in the army – acquaint yourself with the bravery and daring of Vassili Grigorievich Zaitsev.

Marshall of the Soviet Union V. Chuikov[4]

---

[1] The Russian word *zayitz*, rabbit, is the root of the family name Zaitsev. The word translated here as 'gang', *zaichat*, literally means 'baby rabbits.' Medvedev is also derivative: *medved* means bear. MedBelorussian Front, and spearheaded the drive to Berlin. Chuikov had the distinction vedzhata is commonly 'pack,' but it literally means 'bear cubs.'

[2] *KomSoMol* : Kommunistiches - oyuz Molodyozh – Communist Youth Alliance

[3] *kolhoz* : kollectivn xozyaistvo – collective farm

[4] In September 1942, Chuikov was appointed Commander of the 62nd Army in Stalingrad. Subsequently Chuikov's 8th Guards Army was sent to the Belorussian front, and spearheaded the drive to Berlin. Chuikov had the distinction of receiving the surrender of Berlin from General Krebs. After WW II, Chuikov was the Commander-in-Chief of Soviet Military Forces in Germany from 1949-1953.

CHAPTER 1.
CHILDHOOD AND YOUTH

Everyone remembers his or her own childhood. Some recount those early years with bitterness, some with sentiment and pride – oh, what a childhood I had! But I have never had the occasion to hear someone try to define when youth begins or ends. Personally, I don't know. Why? Probably because the initial step into childhood is made without awareness, and it leaves no trace in one's memory; while the exit from childhood to youth happens indistinctly and with the burden of a typically childlike, unreflective view on the world. It's not for nothing that we say, "Grownup children." At which age children are referred to in this way is hard to say. Sometimes of course, you run into 'children' older than twenty, but that kind of childhood is hardly something to brag about.

In my memory, the end of childhood was marked by the words of my grandfather Andrei, who once took me out hunting with him, stuck a bow and some homemade arrows in my hand, and said, "Shoot with a steady aim and look your prey in the eye. You're not a boy anymore."

Children love to play grown-up, but this was no game. The woods are filled with real wild animals, keen and swift - not make-believe ones. Let's say you want to get a look at a goat, for example - what kind of ears or horns or eyes he's got – you must sit camouflaged in such a way that it looks at you like a bush or a scrap of hay. You must lie still, without breathing or batting an eyelash. And if you're making your way towards a rabbit's hutch, try to crawl from the downwind side, so that not a single blade of grass crackles under your weight.

Become one with the ground, press yourself to it like a maple leaf, and move in silence. You've got to hit the rabbit with a well-aimed shot from your bow. Crawl up as close as possible – if you don't, your shot will miss its mark.

Grandfathers love their grandsons even more than fathers love their sons. Why this is so, only a grandfather can explain. My grandfather, Andrei Alekseevich Zaitsev, came from a long line of hunters. He chose me as his favorite, like his own first-born son, Grigoriy – my father, the father of a daughter and two sons. I was the oldest, and grew very slowly. My family thought I would always remain a runt, a half-pint, like a yardstick[5] with a hat on. But my grandfather never gave me a hard time about my height. He always taught me from his vast hunting experience. My failures would nearly bring him to tears. And when I saw how much he cared for me, I repaid him – I did everything he asked, exactly as he told me.

I learned to interpret the trails of wild animals like I was reading a book; I tracked down the dens of wolves and bears, and built blinds that were so well hidden, not even my Grandpa could find me until I called out to him. These accomplishments made my grandfather, the experienced hunter, very happy. Once, as if thanking me for my efforts, my Grandpa took a dangerous risk; while we were tracking a wolf, he waited for the beast to approach so closely that he could kill it with a wooden mallet. It was as if to say, "Look, my boy, and learn how one must bravely and calmly deal with a ferocious adversary." And then, when the wolf's hide lay at my feet, he said, "You see how nicely things

---

[5] yardstick with a hat – the reference is to an *arshin*, an old Russian measure of length, 0.711 meters, sometimes used to denote shortness

turned out? We managed to save a bullet, and the hide is spotless – this skin is going to be first class."

Not long afterwards, I managed to lasso a wild goat. Oh, how that goat raced off when I tossed the rope over his horns! He yanked me from my hiding place and dragged me through the bushes, trying to tear the end of the rope from my hands. But no! - I grabbed on to a bush and held on for dear life.

That goat darted to the left, then to the right; he circled the bush once, then twice, and finally collapsed to his knees. Grandpa was delighted with my success. I was so happy I was crying, and Grandpa kissed the tears from my face.

The following day, in front of my father, mother, grandmother, sister and brother, Grandpa presented me with a gun – a single-shot 20-gauge shotgun. It was a real firearm; military-issue cartridges in an ammo belt held slugs and buckshot, for shooting field grouse. I stood at attention, and Grandpa hung it on my shoulder. I was so short that the butt of the shotgun rested on the floor, but at least I wasn't a kid anymore. Children weren't allowed to touch real weapons like this one.

At that time I was barely twelve years old. I had grown up within the span of a single day. Let them call me a half-pint, I had a real gun over my shoulder! This happened in 1927, in the home of my grandfather, on the bank of the river Saram-Sakal, in the Yelenovskoye *sel'soviet*[6] of the Southern Ural *oblast*. [7]

I became a grownup, or more precisely, an independent hunter. My father, remembering his days fighting under Brusilov[8] said to me, "Use every bullet wisely, Vassili. Learn to shoot and never miss. This will help you, and not just when you are hunting four-legged beasts."

Along with the shotgun, my grandfather gave me the wisdom of the *taiga*, a love of nature, and his worldly experience. Sometimes he would sit on a stump, smoking homegrown tobacco

[6] *sel'soviet* : short for "sel'skokhozyaistvenniy soviet," or 'agricultural district'
[7] *oblast* : district
[8] Aleksei Alekseyevich Brusilov (1853-1926) – Russian general in WWI

in his favorite pipe, staring intently at a single point on the ground. He patiently taught me how to be a hunter.

"Suppose you've entered the woods to catch some animal," he said. "Take off your hat so you can hear everything going on around you. Listen to what's going in the forest; listen to the birds talk. If the magpies are chattering, it's a sure sign that you've got company. Something big, so get ready. Find yourself a good spot, be silent, and wait: the animal is coming your way. Lie perfectly still, and don't move a muscle."

Grandpa took a puff on his long-stemmed pipe.

"When you return from a hunt," he continued, "make sure you go home after sunset, so that nobody spies you with your catch. And never get swell-headed over your accomplishments, let them speak for themselves. That way you'll always remember to try harder the next time."

My grandfather knew how to instill his convictions in us children.

We always took our catch to a hunter's lodge, called an *izba*. Our *izba* was a large dwelling. Only men were allowed to use it. The *izba* was divided into two parts, separated by a log wall. We slept on one side and used the remaining space to store meat. During winter, the storage area was filled with frozen game. Hundreds of birds hung from the ceiling, preserved by the cold.

Grandpa and my cousin and I slept on wooden benches covered with wolf pelts. Beneath the benches we piled up the hides from other game. There was another bed for my grandfather to nap on during the day.

On the eve of religious feast days, all of my relatives would gather in the *izba*. The rule against women entering the lodge would be temporarily suspended.

My grandfather had his own sacred figures and gods, which he honored. He did not believe in the Russian Orthodox saints, or the god that Grandma worshiped, but neither did he throw her icons out of the house. So in our house these two faiths existed, side by side. My grandmother's faith dictated that "thou shall not kill, thou shall not steal, thou shall honor and obey thy elders, and gracious God in heaven sees all." According to my Grandma Duna, we were born with eternal life: "When the soul separates from the body, the body is sent to its penance, while the soul flies like a dove to Holy Judgement. There each of us must account for the way we've lived our lives, and the sins we've committed. Your life in the next world depends your behavior here on earth. Whether you burn eternally in hell, or revel in paradise, depends on what you do in this earthly life."

Of course, my cousin Maxim and I always tried to do everything the right way, so that our souls would be admitted into heaven. Grandpa, however, saw things differently. He said to us, "Nothing can live twice – neither man nor animal. For example, today you bagged a goat, and you did an awful job skinning him, you ruined the hide with two big cuts."

Grandpa would sometimes get angry and digress from his original line of argument.

"If you ever do that again, I'll whip you so bad you'll still have the scars when you're as old as me!"

Maxim and I sat in the corner, holding our breath, as we knew Grandpa's character. He puffed on his pipe, then returned to the reasons behind his rejection of Grandma's religious beliefs.

"So you hung the goat's hide out in the cold, and every bird in the forest came to pick off the meat. Did you see any soul there?"

We sat in silence, blinking like two hamsters.

Grandpa Andrei was working himself up into a proper rage.

"So, all of the sudden, you're speechless! Listen, this soul people talk about, have you ever seen one anywhere?"

I answered that we hadn't seen one.

"Well," Grandpa concluded, "if you didn't see it, that means it's not there. There's skin, meat, and guts. The skin is hanging outside, the meat is in the soup, and the dogs got the guts for dinner. Remember, boys, the soul, the spirit, it's all make-believe. There's no spirits to be afraid of. A true hunter knows no fear. And if I ever see fear in your eyes, I'll whip your backsides!"

~~~

Cousin Maxim wore glasses and was always squinting. Maxim was five years older than me, but when we fought I never gave in to him, and if I was losing, I would start scratching and biting. Maxim would back off, and Grandpa loved it when I stood up for myself. No matter what, I would always remain Grandpa's favorite. Nobody else in the family was allowed to punish me; Grandpa reserved that right for himself. But he would beat me for boasting, for lying, for being a tattletale, or being a coward.

My sister Polina often complained that we reeked like animals. She was right. In the wintertime, we spent more time in the company of wild animals than people. Our hands, faces, clothes, guns, traps – everything was smeared with badger oil. Even iron changed its smell after this treatment. We smelled like animals, and because of this, the animals of the forest were not alarmed by our scent.

Every morning began with a command from my Grandpa – always some piece of advice about how we were to comport ourselves in the woods: "If you've caught a whole lot of rabbits in your traps and you can't carry them back in one trip, hang the remainder up in a tree." Of course Maxim and I had been taught this long ago, but to interrupt Grandpa was strictly forbidden.

We would leave the house at dawn, just as the sun was rising. Fresh powdery snow crunched beneath our skis, the air pure and frozen. We hadn't stretched our legs yet, so we skied at a lazy pace, but our dogs, always ready to go, would tug at their leashes. They begged to be set free, but we had to check our traps first. That is the way the days went by in the *taiga*.

One morning when we started to check the traps, we discovered that a wolf had got caught in the first trap and dragged it off. We tied our dogs up, and Maxim went back to the house for a gun, while I stayed to check out the rest of the traps.

The sun was rising, and a rainbow glowed on the sides of the sun's red ball, with rings of dazzling colors. The cold was unceasing. The dogs started to yelp, their paws freezing in the frigid wind.

Maxim finally came back, and we took off in search of the wolf and our trap. The wind was blowing like mad. In the Urals on days like this, they'd say, "A little freeze is nothing to worry about, but you'd better not stand still!" Maxim's eyes often gave him trouble and the biting wind was causing him to tear up, so we decided that I would take the first shot.

We studied the wolf's trail, and concluded that his front right paw had been caught in the trap, as he was walking on three legs. The wolf wasn't stupid; he knew someone would be trailing him, so he was walking across places where the snow cover was lightest. Wherever the anchor on the trap got snagged, the wolf would retrace his steps, trying to conceal his prints. Then he would take off again, in the same direction he had been heading before. He picked the most out-of-the-way parts of the forest and the frozen swamps, and didn't leave a single hair in his trail.

Maxim and I were so absorbed in the chase, that we did not notice that it was getting dark. I was tired, my back was aching, and I needed something to eat.

Maxim used his hatchet to mark a few trees so we wouldn't lose our way back. I was disappointed and bitter about our failure to accomplish anything that day. I absent-mindedly strayed off the path. My dogs sensed something and immediately started straining at their leashes. I hushed them up and grabbed the rifle. Not fifty paces away from me, standing by some bushes, stood a horned mountain goat. His back was to me, which made aiming difficult. I waited for the animal to turn so I would have a better target. But as if to spite me, the goat stood in place, munching on bits of grass that poked through the snow. Then I took careful aim and pulled the trigger. The goat leaped high in the air, ran a few paces, then stumbled and dropped to its knees. I set the dogs free and ran after them, waving my knife.

When the dogs caught up to the goat, they jumped him. The animal was strong and cunning, and he beat them back with his horns. He fought them bravely, but he was wounded and could not escape. I did not want to use another bullet, but I had no choice. I couldn't get close enough to the rampaging animal to use my knife. So I shot again. This time I hit him in the head and he collapsed in the snow.

Maxim had heard the enraged goat bleating and the dogs barking, and he had caught up with us. He was impressed by the size of the thing.

"Whoa," said my invigorated cousin, "both of us together won't be able to carry that beast. We'll hang him up in a tree." Then he began giving instructions.

"Make a little clearing, we'll have to sleep here tonight. Gather as much firewood as you can, because we want to keep this fire going all night." So I prepared a camp, collected some dry wood, and then spent a long time trying to get a spark with tin and steel. I rubbed them together, but my hands were clumsy from the cold, and I kept having to start over. Finally I got the tinder going and the fire burned brightly, red tongues of flame dancing above the burning logs.

By that time, Maxim had finished skinning the goat. First to slake their hunger were our four-legged friends – Maxim tossed them the steaming guts. Then, using the rifle's ramrod as a spit, we roasted the goat meat. We were both very hungry.

After a tasty supper, I wanted nothing more than to go to sleep. I looped the dogs' leashes around my belt, wrapped my arm around the rifle, pulled my cap over my eyes, and fell asleep as if I were back home in bed.

Maxim stoked the fire, rolled over towards me, and in minutes he was snoring. Our entire camp was in a peaceful slumber, except for our little Siberian husky, Damka. She was curled up in a ball, but one of her ears stood pricked up at attention, keeping guard over the camp.

We were deep in our dreams when Damka began a fit of wild barking. In few seconds, Maxim, I, and the dogs were all on our feet and alert. Judging from the quantity of wood still remaining on the fire, we had not slept for long.

Maxim pulled out a smoldering ember and hurled it into the darkness, so that it showered red sparks. But there was no response. Our dogs grew quiet. I moved away from the fire in order to be able to peer into the dark. About a hundred yards away, two pairs of tiny lights blinked back at me.

"Wolves!" I shouted.

"They must have smelled our little barbecue," said Maxim. Then he teased me: "You scared?" His question wounded my pride.

"Of course not," I replied. I was angry with Maxim for this insinuation. I started hiking towards where we had seen those beady eyes. I had to move slowly, as the snow was up to my knees. Suddenly some instinctive force commanded me: "Stop! Shoot!" I raised the rifle and fired.

The shot echoed through the trees, and the wolves disappeared. I yanked off my fur cap, pricked up my ears, and held my breath, but the forest was totally silent. So I put my cap back on and returned to our campfire. Maxim was calmly shaving meat from the goat's haunch and sticking it on the spit. The fire had turned into a big bed of coals. I wondered why Maxim didn't bother to ask if I had hit a wolf or not, but there was really no reason for him to inquire. After all, it was a haphazard shot in the dark. I had to have missed. As I was thinking this, I fell into a wonderful sleep.

In the morning I woke up, because Maxim was poking me in the side.

"Come on, big-game hunter, time for breakfast."

As I was standing there watching Maxim cook, I decided to take a look in the direction where I had shot last night.

"Where the heck are you going?" Maxim asked, perturbed.

"I want to look and see how many wolves were out there," I answered.

"OK," he said, "but make sure to get back before your breakfast gets cold."

On the snow were wolf tracks mixed with blood. At first I

couldn't believe my eyes. But when I followed the prints, there was no longer any doubt. My shot had hit its mark.

Maxim caught up to me, out of breath.

"So, what do you say, did you get him? Well come on, let's take a look…"

From where I stood, it looked like the near-sighted Maxim was following the trail with his nose, instead of his eyes. Then he straightened up, and peered at me, surprised---like he was seeing me for the first time.

"Nice job, cousin. That wolf's not going to get very far."

We hiked over a rise, following the blood traces. Once we reached the top of the slope, we caught sight of the wolf. He was an old creature and was bleeding from his chest. He was lying motionless. Just to be on the safe side, Maxim set loose the dogs before we approached the wounded animal. Damka circled the wolf and barked; the wolf showed no response. Maxim took a stick and hit the wolf hard on the tip of its nose, and the animal's body twitched and then stretched straight out.

We still had to find the other wolf that had taken our trap. We set the dogs free, and in a couple minutes, the forest erupted with barking. At first Maxim and I thought the dogs were battling with a pack of wolves. But something strange was going on. The dogs were calling out to us, as if begging for us to come and help! We ran to them. Maxim had longer legs than I and reached them first. When I got closer, I was surprised to see Maxim holding a rope, the other end of which was hidden in a burrow.

"What could that mean?" I wondered.

"This is the rope from our trap; the wolf's hiding in that burrow with the trap on his leg. Let's smoke him out…"

In half an hour, the wolf lay at our feet. We finished him off without the rifle, saving a bullet and preserving the hide. We did everything exactly like Grandpa had taught us.

We returned home with our bountiful plunder: two wolf skins, a dozen rabbits, and a wolverine that the dogs had bagged by themselves. And surprisingly, no one in the family - not

Grandpa, father, mother, Grandma or my sister – acted in the least impressed. They looked upon what we'd been through as just an ordinary episode in the lives of two hunters. We had spent an entire night in the woods in a bitter freeze, killed two wolves, and came back home – nothing strange about that. And although one of the hunters was the notorious "yardstick with a hat," nonetheless he was a good shot, and that meant he had the right to be called a hunter.

And thus, without even noticing it, with a rifle slung over my shoulder, I crossed the threshold from childhood to youth.

I had learned the art of tracking in the *taiga*. Later, those skills would pay off in the struggle against the two-legged predators who came, uninvited, to invade our motherland.

Chapter 2.
A Sailor's Shirt Under
A Soldier's Fatigues

Grandma had taught me to read and write. At age sixteen, I went to work as a construction worker on the Magnotorsk project.[9] While I was there I finished my basic schooling, and started taking accounting classes.

In 1937, I was drafted. Despite my short height, I was admitted into the Navy's Pacific Fleet, and I was very satisfied with this.

The blue and white stripes of the *telnyashka*[10] have always been considered a symbol of courage and bravery. A sailor in his *telnyashka* stands out, from far away. You can't lose sight of him, not on stormy seas, or in a crowd of people. The blue and white lines seem to come alive and move, as if the sailor is wearing the ocean on his chest.

Of course, a uniform shirt is merely external, just an object. But just try one on – suddenly you want to straighten up and throw back your shoulders. And unless you're a pansy, or some sort of sickly specimen, you immediately feel the urge to test your strength – to do a couple of pull-ups, or a few bench presses.

---

[9] *Magnotorsk* : a major rural development project from one of Stalin's five year plans, built with the help of a popular communist youth movement.
[10] *Telnyashaka*: navy issue tank-top

And so it starts to have an effect on you, and it is not for nothing that people say that men in *telnyashki* knows no fear, spit in the face of death, and never ask an enemy for mercy.

Telnyashka, telnyashka...I had the good fortune to first put one on in the fall of '37, in Vladivostok. My fellow landlubbers—*Komsomol* members—and I arrived there after the long journey from the Urals to serve in the Pacific Fleet. For a full five years I wore the *telnyashka* with pride. I prepared myself for battle on the open seas...but ultimately, I was called to fight on dry land. However, I couldn't leave behind my *telnyashka*, so I kept its blue and white stripes hidden beneath my army fatigues.

To make a long story short, in September of '42, my fellow seamen and I had to shed our naval garb and don the attire of soldiers of the 284th Infantry Rifle division.

My memory carries me off to the far-away shores of the Pacific. I recall Vladivostok as it looked when I saw it for the first time.

The trainload of us green recruits arrived at the station at dawn, on the morning of February 3rd, 1937. The night was receding slowly, and the outlines of buildings surrounding the city were growing more distinct.

We were eager to leave behind the smoky train cars, and we made our way two by two along the elevated walkway over the tracks. Then we caught sight of the ocean, sheathed in a gray coat of ice.

"Well, where are the waves?" None of us had ever seen the ocean before. We were all landlubbers from the middle of the country.

A chief petty officer was with us.

"Alright, you loudmouths," he snapped, "fall into line."

We trod through the streets for a few blocks and ended up in front in of a pair of red gates with an old sign that read, "Garrison athhouse." The letter B in Bathouse had worn off and had never been re-painted. We stepped inside the building's courtyard, and a truck skidded to a halt in front of us. Seated next to the driver was a pea-coated sailor with a fresh crew cut. He threw open the door of the truck, pushed back the beret on his head, and stood on the running board sneering at us, as if to say, "Look who just showed up – the wannabes!" He came over to me and sized me up.

"How was your trip, *salazhki*?"[11] he asked me.

"It took forever," I replied, "but we finally made it."

"Well, congratulations," he said. "I think you'll be a fine bunch of sailors."

"How can you predict what kind of sailors we'll turn out to be?" This was Sasha Gryazev, a friend of mine who had a build like a gorilla. Sasha was a joker, just like the sailor standing on the truck's running board.

"How can I predict?" the sailor mimicked him. "You sound like a real country boy, my friend. Just wait till they send you to the *Guba*,[12] then you'll get some education."

"What's the *Guba*?" I asked, naively.

"Oh, it's a special resort for seaman," said the sailor on the running board. "They only send a chosen few. If you'd like, I have a friend who can arrange a special five-day vacation for you."

"Just who is it I have the privilege of speaking with?" I asked the joker on the running board.

The sailor pretended to be astonished, and said to me, "You mean to tell me that on your way here from Habarovsk, not one person bothered to inform you that your civilian clothes were to be handed over to assistant laundryman Nikolai Kuropiy? Nikolai Kuropiy – that's me…"

We listened carefully to this comedian, and because we didn't know any better, we joked with him, as if he were not a couple of ranks our senior.

"OK," he said. "So it's not your fault. I'll have to give a good thrashing to the stationmaster at Habarovsk, that's all. But now, I've got a job for you."

---

[11] *salazhki*: young, inexperienced sailor.
[12] *Guba*: Russian navy slang for the brig.

He led us to the bathhouse and ordered, "Strip down to your skivvies…"

After a couple minutes, our bunch of landlubbers from the Urals couldn't recognize each other. Nikolai Kuropiy carried off bundles of our suits, shoes and shirts. In his place appeared a chief petty officer, who introduced himself as Vassili Gregorovivich Ilyin.

Ilyin lectured us: "A sailor is nothing without his *telnyashka*, and yours will be issued soon enough. But in order for them to fit correctly, you first have to wash up, and shave your heads clean as monks. Cleanliness is the mark of good health, and a seaman's strength."

My comrades were handed electric razors. They started shaving each other's heads. Soon my hair was dropping in wisps by my feet. I felt a little sad: "farewell, dear youth…"

I was surrounded by the sounds of splashing water, as my compatriots scrubbed themselves down. I did not have a basin, nor were there enough sponges to go around, so I wandered from bench to bench like a lost man. Everyone was shouting and splashing, and having water fights, as if they were boys in school. I was left out and was feeling sorry for myself. I finally plopped down in a corner, assuming I would wait until the others finished. Then a skinny guy sat down nearby. His body looked withered and bumpy, like the twisted fibers of a rope. This fellow was named Okrihm Vasilchenko, and he was Ukrainian.

"Well, partner," he said, "We got to get washed up. Can you help me?"

After the sauna and shower, chief petty officer Vassili Ilyin handed me my *telnyashka*. And it really seemed that the shirt took a liking to my body. Those blue and white stripes really magnify your feelings of power and destiny. When you wear your *telnyashka*, it is like saying: "Let the seas rage around me, I will hold on and endure!" Sergeant Ilyin was right about the *telnyashka*. It constantly challenges you to prove yourself.

~~~

After five years of service in the navy, I became a rifleman in the infantry. This is how it happened.

The war had been raging for over a year. After many requests to be sent to the front, I was finally included in a list of sailors to be commissioned into the infantry. By that time I had already reached the rank of Chief Petty Officer, which translated into the army rank of Chief Master Sergeant.

Along with the other sailors who had requested combat duty, I was loaded onto a train headed west. At last, to the front! What a long and tedious ride it was – the train's wheels clacking incessantly. I couldn't wait to reach our destination, and the slow progress of the train was infuriating.

As we passed through the Urals, I remembered Grandpa teaching me to track, to shoot, and to camp out in the bitter frost under an open sky. But now was not the time to indulge in sentimental memories. Our country was in peril. To the front, and step on it!

Suddenly the train was diverted onto a dead-end siding at the Krasnoufimsk freight station. There were shouts up and down the platform: "Everybody off!" It was hard to imagine the disappointment on the sailors' faces when this happened. We were asking, "Why are they dragging us out here, in the middle of nowhere?" But it was here, in Krasnoufimsk, that the regiments of the 284th division were stationed. They had been rotated here to take a break and absorb replacements, after some hard fighting at Kastornoye.

My detachment from Vladivostok was enrolled in the second battalion of the 1047th regiment. The commanders and political officers of the battalion greeted us warmly, although our black pea coats and bellbottoms – not to mention our *telnyashki* and berets - elicited a few smiles.

We were soon back on the train, listening to the rhythmic clanking of the wheels, and now with even fewer stops along the way. Whenever I looked out the window, I saw the infinite, oceanic expanse of the steppes.

The inside of the train car was stuffy, and my comrades and I shed our pea coats, so up and down every car one could see the blue and white stripes of our shirts. We had become a ship on wheels, making our passage across an ocean of dry land. Ahead – a mirage made it look as if we really were heading into a stormy sea.

Day, then night, then day again. Russia is a vast country. We wanted the train to hurry up – we wanted to get into action as soon as possible.

But it wasn't to be. The train was brought to a halt. Somewhere up ahead, between us and our destination, Luftwaffe bombers had knocked out a bridge. We streamed out of the railway cars and peered into the distance. We waited an hour, then two, and three. Out there somewhere, on the very edge of the steppe's expanse, something was raging, but exactly what it was, we couldn't make out. One minute, black clouds would totally obscure our view, and the next minute a beam of light would break through, and the sun seemed to split apart into fiery fragments.

That night we marched through the fields, instead of taking the roads, to minimize the possibility of air attack.

The reference point visible to all, the hellish fires at the edge of the steppe, gave us the sensation of walking toward the edge of the world. But those fires were Stalingrad!

As morning approached, the sun obscured the red of the flames on the horizon, but the dark crimson clouds became thicker. It was as if a huge volcano was erupting, spitting forth smoke and lava. And when the sun's rays lit up between the clouds, we could see things circling, like a swarm of flies.

Our company commander, *Starshiy*[13] Lieutenant Bolshapov, handed me his binoculars. I looked through them and I could not believe my eyes. Stukas, Heinkels, ME-109s – it looked like the entire German air force – were flying over the city in formation, stacked three and four layers thick. There were unleashing their explosive payloads on the city below. The dive-bombers dipped

[13] *Starshiy*: First, as in First Lieutenant. *Starshina* means foreman or elder.

down into the heart of this conflagration, and from the ground below them columns of red brick dust would shoot up hundreds of feet into the air.

We were all astonished. Surely our comrades could no longer be fighting there – how could they manage to hold on and fight in that inferno? How could they manage to breathe? Was it possible for anyone to survive?

"Stalingrad has sustained a steady barrage of air attacks," Bolshapov explained, as if in response to my thoughts. "That's where we're headed, but right now, sailors, we have to prepare you for action."

For the next three days our task was intensive training for street combat. We were eager to train. We practiced with bayonets, knives, and shovels. We threw grenades, and we passed through obstacle courses. Everyone understood that this training was crucial, and sometimes our hand-to-hand exercises nearly turned into brawls. In the heat of the moment, a sailor might whack his partner square in the nose. After all, our commander wasn't training us for a walk in the park.

Lieutenant Bolshapov sat on a rise, his legs stretched out before him, twirling his thick red moustache. His boots were dug into the earth, and his sunburned arms rested across his knees.

It was easy to see that Bolshapov was content. Our hand-to-hand training was going as planned: us sailors were now accustomed to catching grenades in mid-flight, and hurling them back into the trenches where scarecrow Germans loomed.

A chubby, college-boy type political officer, *Zampolit* Stepan Kryakhov, was watching the exercises with Bolshapov.

"Against sailors like these, the Krauts won't stand a chance," said Bolshapov, and the round-faced Kryakhov agreed with him.

At that moment I was deep in a trench, learning how to use a shovel to overcome an "enemy" armed with a pistol. My opponent was Private Sasha Reutov. Reutov was a huge fellow, the orderly for Lt. Bolshapov.

The other sailors were watching us closely from a nearby

embankment. Somehow Reutov managed to free his pistol and unload a whole clip into me. Of course, the bullets were blanks.

In order to learn this exercise, all of us were required to pass through the trench and try our luck. After the second run–through, there were very few "casualties."

At the height of these exercises, a staff car pulled up, pennants flying from the hood. A short, frail man with crimson diamonds in his buttonholes emerged – this was our divisional commander, Brigadier Commissar Konstantin Terentyevich Zubkov. He was calmly smoking a *papirosa*,[14] and looking over towards the center of a circle of soldiers and sailors, where two men were battling it out.

Starshiy Lieutenant Bolshapov had joined in the exercises. He was beating back the attack of Midshipman Rovnov. The midshipman was clearly more powerful than the lieutenant; the midshipman was much taller, and he had about a six-inch advantage in reach. Lt. Bolshapov was having a tough time, but his training and his knowledge of self-defense made him virtually invulnerable.

Bolshapov would wind up like a spring, then throw his much larger opponent, and everything would start all over again. It looked like an even match, and we couldn't tell who was going to win.

The seamen were rooting for their midshipman, but the infantrymen were confident that the sailor didn't stand a chance of overcoming Lt. Bolshapov. The two fighters grappled again. Each man had the other by the shirtfront, and their faces were turning red. Suddenly Bolshapov planted one foot on the cuffs of the midshipman's bellbottom trousers, so the midshipman was riveted in place. Then Bolshapov shoved Rovnov with his shoulder, and Midshipman Rovnov went crashing to the ground.

Lieutenant Bolshapov wiped the sweat from his brow.

"Those damned bellbottoms could cost you your lives."

Lieutenant Bolshapov then noticed the Brigadier watching

[14] *papirosa*: unfiltered Russian cigarette.

and called the company to attention.

"At ease, men," said Brigadier Zubkov. "Haven't you received your army uniforms yet?"

Bolshapov wanted to spare us from the Brigadier's wrath, but he had no choice except to make a truthful report.

"These seamen have been issued fatigues, sir, they just haven't got around to changing yet."

Everyone waited for the brigadier's response. He puffed his *papirosa*, blew a ring of smoke, and regarded us in silence. We wondered what he was waiting for, but no one dared to speak. Finally the commissar flicked the ash from his *papirosa*, and said, "So, you're sorry to have to part with your navy get-ups, huh? But what about your warships, which were your home for so long? Did you want to leave them?"

The brigadier's face had turned white, and his left hand clutched at his belt. Then he resumed, answering his own question.

"You eagles have flown out of your nest. You've flown away, but you haven't been forgotten. Your old commanders are all thinking about you. They sent you here as proud sons of the Pacific fleet, men of heroism and discipline. So where's your discipline now?"

We stood, silent and resentful. But we understood that the Brigadier was correct. In the distance Stalingrad was ablaze. Black smoke was rising in plumes above the city. Artillery pounded the earth, and enemy planes were bombing the city mercilessly. The emergency we faced made our obstinate pride in our navy uniforms irrelevant. Within an hour, we were transformed into Red Army infantrymen. The uniforms fit badly and were very uncomfortable. But at least we kept on our *telnyashki* underneath the army fatigues.

CHAPTER 3.
THE CROSSING

We boarded the trucks and prepared to move out.

The commander of the 2nd Battalion, Captain Kotov, was a stocky fellow with a pale complexion, blond hair, and watery blue eyes. He was standing with his bandy legs wide apart, keeping his eye on his watch. A few yards away stood a small group of soldiers, the messengers from each company. I stood among them – I was the newest messenger for the machine gun company. We were discussing Captain Kotov. We had not yet served under him, and none of us really knew what kind of officer he was. Kotov was concerned with getting the trucks loaded on time, and he barely noticed us.

All of us messengers were about the same age, so we felt like equals. After we finished loading the trucks, the Captain and a nurse climbed into the lead vehicle. We were left with no superior ranks around, so I decided as the most senior non-com in our group, that I would take command.

The first thing I thought to do was to break down our group into its respective units.

"Alright, get in the trucks!" I bawled out. "I'll be in the number two vehicle. If you're late, you've only got yourself to blame. This is no drill, this is the real thing."

A private named Pronischev took the seat next to me. He commented with a snicker, "Chief, you've never been in combat, but you're already scaring the rest of us."

This man's words got under my skin. I was flustered, and extremely angry. I shouted at Pronsichev to fall in.

Pronischev and myself got stuck with the worst seats in the truck, sitting next to the rear tailgate, so that we were covered with red dust from the road. I was still angry – at the Krauts, at Pronischev, and especially at the fact that I was stuck being a messenger. I was angry at the world.

Pronischev cleared his throat.

"Look chief," he said, "don't get bent out of shape." Pronischev was a Siberian from a collective farm near Vladivostok. He was a typical country boy, and had a big Adam's apple that rose and fell as he spoke.

"I didn't mean to get your goat," he said, "I'm just tired of hearing people talking about things they don't understand. For example, my profession is driving a tractor. Let's say I started lecturing a pilot about how to fly his plane. That would be ludicrous, eh? As for our job…I'll tell you about being a messenger. Everything is always out of control; everything is turned upside down. You don't know who's who, or where your side is, or where the enemy is. What's a messenger supposed to do? Where do you run? When your side's retreating, that means everyone withdraws together, soldiers help each other to reach safety…but the messenger is always alone."

The dust from the road was making Pronischev's voice grate. He cleared his throat and continued:

"For example, at the battle of Kastornoye, I took a message from regimental command through the forest to second battalion. I managed to deliver it successfully, then while I was heading back, some Kraut motorcyclists cut me off. Thanks be to God I saw them before they saw me. What could I do? I rolled a couple of grenades in their path and blew them off the road. But I couldn't stop to congratulate myself; I had more communiqués to pick up. So that's our job. In battle you've got to be your own commander."

I shut up. What could I say? Here I was, a greenhorn who had never seen action, and I had been stupid enough to belittle the messengers' job, which was vital and dangerous.

I remembered my early days in the navy, and the first test of conscience I had there.

It was a March morning in 1938, a bright day in spring, and Vladivostok's Bay of the Golden Horn was sparkling in rainbow colors - but I was feeling bitter and frustrated. The reason was that my career goal in the navy had been to become a minelayer or a torpedo man, but instead I had been assigned as an accountant and payroll clerk. In hopes of being re-assigned, I would deliberately make my handwriting illegible, and make grammatical errors. For this I was punished by being given extra forms to fill out. My commanding officer, like me, was named Zaitsev, Dmitri Zaitsev.

I was bored and decided to play an adolescent joke, of the type I should have outgrown in high school. While drawing up a claims form, I surreptitiously changed the name of "rammer-discharger" (for the turret of a battleship), into a certain unprintable word. I gave the form to Lieutenant Zaitsev for his signature, and forgot about it. I thought that was that.

But the following day, my little trick blew up in my face. First off, my conscience grew into a heavy weight. I was paralyzed, thinking that command would discover my prank, and that Lieutenant Zaitsev would be held responsible for it. This was no minor infraction either; I had openly mocked the authority of a commanding officer.

Day passed into night. I didn't know what to do with myself. I wandered, depressed, back to my bunk. When you've got a guilty conscience, other things start screwing up, and that annoys you even more.

That night the soldier on guard duty woke me up twice for failing to lay out my uniform correctly. I couldn't sleep and left the barracks before reveille, totally forgetting that this was against the rules. On my way out of the barracks, our sergeant intercepted me.

"What are you doing up, sailor? Reveille's not for twenty minutes!"

Once again, stupidly, I decided to deceive a superior. I slowly straightened up and stood at attention, doing my best imitation of looking deathly ill.

"Sarge, it's my stomach...." I groaned.

"Go on, get out of here," he said, "make a run for the latrine."

At roll call, the sergeant sent me to the clinic, to have my ailment checked out.

Our garrison doctor immediately uncovered my trickery. He examined me and saw that I was in excellent health. The he wrote a note to the sergeant: "For the next week, malingerer Zaitsev is to be woken thirty minutes prior to reveille to engage in cleaning the latrines."

I spent the next week carrying buckets of water. When it was over I was taken back to the doctor. Just like the preceding time, he examined me carefully. By this time I had learned my lesson.

"I feel fine, sir" I told him. "Can you call off my treatment regimen?"

At that moment a messenger from HQ arrived with a note for me, "Report to your commander, Lieutenant Zaitsev." In a flash I was in Lt. Zaitsev's office. It was obvious that he was irritated with me.

"Zaitsev," he said, "how were you ever able to hold a job as a civilian accountant? Did you pull this same type of joke when you worked for the Young Communist League? Look, I trusted you like my own brother, and in return for my faith in you, you pull this kind of stunt!"

The lieutenant's words turned me inside out. He was a kind man, a demanding but fair officer. The year before he had graduated from military school with distinction. Because he had been an exemplary student, he was sent to command our section. Now he was being transferred to another unit, a demotion for his apparent negligence on the job.

"Here's why I'm being shipped out," he said. He laid a claim form on the desk. It was the same form I had used for my prank – I recognized my handwriting.

"This affair's going to have a pretty sad ending. What an idiot you are, Seaman Zaitsev."

I wished the earth would swallow me up so I could disappear. I apologized profusely, and begged for the harshest punishment. The lieutenant regarded me closely.

"I'm not going to punish you, Zaitsev. Let your conscience do that. It will be your ultimate judge."

The lieutenant was right. No punishment is more severe than the torment of your own conscience. I believe the life of every soldier – if he wants to be worthy of that title – depends not only upon regulations and orders, but also upon each man's own conscience. And losing your conscience in wartime is the most heinous of crimes.

~~~

And now with our country invaded by the fascists, with Stalingrad being blown to pieces before my eyes, my ears were ringing with the words of Private Pronischev: "...in battle, the messenger is his own commander." The only thing for me to do was to execute the will of my commanders faithfully and honestly. Otherwise, it was not even going to be worth dreaming about victory.

Our column turned down a county road. For half an hour, we rambled across the steppe. We drove past sleepy marshes and numerous small lakes. It was a hot day in September, and us dusty soldiers wanted nothing more than to take a swim – but that wasn't on the day's agenda.

Suddenly there was an alarm from the lead vehicle, and all our trucks scattered. Soldiers hurriedly camouflaged the trucks with netting and branches. The sky above was clear, and this turned out to be a false alarm. But we were in a very dangerous area, and our gear was quickly unloaded and distributed.

Now everyone was on edge. We formed into three lines and marched down the road. The day was coming to an end. The heat eased off and we weren't so thirsty anymore.

The air was filled with explosions and we could smell smoke, cordite, and something else that was very unpleasant, the sickening aroma of roasted human flesh.

We turned off the road, and marched along some cattle trails in the forest. Suddenly people in civilian clothes – old men, women, and children - appeared from behind the bushes. They could barely walk, and they were bandaged and covered in dust. These were wounded civilians from Stalingrad, trying to reach a hospital. We sailors, who hadn't yet seen the horrors of war, looked on in distress. And at the edge of the forest, where we concealed ourselves, we could see Stalingrad. The Volga lay between us and the city. We could hear artillery fire and the rattle of machine guns. German aircraft, much closer now than those we had seen before, were relentlessly bombing the factory district.

Wounded soldiers were led past us. We wanted to ask them about the battle, but their appearance spoke for them. They walked like zombies, moaning and groaning, their columns led by a nurse or medic. Then we saw a sailor among them. He was a chief petty officer, like myself. His head and left arm were bandaged, and his shirt was filthy with dried blood. His left arm was in a sling. A bullet had creased the anchor on his navy belt buckle.

He asked us for a smoke. We gave him one, and he sat down against a tree, exhausted. Then he looked at our badges and saw we were from the Pacific fleet.

"Do any of you guys know Sasha Lebedev? He's my brother."

"We have a guy by that name," replied Okhrim Vasilchenko.

"Maybe," said the wounded sailor, "it's just another fellow with the same name." Obviously the wounded sailor did not want to risk getting his hopes up and then being disappointed.

"This Sasha plays the accordion. And he's got a fantastic voice," said Okhrim.

"Yeah, that's him!" gasped the wounded sailor. He was very fatigued, but he managed to drag himself back to his feet.

Three soldiers raced off to find Sasha.

Before the fascists had advanced on Stalingrad, Ivan Lebedev had served with the far Northern fleet, in Murmansk, while his brother Sasha served in the Pacific. The two had grown up in Stalingrad. When the Nazis approached Stalingrad, both brothers requested transfers to the Stalingrad front. And now…

"*Tovarich*[15] Ivan Lebedev!" shouted Okrihm. "Look who's here!"

Sasha was running towards us. The two brothers embraced. Ivan said in a trembling voice, "Look what they've done to me… I can't even hug my own brother."

It was then that he held up his bandaged arm and we saw that his left hand and forearm were missing.

The rest of us crowded around them. "What's it like, in the city?" Okrihm asked.

"It's rough, but we're holding." Ivan Lebedev looked at the sailors gathered around him. "We're going to hold to the end, brothers, we're going to make it through, honest. Don't worry about my arm. We made the Krauts pay for it!"

He slid back into a sitting position, exhausted.

"We're stationed by the *Krasny Oktyabr* Factory," he continued. "We're fighting for every street and house. Everything is engulfed in fire – the Germans are using flame-throwers. Sparks shower down everywhere; they fall inside your collar and set your clothes on fire. There's places where it hurts to breathe." Ivan Lebedev winced as his wounded arm brushed against the tree. Then he continued: "I saw a Kraut officer pull out his pistol and draw a bead on our commander. I jumped the guy, but he got a shot off and hit my arm, before I could finish him with my knife. After I took out their officer, the Krauts got confused, and our men charged. We were able to push them back."

Ivan Lebedev fell silent. To us, it seemed as if we had been there ourselves, living through this combat with him.

[15] *Tovarich*: comrade

I didn't notice, but Brigadier Zubkov had been leaning against a tree, listening to Ivan Lebedev's account with the rest of us. He shook Lebedvev's hand.

"Thanks for your story, Comrade Lebedev. You've given these volunteers an idea of what to expect."

The Brigadier noticed that some of us had shed our fatigue shirts in favor of the *telnyashki*. Lieutenant Bolshapov tried to make an excuse for us.

"Right up until dark, Comrade Brigadier, they were soldiers, now they've turned back into sailors."

The Brigadier ruminated a bit. "In ancient times, Russian soldiers put on fresh clothing before going into battle. Let them wear what they wish."

We walked down to the banks of the Volga and lay down on the warm sand next to the water. The battle across the river had exhausted itself for the moment, and things were peaceful, almost like a normal autumn evening. The Volga was rolling over and sifting tiny stones on the shore, and the pebbles rustled as if they were whispering to each other.

This brief reverie was shattered by streams of large caliber machine gun fire shooting off in all directions from Mamayev Hill. We watched a stream of tracer bullets as it tumbled into the middle of the river.

"We don't need to worry yet, we're out of range," said Okhrim Vasilchenko.

By the mooring across the river, the two sides were exchanging fire. Near some large petrol tanks, Tommy-gunners were at work, their weapons tapping out a steady rhythm, while from a ravine across from the fuel tanks, you could feel the earth trembling from exploding shells.

Overhead we could hear the rumbling of German night bombers. They were trying to hit the moorings, but the majority of their payloads fell into the river, and with every detonation, a wave of hot steamy air washed over us. This was the soldiers' worst nightmare: to be attacked and to be unable to return fire.

Okhrim Vasilchenko couldn't keep still. He tossed and turned, then growled: "What are we waiting here for? We should be crossing now while it's dark! If we wait for the sun to come up, we'll all be sitting ducks!"

Lieutenant Bolshapov overheard him.

"We'll be deployed across the river as soon as our supporting units arrive," said Bolshapov. "So what's your hurry?"

We fidgeted in silence. The city truly looked like a smoldering and sulfurous hell, with burned-out buildings glowing like red coals, and fires consuming men and machines. Profiled against the glow of the fires were soldiers on the run. Were they theirs or ours? None of us could tell.

A wagon train of horse-drawn carts from the second battalion approached. The carts were overloaded and bogged down in the sand. The horses were so tired that they were collapsing in their traces, and they were too exhausted to tear the wagons free. A company of machine gunners came up, and helped to pull the carts out of the sand, so the wagon train could continue on towards the moorings.

A tugboat pulled up with a barge lashed behind it. The barge's hull had been heavily damaged by shrapnel.

We quickly loaded the wagons' contents onto the barge. Our machine gunners prepped their weapons for battle, and in the center of the barge they stacked up boxes of ammunition, so they would be ready to deploy as soon as we reached the shore.

A sergeant was loading boxes into the hold, which was filling up with water. The boxes were full of canned meat from America. It was the "second front" after all. The sailors laughed at the sergeant: "What are you doing, Sarge? The second front is going to drown down there!"

Hand pumps had been rigged at the front and back of the barge, and sailors were busy pumping out water, which was seeping in to both ends of our craft. The barge had so many holes in it, it had to be pumped out constantly or it would have been sure to sink. Below decks sailors were busy caulking leaks, and there was a chorus of hammers tapping. But when we completed loading, the hammering stopped in order to maintain silence for our passage.

The tugboat's motor started up with a muffled sound. It shook, the towrope was yanked taut, and the barge creaked forward with a shudder, like a tired old horse. Tiny waves rolled against us, lapping gently against the barge's iron hull, then dissipating with a swish. The opaque darkness was like a blindfold, and all of us were anxiously peering ahead, trying to make out what was in store for us. You could hear the lap of oars to port and starboard as sailors in small boats ferried men and equipment across the water.

Sailors' luck was with us that night. The crossing went off without a hitch. Every one of us sailors from the Pacific fleet made it across the Volga, towards the fire-spitting ruin of Stalingrad.

This took place on the night of September 22nd, 1942.

CHAPTER 4.
FIRST COMBAT

The tugboat's bow slid into the sand of the opposite shore. Its motor puttered for the last time and then fell silent, waters continuing to guzzle astern. So we had made it – the long-awaited left bank!

A flare flashed overhead. Its bright light sent a reflection across our steel helmets, and we all froze. I can not describe the feeling we had looking at each other as we waited to be hit with a fusillade. Fortunately nothing happened, the flare went out, and the shore came back to life. By about five that morning, our entire 284th Rifle Division had crossed the river.

I still can't understand why the Germans did not fire a single round at us as we crossed the Volga. Perhaps it was because the night was exceptionally murky, and we had been careful not to betray our presence with unnecessary sounds or movements. Perhaps they thought that we had given up sending in further reinforcements. More likely, the Germans simply let their guard down, presuming that the Russian army at Stalingrad was already broken, and that among the city's ruins there only remained isolated bands of "kamikaze" communists. The Nazis must have believed that all that remained for them to do were a few wipe-up operations, and the Red Army in Stalingrad would be *kaput*.

Anyway, I will never know why or how, but the fact was that our division succeeded in crossing without a single casualty.

Now there was no longer any doubt – we would soon enter the battle. The baptism of fire for us sailors was going to commence on dry land, in a devastated city. Who would begin it, and which of us would survive to see to the end? I was resigned to whatever was going to come. I had been repeating to myself that I was not going to retreat, even if I was staring death in the face. I knew that my comrades from the Pacific fleet were thinking the same thing.

As I turned all this over in my mind, I remembered my days in Vladivostok, and a radio announcer reading out the regular news update from the *Sovinformbyuro*: 'Our forces have abandoned Sevastopol'…."

I had heard that discouraging piece of news while I was at the bank, picking up the pay stipends for the month of May 1942. And there, while standing at the counter, from behind my back I heard a condemnation that for me was no less hard to deal with, than the announcer's proclamation about Sevastopol. It was preceded by much coughing and hacking from one of the old fogies that worked at the bank. It went like this:

"So what I'm saying is that any old woman with half a brain can fetch money at the bank; it's time to call up bell-bottomed sissies….like this one…… to the front."

"You're right about that, Luka Yegorovich," chimed in the familiar voice of Uncle Fedya, a mechanic who worked in the bank's boiler room.

"Take me, for example," continued Fedya, "I hold two different positions, so on top of my job here, the upkeep of an entire bathhouse rests on my shoulders. What if the boss were to ask me, Fedya, to hop over to the bank and pick up paychecks for the staff - what's so hard in that? They shouldn't hand these loafers women's work, I tell you…."

From that moment on it hurt me to keep serving in a peaceful city, so far from the front. When I returned to the base I felt ready to toss all the rubles to the breeze, just so I would be sent to the front with a penal battalion. And that's exactly what would have happened, but precisely at that moment I ran into our base commander, Nikolaev, who informed me that my replacement was arriving, and that the fleet command had granted the request of the *Komsomol'tsi*. We were to form a volunteer company of sailors to be sent to the front.

I was so stunned I had to catch my breath.

The commander grinned at me, pulled out a pack of Belmoras, and handed me a cigarette.

"I envy you and your *Komsomol* friends," the commander confessed to me. The base commander was a nervous man by nature, who took to heart the most minor snags and screw-ups. He often worked for days with no sleep. He had a scar that crept like a snake from his brow to his cheek, and his worries made it stand out from the worn flesh.

"I've put in four requests of my own to be sent to the front," he said. "The last time I made a submission the Military Council[16] finally gave me my response." The commander pulled out a copy of the letter, with its official stamp, and showed it to me. It read as follows:

"Please explain to Comrade Nikolaev that he must understand we are not on a holiday, and that the Pacific fleet has a mission to accomplish here in Vladivostok. If Comrade Nikolaev doesn't come to understand this, the matter will be sorted out at the next staff meeting, if necessary right up to expulsion from the party, and dismissal from command."

Nikolaev knew he could not pursue this matter any further. The decision of the Military Council was final. He was a wise commander who had given eighteen years to the service, and at that moment he appeared to me almost like my own father – and

[16] Military Council: the Soviet Military Councils on the different fronts were a mix of high-level communist party officials and ranking military officers. These Military Councils held ultimate authority in their areas of control. Their decisions could not be appealed, short of going to Moscow.

in his way, disappointed, as my father had been in his military career. My father's wound had sidelined him, and kept my father from fighting for the Revolution during the Civil War. Now Nikolaev had been sidelined by circumstance, and stuck here in Vladivostok, when he wanted to be in the thick of things.

Commander Nikolaev counseled me on how to comport myself in battle: the most important things were never to lose courage, and to always be alert.

I was the most senior volunteer and therefore was appointed commander of our detachment of sailors, which was to be part of the Pacific Fleet marines battalion.

Time dragged by slowly while I waited for my replacement to show up. I was counting every second. One night I made the special effort to review all of our unit's books. I managed to draw up a complete financial report to hand over to my replacement, and early the next morning I took a walk down to the ocean.

Dawn was breaking over the sea with exceptional beauty. It began with the appearance of barely noticeable point of brilliant light. It was the *zarnitsa*, the pathfinder star for the sun. The *zarnitsa* is as tiny as a mouse's eye, but at dawn it shines so brightly that it lights up everything around it. This little light was no ordinary star; it was more like a scout, laying out a path for the sun to travel. When that little star flared up, the sun soon followed it.

On that particular morning, I thought of it as the star of good fortune. As the sun rose, the flowers, the trees, the birds singing, and the peaceful, grazing animals – every living thing I saw, was rejoicing and turning towards the sun. And, of course, I too was rejoicing: how could it be otherwise, considering what lay in store, tomorrow I was going to leave, to serve my country at the front!

After a swim in the chilly ocean, I trotted back to my barracks. By that time, everybody knew that a detachment of twenty *Komsomoltis*, myself included, was heading for action. Time was running out, and they gave us a send-off in the true Pacific Fleet fashion.

~~~

Now we had finally arrived at Stalingrad, on the left bank of the Volga. Was the *zarnitsa* going to be the same lucky star for us sailors from Vladivostok? You couldn't find it in the sky here over the Volga – the stars of the steppe looked completely different from those over the Pacific.

We disembarked from the barges and waited for the order to engage the enemy. Until orders came down, we were to stay put, near the moorings. A few hours passed. Sailors can normally tell time by looking at the sky, but in the city it was impossible. The sky was completely blanketed by smoke.

We could see that our officers were getting jittery, and this made us even more nervous. It became obvious that we were going into battle at any minute. But where was the enemy, where was his front line? It seemed like no one wanted to find out. The idea of sending out scouts had not even occurred to our battalion commander, Captain Kotov. He was lying on his stomach, next to me. To my other side was *Starshiy* Lieutenant Bolshapov.

As the sun rose, the outlines of distant objects in the city's factory district began to take shape. We could see giant petrol tanks to our left. What was behind them, and who was out there?

Beyond the tanks was a railroad yard scattered with empty cars, where God only knows what lay hidden. A few minutes passed, and German scouts spotted us and called down a mortar strike on our position. Then ME-109s appeared overhead, and incendiary bombs began raining down, with a steady pattern of concussions, each one of which rattled our teeth. Turmoil reigned amongst us – sailors rushed back and forth, not knowing what to do.

Kotov, Bolshapov and myself leaped into a deep bomb crater. We were stuck there, glued to the earth, as we waited for the bombardment to slacken off. To all sides, we could hear groans and pleading from our wounded. A messenger leaped in with us. He reported that the division's #2 commander had been killed. This was horrible. Things couldn't have been any worse.

Exactly at that moment we heard the whoosh whoosh whoosh

of our katyushas, firing from the opposite bank. Nice job, boys, and right on time!

We could see the katyushas pulverizing the Krauts' mortar batteries, with Krauts being blasted into the air as every salvo hit the ground. What a sight this was, the yellow flames of the katyushas' explosions, then men and pieces of men thrown into the air in every direction....

Lieutenant Bolshapov ran up a rise, and raised his pistol. He shouted "*Rodina!*"[17] He dashed towards the huge petrol tanks where the Kraut machine gunners had taken up positions.

It was as if a spring had shot me to me feet – and I don't recall how, but I ended up at his side. I urged my fellow sailors to follow me. Our line – which had been wavering - suddenly pulled back together. Every one of us leaped to our feet. Our fear and hesitation had been eradicated. A united attack can embolden even the most timid.

The Krauts opened up with machine gun fire from our left. Their machine gun nests were well camouflaged, somewhere in the ruins by the Dolgiy Ravine. Our waves of advancing sailors dropped to the ground and the attack stalled.

Starshiy Lieutenant Bolshapov ordered me to run up to the shattered buildings and take out the machine gun nests with grenades. I obeyed his orders at once, without hesitation. Fortunately the enemy fire flew past me, leaving me unscathed. As soon as the German machine gun fire was halted, our sailors again leaped to the attack.

When the Krauts caught sight of us and realized we were close to outflanking them near the petrol tanks, they called in another artillery strike. They were able to coordinate it with an air strike by the Luftwaffe. The German incendiary bombs lit a huge fire, and the petrol storage tanks began exploding. Everything was showered with burning fuel. Above us were gigantic tongues of flame, dancing with a deafening roar. Another minute and we would have been turned into so much smoked meat.

[17] *Rodina*! : Motherland, for the motherland.

The soldiers and sailors who were engulfed in flames ripped off their burning clothes, but none of us halted our advance, nor did we drop our weapons. An attack of naked, burning men – what the Germans must have thought about us, I can only guess. Perhaps they took us for demons, or maybe for saints that not even flames could stop. This might explain why they abandoned their positions and ran like rabbits, without even looking back. We beat them back from the road adjacent to the petrol tanks, and they didn't stop running until they reached the city's westernmost avenues. Then we took cover among the tiny freestanding houses that lined the street.

Somebody threw me a tarp to cover myself. We stood around naked, some with tarps draped over us, waiting until new uniforms were brought up.

A bunch of naked Russian soldiers had come through their baptism of fire.

~~~

Regimental commander Metelev directed our fire towards three targets: the Metalworking Factory along the Dolgiy Ravine, the city's Ice House, and Mamayev Hill, which long ago had been a burial ground. In the Dolgiy Ravine, we made contact with a machine gun company from Rodimtsev's 13th Guards' Division. They had been decimated by fierce fighting at the city center.

German planes continued to circle above. Some ME-109's were hitting the *Krasny Oktyabr* Factory and the northern slopes of Mamayev Hill. They were using incendiary bombs on other targets as well, and in some areas the earth was on fire. The air had been superheated, so that our lips cracked from the scorching temperatures. Our mouths went dry, and some men had their hair fused together into a mass no comb could separate.

Our battalion commandeer, Captain Kotov, was happy because our first advance was successful. The petrol tanks had been taken, and we now occupied a nearby unfinished red brick house. We had captured the Metalworking Factory's office, and were inside the factory itself, fighting for the huge workshops of the Metalworking Factory and the adjacent Asphalt Factory.

Command gave us a breather. I looked around, and in every direction I could see the city burning around me. Flames were rising over homes, over the Metalworking and Asphalt factories, and in the distance, over the Tractor Factory.

I ran my hands over myself. It was a reflex action. I was checking for bullet holes. Above me a thick black column of smoke was rising high into the air. It moved noiselessly along the shore to the west. Like a black veil it drew tight around Mamayev Hill and completely obscured the fighting there. The smoky clouds sank ever closer to the earth. The smoke crawled into the ruins of the buildings and into basements underground, it seeped down into the trenches, and pushed away the breathable air. Rain was drizzling down, and the smoke drifted through the rain and out towards the Volga.

German aircraft continued their bombing runs. At first we hid among the ruins, in craters and at the base of stone walls. None of these provided enough protection, so we ran across to the plant's farthest workshop to take cover beneath tables supporting presses and lathes. The bombing and artillery exchanges stopped again, and we were once more on the attack. Hand-to-hand combat ensued, hundreds of men locked in mortal struggle. I saw the sailors around me wrestling with the Germans. Suddenly a big German was on top of me. He hit me with the butt of his gun. Fortunately the blow glanced off my helmet instead of my face.

This was where our training on the other side of the river came in handy. I slipped behind him and got my arm locked around his neck, then managed to choke him while he thrashed around trying to shake me off, like a buffalo trying to dislodge a tiger from its back.

Finally the Kraut stopped struggling, and I smelled something foul. He had shit himself at the moment of death.

The enemy soldiers melted away and there was another lull in the fighting. We inspected the ruins of the Metalworking Factory -

everywhere there were heaps of brick and twisted metal.

Suddenly I spotted a young girl, very thin, with feeble legs that were scraped and bleeding. She was in a torn blue dress, too big for her, and on her bare feet she wore little red boots, that were ripped like her dress.

She was walking at the head of a line of our wounded soldiers, leading them through an abandoned ravine toward one of our aid stations. A shell burst nearby, and fragments and clumps of dirt showered the wounded men. Then the Nazis' explosive bullets began whizzing by. The Krauts were targeting our wounded! But the little girl just kept on leading them, ignoring the danger. I took cover and fired off the entire drum magazine of my Tommy-gun in the general direction of the fascists.

I will remember the courage of that little girl as long as I live.

Lieutenant Bolshapov wondered out loud, how did that girl figure out a path through our lines, back to the aid stations? What if the Krauts discovered the path, and were able to outflank us from the rear? Bolshapov ordered me to go with Sasha Reutov and to find out where the path led, and to see if the fascists would be able to use it to infiltrate our lines.

We grabbed our Tommy-guns and a few grenades each, and ducked into the ruins. I was in the lead, with Reutov behind me, lighting our path with his flashlight. We stumbled through the destruction and shrank beneath the bent girders. We approached a massive steel door, opened it, and were immediately choked by the reek of kerosene, along with some other heavy, unidentifiable stench.

Reutov covered his face with his shirt.

"Whew!" he said. "You could hang an axe[18] on that!"

There we were in a long, narrow corridor, and to the right was another door. We could hear voices and groans from behind it. Who was there – the enemy, or our guys? We pushed against the door, but it wouldn't budge. It was locked from the inside.

---

[18] "You could hang an axe on that": a Russian expression pertaining to a bad or heavy odor, similar to the American expression "you could cut that with a knife."

Reutov put his ear to the keyhole and listened. "It sounds like Russian," he said, and then he pounded on the door. In the closed space, his knock echoed like cannon fire.

From somewhere behind the door, a deep voice demanded: "Who's there?"

I recognized the voice as one of our fellow sailors, Nikolai "Kolya" Kuropiy.

"Kolya," I shouted, "open up, it's me, Vasya, and Reutov!" We waited for what seemed like several minutes. The ground shook from time to time, reminding us that there was a bombardment going on outside. Finally, we heard the screech of an iron bolt, and the door swung open. In front of us stood a half-naked man. His face and chest were covered with burns. His left arm hung in a kerchief that was tied around his neck. This was my navy buddy Kolya, former laundryman and more recently, the bookkeeper on the *Poltavschina*. He was a loudmouth and joker.

There were nineteen other men in the cellar; all of them wounded more seriously than Kolya. They had already received first aid; nurse Klava Svintsova and two helpers were taking care of the wounded. But the wounded needed to be immediately evacuated across the Volga, to a real hospital.

It turned out that from this basement you could reach the Volga by a hidden route - first by a labyrinthine path through some ruins to an area of free-standing homes, then down into the Dolgiy ravine. From there, the moorings were a stone's throw away. Medical personnel had used this route to get here, but had been disrupted when the Germans took over the plant's workshops.

Up above – the Nazis; down in this dank and moldy basement – our wounded.

"A perfectly neighborly arrangement," Kolya cracked. He had found the spirit to joke, despite his burns. "Foxes in the hen house! If only we could find a way through for the battalion, to drive out the Krauts from upstairs so we could move these casualties …"

Sasha Reutov had found something and he called me over.

I turned to look – it was a large rectangular air duct, over two yards in width. It was about five feet high. I stand 5' 3," so I was able to walk through it with only a slight duck of the head. The air inside was clean, breathing was easy, and I could even feel a slight draft. I passed through it in the darkness. With my left hand I held on to a thick braided cable, which was hanging a few inches down from the ceiling. I kept my right hand on the butt of my pistol. The cable made a sharp vertical turn, and within fifteen feet, I smacked into a brick wall. I fumbled about until I found a short set of wooden stairs. The four steps led me up to an exit: a square opening covered by a thick sheet of iron. Light was shining through the chinks in the metal. From this vantage point I could hear a firefight immediately above: machine guns chattering, shells exploding, but exactly where was I was going to be, when exiting this passage? I decided to look around, and tried to budge the sheet of iron with my shoulder. It was no use. The sheet seemed to have been welded to the spot.

Sasha Reutov called from somewhere behind me, "Vasya!" He was like a big clumsy bear trying to squeeze himself through this passage. He was panting and out of breath.

We both braced our shoulders against the iron cover, and we were preparing to shove it to one side when two powerful explosions thudded nearby, one after the other. Sasha and I looked at each other. Our ears were ringing. We waited but we didn't hear anything more from above.

I muttered "one, two, three!" and we pushed up together. The cover budged, but it made a screech that could easily have betrayed us. Fortunately the sound didn't draw any fire to us.

We had managed to create an opening, but it was so small that only I was able to squeeze through. The bear-like Reutov was several sizes too large to follow.

So I poked my head up like a mole, and glanced back and forth. We had found our way into a storeroom for the machine shops; all around me were shelves filled with appliances and tooling.

I could also see what was going on in one of the adjacent

assembly workshops. It was full of Germans, maybe a whole company. They had gathered for lunch; they had their bowls and thermoses in their hands. A cook from a field kitchen had delivered a pot of stew for them, and the cook was ladling it out. The Germans were acting relaxed, as if they were back in a mess hall in Munich or Cologne. They were oblivious to me, the Russian sailor, who was counting them one by one like sheep.

I made a rough drawing of their positions, their firing points, the windows, and the Krauts' possible routes of escape. I gave the diagram to Reutov, and told him to run back to report to Bolshapov, while I remained to keep an eye on things.

A little slip of paper fluttered into my hands: it read, "PASS" in Russian. The reverse had some writing in German I couldn't understand. Later I had it translated. It read: "To all soldiers of the Fuhrer, disarm without delay, and send to a POW camp all Russian soldiers and officers bearing this ticket of surrender."

For the next 20 minutes, I watched the Nazis eat their lunch. I counted sixty-five of them. After they finished, I heard the click of lighters as they broke out their cigarettes for a smoke.

Two of the Krauts wandered in to my corner of the workshop, and I popped my head down. They were smoking and laughing as they talked. They were so close I could smell the cabbage stew on their breath. I was sure they would notice the bent metal cover, but fortunately they ignored it, as they were absorbed in their conversation. They were laughing at some private joke. I stole a look at them – they were tall and hearty, their faces full of arrogance - the arrogance of the conqueror.

Where the hell was Reutov? Here we had the Nazis with their pants down, and Reutov had disappeared. I had no idea if he had got the message through to our company our not. I imagined that his fat behind had been caught in an air duct, and that he was still stuck there.

As I was thinking this there was a clattering noise from the opposite side of the building, and the Germans began shouting and rushing about. Then I understood that this clattering was intentional. Our soldiers had managed to slip into the instrument storeroom via the adjacent basement, and they were waiting for the Germans to be distracted by the noises they made.

Then I heard Bolshapov's voice shout a command, and grenades were heaved into the Nazi's makeshift cafeteria. I counted thirty-odd explosions in the space of a few seconds. The two Krauts by me took cover, and I rolled a grenade up to their toes. When they noticed the grenade rolling across the floor they glanced in my direction and our eyes met. When they saw the grenade coming they didn't look so arrogant anymore.

I ducked and heard them scream as my grenade exploded, then heard ricochets as streams of machine gun fire tore up and down the room. In less than two minutes, not a single Kraut in the workshop was still breathing.

That evening we finished mopping up the remaining German positions in our section of the factory.

The Germans still held the Asphalt Factory, the northwest section of the Metalworking Factory, the Transformer Room, and a part of the boiler room. In addition, they continued to hold the bridge and a railroad embankment that skirted the northern edge of Mamayev Hill.

We cleaned ourselves up and carried the wounded out of the cellar, then helped to prepare a field hospital for Nurse Klava Svintsova. Then we sent the wounded back to the docks at the Volga.

Thus ended my first battle, or more precisely, my first day of battle, in Stalingrad.

CHAPTER 5.
BURIED ALIVE

For the entire week of September 23 to September 29, five to six times daily, the Nazis would make full-force attacks on the Metalworking Factory. Some parts of the factory changed hands several times daily; the Germans would hold them in the morning, we would win them in the afternoon, then at night the Germans would grab them again.

The worst days were when the enemy held an unopposed position on top of Mamayev Hill, and used it for an observation post. From this spot, they could watch our ferry crossings and aim their artillery fire at us at will.

From Mamayev Hill, the Krauts could keep all the approaches to the offices of the Metalworking Factory under surveillance. In addition, less than a hundred yards from our bunker there was a tower used by German forward artillery observers. They had even ranged in on the entrance to our bunker.

At eight AM Monday morning, an artillery bombardment began. Shells were exploding by our bunker, blowing everything above it to smithereens. Trees growing along the trolley lines had been turned into stiff charcoal posts. Rails were torn out of the ground by the shockwaves from the explosions, and the rails were mangled into twisted steel balls. Trolley cars lay without windows or doors, scattered like broken children's toys. In the yard, among the tangled rails, you could see helmets, spent cartridges, abandoned crates of ammo, and torn gas masks and medical packs. Corpses lay half covered in dirt, no longer caring which side they had been fighting for.[19]

I barely paid attention to any of this. I had one goal in mind – to reach the safety of my bunker and fall asleep. I was passing out on my feet, and I wandered past this nightmare scenario like a sleepwalker. When I reached what I thought was our bunker, I heard the muffled sounds of German artillery returning to work on our front lines. The earth was aching and groaning with the violence being done on its surface.

Exhaustion pressed me against the wall of the bunker. I squatted down, then leaned back until sleep overpowered me. What a strong force it can be – neither the sound of pounding fists nor of shooting guns can call you back, when sleep wants to carry you away. I crawled to the center of the room and felt something soft underneath me. Explosions were shaking the bunker but I paid no attention to them. I had slipped into a dream about the train ride from Vladivostok, and to me the explosions were like the shaking of the train on the tracks.

We were somewhere near Omsk, and I had been summoned by our CO to his car. I took a seat on a bench, next to a young woman. She was smiling; a beautiful woman dressed in uniform, with four triangles on her lapel, which meant she was a nurse. I could feel the warmth of her shoulder against mine, and as the train moved it tossed us against each other. How enjoyable – and I could see the nurse was enjoying this too. She had depthless blue eyes, like a mountain lake, and her gentle gaze began to stir my heart.

Meanwhile, our CO was pacing up and down the car,

---

[19] In the early days of the battle the Germans had immense air and artillery superiority. To meet this challenge, the Red Army approached the German front lines as closely as possible, even digging their entrenchments next to the German entrenchments, so that the Germans could not use air or artillery strikes against the Russians without hitting their own troops.

pontificating about the dangers of our mission. "The enemy can derail us, if we let our guard down," he said. "To make sure that doesn't happen, don't allow any unauthorized personnel into your car. You can allow access to railway personnel to clean up or deliver food, but pay careful attention to their activities…" and so on. The CO thought Kraut saboteurs might be riding with us, posing as soldiers or railway employees.

The train slowed as it approached the station, and we got up from our seats. I stood up to let the young lady exit first, then took her by the hand, and we strode through the crowd of sailors on the platform. I introduced myself and she told me her name was Maria Loskutova, but everyone called her Masha.

Then she said: "I'll call you Vasya. It's nice to meet a Vasya."

I had to laugh. "Russia's got a million Vasyas," I said.

"That's true," she replied, "but you're the first sailor I met named Vassili, and I think your name will bring me luck. Let's take a vow to help each other through the war, like brother and sister."

I looked into those depthless blue eyes, and wondered, "Why does this beauty need me for a brother?"

But I gave her my word as a sailor that I would take care of her and protect her, as if she were my own sister. She gave her word that until the war's end she would obey me like her own brother.

With those words, we found ourselves back on the train. The brakes were screeching as the wheels skidded on the rails. At this moment, I was distracted and half woke up, and the dream encounter with Masha Loskutova went out of my mind. I was in a dark space and noticed a multitude of fellow sleepers, but my dream was so pleasant, that I was able to push back wakefulness and return to the bliss of sleep. As I nodded off I thought it unusual that no one around me was snoring. Then the dream returned, with remarkable continuity.

When we reached a station, my friend Kolya got the nail on his left index finger torn off in a sliding door. Myself and sailor

Nikolai Starosin were called to escort Kolya to the medical aid car. I was not going to miss the opportunity to pay a visit to Maria Loskutova, as I knew she would be on duty at the medical station.

The train halted at a signal post, and Kolya, Nikolai and I hopped out and ran back along the tracks towards car No. 15. No 15 was the only car in the train with private passenger compartments. It contained the division's HQ, along with the hospital and surgery.

The three of us jumped onto No 15's running board as the train began picking up speed. We were hanging from the door, and Nikolai Starosin was knocking. At first there was no response, then the guard on duty sternly shook his finger at us. He only opened the door when Kolya displayed his blood-spattered hand and shouted about having been sent by our CO to get patched up.

When we reached the aid station, Nikolai Starosin pounded on the door. Nikolai, like myself, had fallen head over heels for Masha.

"Nurse, we have a wounded sailor here!" he hollered.

The door to the compartment opened, and Masha came out, from behind a dull green curtain.

She looked radiant, and us sailors were all grinning at each other. She knew what was up, of course, but she immediately concentrated on Kolya's injured hand,

"Sit down," she told him, "while I prepare a clean dressing for you."

Kolya sat by a metal table, while Nikolai and I hid behind the doorway of the dispensary.

Masha put on a white robe and tied on her snow white nurse's cap, while we feasted our eyes on her beauty. Even her starched uniform couldn't hide her curves. As she bandaged Kolya, she looked like a saint on a stained glass window. None of us could tear our eyes away from her.

Then Masha opened up her notebook and asked Kolya's name.

By now, of course, Kolya was as much in love with this girl as Nikolai and me.

"I'll tell you, but you have to tell me yours first," he said.

Masha was exasperated.

"You sailors are all alike!" Her voice had taken on a sterner tone. "Just give me your hand."

"Sister," said Kolya, "just tell me your name, and I'll give you my hand, and my heart as well."

Masha frowned. "You mean Vasya hasn't told you about me?"

"Vasya say something about you? Not a word," Kolya lied.

"Never mind," she said. "You keep your heart to yourself. But put your hand on the table, and hold still, please."

As Masha finished bandaging Kolya's hand, something began to rumble and thunder. It was like a thunderstorm over the steppe.

I reached around me but nobody was there, and I was very hungry---so hungry I woke up, thinking that I had to eat something.

It was quiet and dark. I sat up, leaned back against a wooden wall, and tried to remember where I was. I pulled out a packet of tobacco and rolled a cigarette. I couldn't find any matches, and I remembered that early that morning, I had loaned my matches to the sailor Mikhail Masayev. I was almost positive that he had not returned them. I cursed him under my breath—Masayev had a bad habit of keeping everything you lent him. Things went into his pockets and you never saw them again. As I was thinking this, and fumbling through my pockets looking for matches, one of my hands brushed something nearby.

It was a face. I felt a moustache, and then sticky congealing blood.

I finally located my matches and lit one. My hands were shaking. In the flickering light I saw what at first looked to be men sleeping, but their legs and arms were frozen in odd angles. When I leaned forward, I saw that they were the slain bodies of Russian soldiers, dozens of them, tossed into this abandoned bunker. I lit another match and continued to look around. It was a walled wooden pit; it had been constructed solidly, a concrete bunker braced with heavy beams and tons of earth.

I tried rolling another cigarette, but by now my hands were shaking so badly, it took several attempts to roll the cigarette right. By the time I finished it and got it lit, my heart was beating like a hammer.

I realized that somehow I had been sleeping amidst corpses. My comrades must have taken me for dead and tossed me into a mass grave! I broke into a cold sweat, and the sleeves of my shirt became sticky with perspiration.

"Snap out of it!" I told myself. I crept forward along the wall. It ended at a heap of sand. I rested for a moment, then composed myself, and crawled off in the opposite direction. Then I ran into another wall. There was no way out. I crawled and scratched on the concrete walls in vain. Around me there were only walls and mounds of sand. There was no way out anywhere!

I had seen a shovel lying to one side of the pit when I lit my cigarette. A soldier in the graves detail must have dropped it in when they finished burying these bodies. I fumbled my way over to the spot where I had seen the shovel. My hands closed around the shovel's handle, and I immediately began digging. I was thinking "just let me out of here, fast!" But no matter where I dug, the blade of the shovel struck wood. This pit had been walled up on all four sides.

I had been buried alive, and it was impossible to control my reactions. I began to hyperventilate, and then I realized that the air was getting stuffy. If I did not make my way out soon, I would suffocate, like a bug in a glass jar.

The tip of the shovel hit a wooden crate, and I stopped to see what was inside. Grenades – a whole box of them. Nearby I stumbled over abandoned weapons and ammunition. I backed away from the boards and beams and began shoveling again. I tried to think methodically, to figure out a way to keep from digging in spots where I had already been. This was difficult, in the dark, as I was panicking, terrified as my air supply diminished. I was throwing dirt towards the center of the pit, as I kept digging away.

"Let me get to freedom, let me see the sky, let me see my buddies again!" I muttered to myself. I would rather be killed in battle than buried alive!

I put all my strength into the job but I hit wood everywhere I turned. What can you do with a little field shovel? I collapsed onto the cool sand, and tried to figure out which direction would get me out. I couldn't think straight; my ears were ringing, and with every passing minute, breathing was getting more difficult.

It looked like I was doomed to suffocate, and the longer I sat there, the sooner death would come. I had to reach fresh air!

I grabbed the shovel and crawled back over the beams, to the hole that I had begun digging. I worked non-stop, flinging shovel-fulls of dirt behind me. Piles of sand were falling on my legs, lying heavier and heavier. I could barely breathe, and a lump was building in my throat. I couldn't inhale and couldn't exhale. I started seeing stars and rainbow-colored rings. With my absolute last strength, I shoved my legs against the wooden beams, and bashed at the wall with my shovel. I hit the wall three times. On the final thrust I broke through to emptiness, like a swimmer breaking the surface.

I collapsed face-first into the sand. I was still having trouble breathing, and I was surrounded by darkness. But this was the darkness of the night sky, and not that of the tomb.

When my eyes became accustomed to the dim light, I saw that I had managed to burrow out a pretty respectable tunnel, in between the timbers of the abandoned bunker.

Less than fifty yards away, from the lower windows of the Metalworking Factory, German tracer bullets were flying towards the Volga. The bullets arced out through the night in streams, one stream going to the west and the another to the east. Parachute flares were shining overhead, illuminating the twisted rails of the tramlines.

I saw that the only way I could return to the Russian lines would be to eliminate both the Kraut machine guns at the Metalworking Factory. I crawled back through the tunnel I had just carved, into the burial pit. I had to locate the box of grenades. It was dark, and I had run out of matches, so I fumbled through the pockets of a corpse. This was a disgusting task, but necessary.

In one guy's pocket, I felt a matchbox and a pouch with *makhorka*[20] inside. I immediately rolled a cigarette. Then I started tearing through the sand. I kept lighting matches until I located the box of F-1 grenades. I stuffed my pockets and an empty gas mask bag with as many grenades as I could carry, then crawled back out of the bunker.

The Kraut machine guns kept up their staccato firing of tracers. A flare exploded, hanging overhead, and I froze. I was so covered with filth, that no one would have been able to distinguish me from an inanimate object. I pressed my face to the ground.

Another flare popped above me, and both machine guns began firing in synch. Meanwhile everything was lit up by the artificial suns overhead. More flares continued to go off non-stop. I saw then that the German lines had edged into the factory office, turning it into a Kraut outpost. It was an enemy beachhead that threatened our lives.

One of their guns was set up on the ground floor, and the other was on the second floor, a few feet directly above. The guns rattled to life again. I inched along the wall until I was immediately below the sputtering gun on the first floor. I heaved a grenade through the first floor window, then without waiting for it to detonate, I tossed a couple more through the second floor window just above. The Kraut gunner on the first floor spotted me and tried to depress his gun so he could fire at me. That was when the first grenade I had tossed detonated, and blew him out the window. The subsequent grenade explosions destroyed the gun and the crew on the second floor.

[20] *Makhorka:* a cheap grade of Russian tobacco

From the eastern and western side of the offices, I heard the Russian charge ring out – the "ooorahh" – and Soviet soldiers flew into the attack. Later I learned that it was our second and fourth companies. The Krauts in the Metalworking Factory office were overrun, and that wing of the building was returned to our control.

When our commandos and officers reached the office and inspected the German's shattered machine gun positions, they began trying to figure out who it was who had knocked them out. These German gunners had our troops completely pinned down, so that no one in the company had been able to move a hair, neither an inch forwards or backwards.

No one thought of me. I was still covered with filth, and stood like an apparition against a wall, eavesdropping on our officers as they spoke. I was too worn out to interject a word. Then Captain Kotov's adjutant, Nikolai Logvinenko, bumped into me.

Logvinenko was a pudgy fellow with wire-rimmed glasses, long dark hair and a droopy moustache. He had been questioning the soldiers and collecting material for an account of the battle. Logvinenko had already filled up a dozen pages of his notebook with his scrawly handwriting.

When he caught sight of me, he wiped some filth off my face, then froze, dumfounded. He grabbed me by the sleeve and hauled me off to see Lieutenant Bolshapov.

We entered into a deep bunker, lit by its own generator. Lieutenant Bolshapov turned away from a map, and looked up to meet us.

I regarded Bolshapov with surprise. Why was he staring at me so intently? Finally he said, "He's alive, he's alive!"

I glanced behind me, to see who the hell he was talking about. Lieutenant Bolshapov vaulted to his feet and ran over and embraced me.

"Vasya," he exclaimed, "I thought we had buried you!"

Nurse Masha Loskutova was in the bunker, treating the wounded.

"You look ghastly," she said. She took a small mirror out and handed it to me.

It was true; I looked like recently exhumed corpse. My face and uniform were smeared with blood.

Captain Kotov came in. He took one look at me and then turned to Lt. Bolshapov.

"What's up with this guy?" Kotov could not recognize me under the filth that was covering my features. "Is he wounded or something?"

"No, Comrade Captain," said Bolshapov, with a grin. "This is Chief Master Sergeant Zaitsev. Zaitsev has been resurrected from the dead."

Kotov took another look at me.

"Get yourself cleaned up," he barked. "Then come back and make a report."

In the corner of the office stood a big barrel of water. No doubt the fascists had been using it, and it repelled me to have to touch it, but at that moment there wasn't any choice. Nikolai Logvinenko showed up with a safety razor, and someone else discovered a blade – ancient, but serviceable. A torn piece of bandage was my shaving brush.

After I cleaned up I reported to Captain Kotov's office, and recounted everything exactly as it had happened.

CHAPTER 6.
WITHOUT CATCHING
MY BREATH

German bombers were again circling overhead. They continued to bombard the Metalworking Factory, the Meatpacking Plant, and the Fuel Depot.

We had already grown accustomed to their tactics. Their first sorties would drop huge demolition bombs. Some of these were converted naval mines. These demolition bombs were fused so they would sink into the earth and then explode, ripping apart whole city blocks.

They were so powerful that a close hit could collapse our bunkers on top of us, so during this phase of the bombing we had to exit the bunkers, and take shelter in open trenches.

I witnessed one of these blockbusters as it raised an entire wall of the Meatpacking Plant from the ground, and broke it up into small fragments. The air grew dark with a mixture of dust and smoke, and breathing became difficult. When the dust settled, we saw that the explosion had tossed a slaughtered German soldier next to the body of one of our fellow seaman, Leonard Smirnov. The two men lay with their unfeeling arms wrapped over each other, like children's' rag dolls that had been tossed randomly into the dirt.

Some of these huge bombs also hit the fuel depot. The sheets of steel making up the storage tanks and cisterns were ripped and torn as if they were made of cigarette paper. Delayed action anti-personnel bombs had also been dropped. Their tails stuck up out of the ground for everybody to see. These were disgusting objects. They were something you would not relish discovering, that was for sure.

Shortly after one of these attacks I was sitting next to Sasha Lebedev, the brother of the wounded sailor we had met on the opposite bank of the Volga.

Sasha had just returned to our company from the field hospital. During our first day of battle, he had been scorched by a wave of burning gasoline.

The air around us was getting hotter. The Krauts had occupied the Transformer Room again, and they were firing explosive bullets. And their mortars were showering down shells on us like pears from an overturned basket. The smoke and dust were becoming worse by the minute.

I heard Sasha cough and looked over at him – sweat was dripping down his forehead. I asked him what was wrong.

"I'm fading," he said, "I can't breathe." Just as he finished saying this, a fragmentation bomb hit nearby. Sasha was thrown to the bottom of the trench, landing with his head by Lt. Bolshapov's feet. Sasha was OK, merely shook up.

Bolshapov looked down at him and said, "No worries. You'll get used to this."

They stared at each other. Sasha mouth hung open as he tried to catch his breath.

"Listen, sailor," said Lt. Bolshapov, "the Krauts will shell us, shoot at us, then finally they'll charge. We'll greet them, smooth them out, and iron them flat. In other words, we're going to send them back empty–handed."

A messenger from the fourth company arrived, his uniform smoking, his eyebrows scorched, his hair practically singed off.

Through his torn pants you could see bleeding abrasions all over his legs.

This messenger reported to Lt. Bolshapov that Kraut submachine gunners were moving against our positions in the Dolgiy Ravine, and that the lieutenant of the company there had requested backup from us.

The Nazis were advancing in three orderly lines, one after the other, like waves marching towards a beach. They were steadily inching closer to the Volga.

Leonid Seleznev the medic, Nikolai Logvinenko, and Sasha Gryazev dragged out one of our Maxim guns, and set it up among some bricks. The Maxim gun worked like a charm. It stopped the first two waves of Krauts, but then we saw that the surviving enemy soldiers were still creeping forward, crawling closer and closer. The Maxim gun's crew could not depress their angle of fire enough to shoot at these crawling Nazis; they were too close, like an army of slugs. Nikolai Logvinenko grabbed a Tommy-gun, hung two grenades from his belt, and ran to cut them off. The grenades flew – the Germans had not been expecting this type of greeting. Their assault ground to a halt and Nikolai Logvinenko ran up to them and raked them at close range, emptying his entire drum magazine.

Now the momentum of the battle had reversed. We had recovered the initiative. We inched forward in small groups, towards the Icehouse of the Meatpacking Plant.

The Germans chose this moment to unleash their surprise. Two heavy caliber machine guns had been positioned on top of the Icehouse, and they opened fire on us. The bullets lashed around us like whips. We had no choice except to stop and hug the ground. Any movement could be fatal, so each of us did our best to make ourselves invisible.

To my left was Seaman Okrihm Vasilchenko, and to my right I noticed a skinny little runt of a soldier. He wore ragged puttees, and his helmet was falling down to his eyebrows. I have already mentioned that I am not very tall myself, but this fellow was half-a-head shorter than me. He crawled towards a mound of cobblestones, as dozens of bullets whistled past his ears.

I was busy clawing at the earth with my fingernails, trying to scrape some sort of shallow foxhole. The other men around me had been also been reduced to groveling in the dirt. But the short fellow in the puttees was relentlessly crawling forward. He reached some cobblestones and shifted his rifle to his right arm. The rifle had some sort of strange little pipe on top of it.

The next second the short guy was aiming, and WHAM! He shifted his weight, and a few seconds later he fired again, WHAM, and suddenly, both machine guns were silent!

The rest of us charged, showered the Germans with grenades, and captured the Icehouse. The Germans had been depending on their machine guns to keep us pinned down. They had not set up any fallback positions - so we caught them unprepared. The short guy's taking out the machine guns had made this an easy conquest. After the battle I caught up with Okrihm Vasilchenko.

"Who was that midget?" I asked him.

"Chief," said Okrihm, "that's no midget, that's a sergeant, the sniper Galifan Abzalov."

My curiosity got the better of me, and I took off, to try and meet with the sharpshooting Sergeant Abzalov. He had already taken up a new position, and I slowly approached his hideaway in the rubble. I was eager to talk with him, to express my admiration, and to inquire about how he had managed to get this assignment. To be honest, I was envious. And after all, I was a good shot myself, and I was thinking that Abzalov might help me get assigned to his unit.

I saw the little guy scrunched up, with what I would learn to be his perennial foul temper twisting his mouth into a sneer. He spotted me as I approached, and before I could say a word, I caught sight of his slanting green eyes.

"Hey you, sailor," he hissed, "piss off! Can't you see you'll draw fire to me!"

I crawled away. Had I ever been stupid! No doubt Abzalov

thought I was some sort of cretin. I told to myself that I would search him out again that night, and then we could talk.

All the soldiers – theirs and ours - who could still walk, had left the battlefield. The area around us was strewn with enemy dead and wounded. Their medics and stretcher-bearers crept about, providing aid to the wounded.

My blood boiled at the unfairness of this spectacle. The enemy medics weren't helping all of their wounded, but only a chosen few: officers and "specialists" from their Pioneer companies. They were leaving the rest of their men crying out, waving their arms, and making desperate but futile pleas, as they tried to awaken some compassion in these so-called medics. It would have been no trouble at all for us to pick off their medics, but we wouldn't stoop to targeting German medical personnel – not even those who were acting so despicably.

Meanwhile our fourth company, under the command of *Starshiy* Lieutenant Yefindeyev, mustered a final bust of strength. They started a firefight with a detachment of the enemy that had been withdrawing along the Dolgiy Ravine.

Nazi planes returned to plague us again. They were like vindictive wasps. Their formations came in over the Volga, and then one after the other the aircraft would peel off to dive bomb our positions in the *Krasny Oktyabr* Factory, and our recently established bridgehead at the base of Mamayev Hill.

In the meanwhile the Krauts had brought up some fresh meat, new replacement troops. As soon as the aerial bombardment halted, they threw these soldiers at our positions along the Dolgiy Ravine.

I was to hear later that Hitler had stage-managed this battle personally, down to the company level, with his lackey Paulus always keeping him informed on developments. So it may have been Hitler himself who was ordering company after company to throw away their lives against the jagged wall of our defenses.

The German trenches, and the adjacent ruins, were brimming with gray uniformed, freshly shaven young soldiers. How many of them were there - tough to say. It didn't make any difference to us; our job was to wipe them out. We knew we could not let them reach the Volga!

A katyusha barrage from a battery on the far side of the Volga got range on the advancing German infantry. The katyushas hit the ravine mercilessly, and the German attack was stopped before it began. The Nazis there were liquidated, blown into bits. We inspected the ravine afterwards, and it was impossible to determine how many bodies filled it.

Despite this victory, it was a sad day for us, because several of the katyushas fell short and hit our own men. Midshipmen Itkulov was killed, and my fellow countryman from Krasnoufimsk, Kuzma Afonin, was struck down by a fragment from a rocket that hit him in the head.

Kuzma and I had served together at the same naval depot. When our group of 20 volunteers had been mobilized to go to the front, we had a stopover in Krasnoufimsk. It was there that I saw the real beauty of his soul.

It was early morning, and a light drizzle was falling. The cobblestones of the city were glistening, wet with the rain. Our group was ambling through the town, en route to the train station. We walked about haphazardly with our rucksacks slung over our shoulders. We were barely in formation, walking idly, rather than marching.

We saw some housewives, wearing headscarves and carrying empty shopping bags, as they trudged to the market. When they saw us they stopped, each of them running their eyes across the rows of sailors, searching for familiar faces.

Kuzma did his best to stand out. He raced around our formation, peering to the right and to the left, as he searched for his mother, was she among them? He tried to run ahead, but the commander of the column ordered him back in line.

Our commander that day was Captain Filipov, a captain 3rd class. Filipov was strutting a bit for the residents of Krasnoufimsk. He held his head high and thrust out his chin.

And he ordered the rest of us to look smart.

We were in a neighborhood of single-story houses with verandahs and beautiful wooden gates. The rest of us sailors regarded Kuzma with a mixture of sympathy and envy. Here he was in his hometown, walking along a street he had run up and down a thousand times. At each house we passed, he would rattle off the names of its residents, as if to check his memory.

Suddenly he grew pale, and shouted with excitement.

"There's my house, and that's my mother!"

There was a short gray-haired lady standing at the gate, by the wickets.

Excitement ran along our entire column like an electric shock. Kuzma requested permission to break formation, then he ran across the street. Meanwhile, the column stopped as the rest of us sailors watched the reunion.

Kuzma's mother was wearing a dark blouse and a cardigan, with the sleeves rolled up to her elbows. The cardigan hung lopsided on her shoulders, her black skirt was tucked up under her belt, and her frayed boots were covered in dirt. Obviously she had been working in the garden.

When she saw Kuzma running towards her, she cried out,

"Kuzma, my son!"

We could see that she wanted to run to him, but her legs would not obey her.

Mother and son embraced. Tears were running down Mrs. Afonin's cheeks.

"Tell me I'm not dreaming," we heard her say.

As we witnessed this, each of us was thinking of his own mother.

Mother – it is a sacred word. It is the honor and root of the family. A mother represents the family's immortality. Our very first word is directed to her: "Mama." And when a soldier is about to leave this world, the words that escape his lips are also spoken to her. There is no deeper, or more noble thing on this earth, than a mother's love for her children.

Kuzma was a tall and strapping fellow. He towered over his mother. He took her in his arms, and in plain view of the whole column, rocked her back and forth and held her to his chest, as if she were a little child.

Kuzma understood that this was no picnic we were headed into. There are no wars without casualties. He knew that this could be the last time he'd press close to his mother's heart, and he was crying. I don't know if they were tears of sorrow or tears of joy, but they were heartfelt and genuine.

Our whole column stood there, holding our breath. Kuzma kicked opened the gate and he and his mother stepped into the yard, where we could no longer see them.

When he returned to his position the column started moving forward again. We stood up straight and got into proper formation, as if we were on parade. As we marched the street echoed with our stamping feet.

This was our salute to Kuzma's mother. As we turned the corner, she was standing in her garden, next to a big birch tree. Mother and a birch tree: the two symbols of *rodina*, the Russian motherland.

Kuzma was in formation behind me, and he whispered, "It's OK Vasya, we're going to get through this alive, my mother told me so."

But now Kuzma was gone. How was I going to explain to his mother that "friendly fire" had killed her son? It had been an accident of war. Our commanders had no choice but to call in the katyusha strike as close as possible, and a katyusha is not the most precise of weapons. But would any of this make a difference to Kuzma's mother? As I tried to write a letter to her, I couldn't make myself explain what had happened, and I ended up crushing the paper into a ball. I would have to write her at another time, when I could control my emotions.

Now it was up to me to seek retribution. And the ones who were guilty of Kuzma's death were the invaders. I picked up my rifle and left the bunker. I would avenge Kuzma. The enemy would find no mercy from me, here in Stalingrad.

~~~

Despite our best efforts, a group of German "Pioneers" had forced their way through to the Volga. They cut off our 13th Guards Division – or what was left of it – which was commanded by the Soviet general A.I. Rodimtsev.

By the direct orders of General Chuikov, of the 62nd army high command, a reserve battalion of Guards from his headquarters, and a reserve tank company, were rushed to our sector. They were given the task of taking out the enemy "Pioneers."

The commander of our regiment, Major Metelev, ordered a group of us Tommy-gunners to that sector, under the command of *Starshiy* Lieutenant Bolshapov.

This battle dragged on for several hours. A secure path between our regiment and the 13th Guards was finally established. Only a brick three-story building remained under German control.

A brief pause in the battle allowed us to replenish our ammo, install new barrels in the machine guns, and lay minefields.

The Germans were not interested in allowing us to consolidate our gains, or in leaving us to have a peaceful night. Just before dusk, their Stukas returned. Now we were holding Dolgiy Ravine again, and the Stukas scattered their payloads into it.

Everything hit us at once. All our survivors of the 13th, plus our unit and the special guards unit from HQ, raced to take shelter in the same place.

I counted heads: we had suffered a lot of losses. Our strength was really down. I didn't know if we were going to have enough firepower to repel the attack that we knew was sure to follow the aerial bombardment.

This time the Germans were employing their allies, the Romanians, as proxies. Probably they were tired of burning up their own troops. So they had ordered the Romanians to advance on the Volga. We had learned that Romanian officers would roar at the top of their lungs when they attacked, they must have thought it would strike terror into us. As soon as we heard them screaming, we knew who was on the way, and we saw the first wave of attackers as they made their approach.

All through this early period of the battle we had very thin air support. Our air force could only muster night flights with plywood biplanes that were as slow as the last dregs of tea being poured from a samovar. These noisy biplanes would drop supplies for us, circle, and bomb the Germans and their allies.

These biplanes were so slow that they were sitting ducks for ground fire. The enemy gunners could target them merely by the noise they made. And they were crewed by young women, by brave Soviet girls. The Nazis had succeeded in knocking down several of these biplanes, which crash-landed in the Romanians' sector. We had reports of the Romanian soldiers raping and torturing the captured Soviet pilots. So you could say that we were sharpening our knives for the Romanians. We could barely wait for the opportunity to confront them. And now these fools were rushing at us, their officers shouting, as if their shouting would frighten us into surrender.

Suffice it to say that very few Romanians left the field that day. Our sacred Russian steppe was fertilized with their corpses.

CHAPTER 7.
A QUIET DAY

At that time the only thing I had to put on my feet were tarpaulin boots meant for someone else. The boots were too big for me and kept flopping off. These boots had been made with iron caps at the toe and heel, so they were very loud. Anytime I stepped on a hard surface, the boots announced my presence to the world, including any enemy soldiers who might be in the vicinity. Fortunately, no Krauts had been around at an inopportune moment. In the factory workshops, it would have been easy for them to hear my steps.

I was stomping down the steel staircase of the Metalworking Factory office, and got the feeling that someone was watching me. I had unholstered my pistol, when I saw that this someone was a shy young woman in a nurse's uniform. She emerged from behind a column at the base of the stairs. She had a medical bag thrown over her shoulder. This nurse, whomever she was, was about my height.

"Your ears can surely play tricks on you!" she said. " I thought you were somebody else."

"How's that, my dear?" I asked.

She was clearly irritated with herself. "How could I ever manage to have confused you with him?"

She flashed a smile at me, took me by the hand, and led me to a better-lit side of the cellar. I followed her obediently, observing her profile. No, it wasn't Masha Loskutova. Masha had been moved across the Volga, with the medical battalion, and I was sure she had already forgotten the oath we had sworn to each other on the train. Well, enough about Masha. The other side of the Volga may as well have been Mars, for all the likelihood I had of ever seeing it again.

The young woman and I finally made it into the light. She had beautiful long brown hair, and warm hazel-colored eyes. I was sure I had seen her before, but I couldn't place where or when. Now she was taking a good look at me.

"So," I said, "I presume I'm not the guy you were expecting?"

"Your boots on the stairs sounded exactly like his, and I expected to see a tall, dark, fellow, so I got excited and hid behind the column." She said all this matter-of-fact, by way of explanation. Clearly I was not in the running for her heart, my mysterious competitor had already staked out that territory. But I couldn't resist poking a little fun at her.

"So," I asked her, "does Mr. Tall, Dark, and Handsome, know that you're carrying a torch for him?"

She stared at me, irritated by my impertinence. "Do you think I'm so naive, that I would let him know?" she asked.

"Well," I protested, "you told me."

Then she realized I was teasing her. Her long eyelashes fluttered. "You're a complete stranger, why shouldn't I tell you?"

Now that we were in the light, she inspected me from head to foot.

"How did your uniform get so torn up?"

I had been on patrol the previous evening.

"I had a rude encounter," I explained, "with some barbed wire."

A needle and a piece of long green thread appeared in her hands.

"Sit down sailor, and take off your shirt."

I didn't object. I was enjoying the company of a beautiful lady. Meanwhile she sewed away like a professional tailor.

I couldn't take my eyes off her. She was growing more beautiful by the minute.

"Stop staring at me!" she exclaimed. "You're acting like a lonesome dog. And don't get any ideas. You know I'm taken."

I protested: "But that guy doesn't even know you exist!"

"I can't stand short, snub-nosed, blue-eyed men," she said. "As soon as I finish this, you bug out. Go crawl under some barbed wire."

I felt obligated to make some reply. "You can hang a dog on a tall guy,"[21] I said.

"Cats can be stuck to shrimps like you," she said, "and I can't stand the smell of cats."

"Of course," I conceded, "you're right about that."

"What, you goof, you're agreeing with me? Well, don't just sit there with your mouth hanging open, what more have you got to say?"

I had to come up with a proverb that would make a sufficiently witty reply.

"There's a saying that goes, "great is the figure of a fool, small is the piece of gold, but precious….""

She was working quickly and had almost finished patching my shirt. My companion backed away as if she had been scalded with boiling water, and she hurled the shirt, needle, and thread into my face.

"You're so clever, finish it yourself. I'll find my own "precious thing," thank you!"

She ran upstairs and vanished. I tried to follow her but she had disappeared among the city's ruins. I sat down in the spot where she had just been sitting, and sewed up the last hole in my sleeve. Then I tucked the needle and thread into my pocket, and with a bitter taste in my mouth, thought to myself: "Matching proverbs isn't my forte."

And that is the way the seventh of October, 1942 began for me.

~~~

[21] "You can hang a dog on a tall guy" – a Russian proverb with no English equivalent.

This was a relatively quiet day. We repaired the housing on our Maxim gun, installed spare barrels on our Tommy-guns, filled our bandoliers with bullets, and laid out and sorted the various grenades we had: Russian, captured German ones with long handles, and donated American "pineapples."

As for the Germans, they were keeping to themselves and weren't making any moves.

That night passed in tense expectation of what was to come.

Dawn broke with the crackling of machine guns. Once the sun rose, street fighting broke out near the *Krasny Oktyabr* Factory and the Meatpacking Plant. The earth by Mamayev Hill boiled and bubbled with artillery and mortar explosions. But in our battalion's sector, in the portions of the Metalworking Factory that we held the enemy was silent. I felt like shouting: "What are you bastards waiting for, come out and fight!"

The Germans finally got to us, about ten AM. First was the artillery, then came the mortars. Then the Luftwaffe arrived to finish the job. Bombs were exploding everywhere.

Suddenly everything stopped: their planes disappeared and their artillery re-directed its fire at targets deeper in our lines. We were sure an attack was about to come, and some of us kept busy by digging in deeper. Others lay motionless, with their eyes wide open, not knowing what would happen next.

But no attack followed.

What had happened was, that the Krauts had come off worse from their last bombardment than we did. The night before we had not prevented them from approaching our front lines, and many of them had slipped through, but they hadn't had any opportunity to dig in. Now their own heavy weapons had blasted their infantry to smithereens. They were unable to regroup and get up the momentum for another attack. They let the opportunity for a new attack slip by, and, in the interim, we managed to advance, unopposed, to new positions.

Lt. Bolshapov had some of our guys set up the Maxim gun in the boiler room of the Metalworking Factory office. It was next to the office where I had taken out one of the Kraut's machine guns not many days before. But now the location was an even better firing position: the most recent Kraut artillery barrage had flattened all the rubble and ruins, increasing the Maxim gun's arc of fire.

Meanwhile the Krauts had moved up some fresh units and with these new replacements, gone over to the attack. The distance between us was less than 150 yards. Our machine gun halted their first wave, but not before they reached the factory boiler room.

In order to suppress our heavy machine gun, the Krauts rolled out a small field piece, positioned it by a railway engine and opened fire at point-blank range. Shells were exploding inside the boiler room. Our machine gunner and his loaders were forced to take cover.

We had to destroy the cannon and its crew. But how were we going to do this, with a sniper or with grenades?

I caught sight of Galifan Abzalov, the "midget" sniper. Abzalov was always turning up unexpectedly, at critical moments. He was up on the roof of the Metalworking Factory. How he got up there, under such withering fire, I'll never know. Abzalov shot three times, and then the Krauts noticed him. He scooted to the side of the roof, then sprawled to one side, his rifle hanging over the edge.

They couldn't have got him!

Leonid Seleznev, our medic, a fellow who wore thick glasses and was too near-sighted to shoot at anything, gritted his teeth and made it up to the roof. He crawled across the tiles and hollered: "Abzalov, are you alive?"

Abzalov replied: "Two snipers have me pinned in their sights. I'm stuck here 'till dark. Whatever you do, don't come any closer!"

The medic beat a quick retreat and reported Abzalov's situation to Lt. Bolshapov.

"Alright," said Bolshapov, "then we've got to take out the cannon with grenades. I need a volunteer."

A messenger from the 4th company, Pronischev, the Siberian tractor driver – immediately stepped forward.

"Look, Pronischev," said Lt. Bolshapov. The two men were peering just above the slit trench, wincing as Kraut bullets flew nearby. "…run across the courtyard and hide by the foot of that wall. Then wait and check the direction of fire, don't move until you're sure you've located the Krauts. Then, as soon as their fire slacks off, crawl into the crater by the wall, and from there you can proceed to the railway engine. Once you're behind the engine, you can hit the cannon with grenades. We'll be giving you covering fire all the way. Don't take any foolish chances, understand?"

"This is my second year on the front, sir," said Pronischev, "*kak dva pal'tsa obossat.*"[22]

Pronischev hooked two grenades in his belt, put a fresh clip in his pistol, saluted, and vaulted out of our position, running past the trenches in a zig-zag.

Misha Masayev, another sailor, was lying next to me.

"Do you think he can pull it off?" Misha asked.

As Misha asked me this, I was blasting away at any spot the Krauts might put their heads up.

"If we give him enough covering fire," I replied.

Pronischev had made it across the courtyard, and he was supposed to continue following the lieutenant's instructions and creep along the wall to make his approach. Instead he stood up and took off in a bee-line, straight for the railway engine.

Bolshapov stood up and shouted at him: "Get back, you fool, I order you, get back!"

Pronischev ignored the lieutenant and continued barreling forward like a football player intent on making a goal. The lieutenant was shouting himself hoarse. The rest of us held our fire, because we were afraid of hitting Pronischev.

Pronischev ran across the open bridge and skirted the boiler room. He came up on the Transformer Room. The Germans held

[22] *"kak dva pal'tsa obossat"*: "..it'll be a piece of cake."

their fire. They must have been astounded, either that or they thought that Pronischev was running over to surrender to them.

He reached the Transformer Room, and had only another few yards to make it to the vantage point behind the train's engine. Then the Germans came out of their stupor and opened fire, and Pronischev halted, turned his face to us, and collapsed.

We all grew numb. Lt. Bolshapov turned pale. For a minute he was silent, then he spoke up: "That's what taking a stupid risk will get you!"

The lieutenant looked like he was ready to tear out his hair. He turned to the rest of us, his eyes glaring, and asked: "Who can rid us of that damn cannon?"

Misha Masayev and I exchanged a glance. The look Misha gave me told me to proceed.

I cleared my throat.

"Lieutenant," I said. "Permit Masayev and me to execute the order."

Misha Masayev was a tall and powerful Tartar with long arms and a smartly curled moustache. He was one of the larger men in our company.

Political officer Danilov had joined us. I overhead him ask Bolshapov, in a low voice: "Are these sailors for real? Can they pull this off?"

"They'll come through for us," Bolshapov replied.

Danilov studied us, then asked: "*A eto smozhesh?*[23] So what's your plan?"

"First we'll transit the wall by the workshop, next…" and I pointed to a trench that stood by the wall.

"That trench is full of Kraut corpses," protested Bolshapov, "and that route will leave you exposed to enemy fire. There'll be no stupid heroics!"

"Sir," I said, "allow me to explain. When we held that position a few days ago, I reconnoitered it. The trench abuts an underground heating duct. We can crawl through it. We go

[23] "*A eto smozhesh?*": What about this, can you do it?

through the duct, we exit by the engine, and voila! The Kraut's cannon will be in grenade range."

Lt. Bolshapov and political officer Danilov held a brief, hushed conversation.

"Alright," said Bolshapov. "But don't rush it, remember we can't help you from here. Everything is riding on you guys, so don't screw up."

Misha Masayev and I took off through the Germans' abandoned trench. Because of the intensity of the battles of the past week, the Germans had been unable to retrieve any of their dead, and the corpses were soft and rotting. Neither Misha nor myself had anticipated how bad the stench was going to be, and we were practically choking. We had to tread carefully. If you planted your feet on one of the bodies it would push right through.

When we reached the heating duct we crawled in on all fours, first me, then Misha. It was dark, wet, and stifling. The floor beneath my hands was slippery and sticky. It was big enough to enter but once you were inside, because it was so narrow, it was impossible to turn around. Misha, with his wide shoulders, was having trouble. I could hear him gasping and grunting behind me, and I had to stop and wait for him. Misha finally caught up to me.

"Keep crawling!" he admonished me, "what are you waiting for?"

The heating duct changed directions, and we were relieved to have some fresh air coming through. There had to be a fracture or some outlet nearby, as our breathing became easier.

We reached a fork and I guessed that we should make a right. After five more minutes of crawling, we ended up in a brick-lined pit, covered by an iron roof. It was one of the inter-workshop drainages that linked the factory's plumbing system. We sat there and tried to figure out if we were beneath the part of the factory occupied by the Germans, or under the boiler room where our Maxim gunners were stationed.

I tried looking through some slits in the iron cover. We were impatient at being cooped up. I knew we had to get on with our job as soon as possible, and our job was to take out the Kraut cannon.

"What's up?" Misha asked.

"I can't see a damn thing!" I responded.

The two of us heaved off the cover and it clattered to the floor. We saw that we had found our way into an enormous workshop. Its walls were charred by the ferocity of the battles within. It was full of lathes and unfinished machine components. Everywhere dead soldiers lay across them, dead sailors from the Pacific fleet and dead Nazis, lying next to each other. The bodies were on their backs, their stomachs, and curled up on their sides.

Misha and I clambered up into the workshop, crawling past a turning machine, and pressed close to the floor behind it. There was no roof to this room. It had long since been blown away, and we could see the sky. Planes were circling overhead, engaged in an air battle. Soviet fighters had finally been moved up, and were starting to chip away at the enemy's air superiority.

After we caught our breath, Misha and I started sliding towards the boiler room. Misha bolted and rolled, making it safely.

"Vasya, come on!" he called. He was pressed against the wall, waiting for me.

I made ready to dash after him, but the enemy had spotted us and opened up with rifles and submachine guns. Something scorched my right leg, and immediately the leg felt much heavier. It was difficult to drag it across the floor. I inched slowly over to Misha, while the enemy kept on shooting. By the time I reached Misha, my trousers were drenched in blood.

"You're wounded?" he asked.

My leg was not hurting, so I shook my head, no.

Inside the boiler room were six of our Tommy-gunners and one machine gunner, the sailor Plaksin. Since their group had been cut off from our battalion, they had turned the boiler room into a fortress, from which they had been able to repel one

German attack after another.

Misha and I were amazed by their cunning and ingenuity. They had taken several of their Tommy-guns and aimed their barrels through breaches in the wall. The Tommy-guns had been bracketed in place by twisted pieces of water pipe. They had run wires from the triggers back to Plaksin, who at this stage was the only soldier left with injuries minor enough to be able to fire anything.

I asked Plaksin how it worked, and he demonstrated by jerking on the wires. The infernal racket in the closed space made Misha and me cover our ears.

Judging by the amount of incoming fire we were taking, the Germans must have thought we had an entire company in the boiler room.

Plaksin, Misha, and I decided on a plan to hit the German's mobile cannon. Misha and I would approach the railway engine while Plaksin covered us with the Maxim gun.

We started off crawling, explosive bullets whizzing and cracking inches past our faces. A green flare shot off and Misha and I slid into a crater.

"Misha," I said, "did you see that? It's Bolshapov's signal that he's seen us!"

Our troops began to direct heavy fire at the Krauts around us, but it wasn't enough to pin the Krauts down.

Misha hissed like a goose. "Lt. Bolshapov can't do anything for us out here. This is up to us." He thumped his big fingers against his chest. "Listen," he said, "..this Tartar from Kazan doesn't scare so easy. I'll show them what sailors are made of..."

Misha started crawling out of the foxhole and I yanked him back just in time, as an explosive bullet shattered inches from his face. We spotted the German riflemen and directed Plaksin's fire to them by shooting a red flare in their direction.

Plaksin opened up – the pounding of the Maxim was right behind us. He turned the Nazi riflemen into shredded limburger.

Plaksin had bought some time for us, and I crawled out of the foxhole, pulling myself forward with my elbows. My right leg had stopped bleeding, but it was dragging behind me. When Misha saw that I had made it, he set out to follow. But Misha didn't flatten himself out enough when he crawled, he looked like a beached whale. A German rifleman spotted him and opened up on him from a window of the Transformer Room.

I was in a dilemma. I was close enough to toss my grenades at the cannon, but I had to rescue Misha first. And as I was trying to figure out my best course of action, I stumbled across Pronischev. The Siberian was still breathing, but he was badly wounded.

I snatched up Pronischev's pistol, took cover behind the engine's wheel, aimed and fired. One German gun barrel vanished from the window of the Transformer Room, but another rifleman leaped up immediately to replace him. He was over-excited, and fired wildly at Misha, who was pinned down by the hail of bullets.

I checked how many shots I had left in the pistol's clip - only one remained. My wounded leg was giving me trouble. I dragged myself along the rubble, one elbow after the other, until I was directly under the window the German rifleman was firing from. I tried to get up, but with the muscles in my leg cramping, standing was difficult. So I rolled over on my back. I could see the arms of the enemy rifleman jerking with every shot, and he was cursing as he missed. Then he leaned forward to get a better angle. That was when I pointed the pistol at the base of his chin and pulled the trigger.

The slug went through the top of his skull and hit his helmet with a clang. The Kraut tumbled out of the window, his nose smashing against the concrete.

Misha saw that I had created an opening for him, and he leaped behind the train engine. Finally, one of us had achieved the vantage point! From this position, the Kraut cannon was less than a dozen yards away. Misha stood up straight. He had exceedingly long arms, like some tree ape. He scooted around the engine. He wound up and pitched a grenade, while shouting at the cannon's crew, "Here Krauts, catch!"

The grenade detonated in mid–air and knocked the cannon on its side. The cannon's crew was sliced up by the flying shrapnel, and they were screaming like pigs in a slaughterhouse. Misha's face was full of fury. He threw his second grenade at the screaming Nazis. It silenced them. Then Misha ran up and spiked the cannon by exploding a grenade in the breech. No Nazis would be using it again.

Although the threat from the cannon had been removed, our guys were still in too much disarray to move over to the attack. And the surviving Nazis in our vicinity took this chance to surround me and Misha. Maybe they were planning to capture us alive. The Nazis took great pleasure in torturing their captives publicly, so that other Russian soldiers would be compelled to see their comrades writhing in agony. But Plaksin spotted the Germans who were advancing on us and opened fire with the Maxim gun.

This gave Misha and me a chance to retreat. I ordered Misha to grab Pronischev, and he heaved the wounded sailor over his shoulder as if Pronischev had been a sack of potatoes. I jumped into the foxhole and Misha tried to follow me, but as soon as he left his cover behind the train engine, something flattened him. Misha and Pronischev had fallen into a heap, and I thought Misha was finished, but then he raised his head. A bullet had hit his helmet and stunned him, nothing more.

I knew we could not hold out in this isolated position much longer, so staying put was not an option. Then I saw two Nazis crawling our way. I heaved my last grenade towards them and they retreated.

Misha and Pronishcev had made it to the foxhole, and Misha was bandaging Pronischev's chest as Pronischev groaned and called out for water. By then it had turned dark. Our comrades in the boiler room were waiting for us to return.

Misha hoisted Pronischev onto his back and crawled off as I

followed. We were both extremely fatigued, and our exhaustion showed in our sluggish movements.

Tracer bullets whistled overhead, as if to point us out to the enemy.

Neither of us thought Pronischev was going to survive, but we had to get him back to our lines. The boiler room was silent and dark. Plaksin had been wounded and was lying next to the Maxim gun. Misha started to move him, and Plaksin woke up. He mumbled: "…the Germans are here," before passing out again. Plaksin was the only man from the original detachment in the boiler room who was still alive.

Misha and I could hear voices speaking in German on the other side of the wall. Obviously, we could not make our escape in that direction.

Pronischev muttered something incomprehensible. We lay him next to Plaksin. The German voices sounded farther away.

Misha and I cooked up a plan. He would head back to the battalion by passing through the heating ducts, the same way we had come, while I would stay and guard the wounded. So Misha took off down the tunnel and I lay still, listening for movement.

My leg had really started to ache, and I lay down next to the wall. I had scoured the floor of Plaksin's boiler room and found two grenades, and one clip for the pistol. So I was ready for whomever or whatever was going to come.

My leg started bleeding again, and I was passing in and out of consciousness. When I woke up, I could see that the night was almost at an end, and a blood-red dawn was breaking. The thump of grenades and the rattle of machine guns started to the east.

I heard the rush of footsteps and I pulled the pin on one of my grenades.

Plaksin had awakened as well. He said through his cracked lips: "Who's there?"

I put my hand to his lips to silence him, and huddled closer to the wall. Suddenly I heard voices speaking Russian. With all my remaining strength, I shouted: "Comrades, we're alive!"

Someone shouted, "We hear you!"

Lieutenant Bolshapov and Misha entered the room. Misha Masayev had reached our lines and brought our troops to rescue us.

CHAPTER 8.
I BECOME A SNIPER

For five days in a row, from the morning of October 16th, through to midday of the 21st, the Germans attacked our positions in the factory district. Bombers, artillery, tanks and infantry – they threw everything they had at us, to try and break us. The German high command was committed to pushing through to the Volga at any cost.

The enemy soldiers advanced ruthlessly, with no concern for casualties. At times, it seemed that Hitler had decided to drown his entire army in blood.

We were defending the Metalworking Factory, the petrol storage yard, the Meatpacking Plant and half of Mamayev Hill. In the beginning, we sustained the heaviest hits around the Tractor and *Barrikady* factories.

I can't say exactly what happened around the Tractor Factory, since I wasn't there. But even from a distance of several kilometers, things looked horrible. Hundreds of German planes were circling the Tractor Factory non-stop. We heard later that on the 17th of October alone, the Luftwaffe carried out seven hundred sorties against the Tractor and *Barrikady* factories. I calculated that the enemy dropped 6 bombs per Soviet defender, in a single day.

At the time, the Tractor Factory was being defended by three reduced strength divisions, all of them badly mauled. (One of them, the 112th, later had its 600 survivors converted to a regiment.)

The fascists met with fierce resistance. Our soldiers managed to defend and hold that area. We had learned to live under fire, and to the enemy, it must have seemed that the stones, the bricks, and even the dead were firing at them. The German response was to unleash relentless bombing and shelling, in an attempt to turn the city to dust. They even destroyed our dead, by running over them with the treads of their tanks, so there would be no bodies to recover.

It is difficult to sit by and watch, while your comrades are suffering. You feel as if you should be there in their place; that is just the nature of the Russian soldier. And so we appealed to our division commander, Nikolai Batyuk, to send a detachment of us sailors to the Tractor Factory as reinforcements. But Batyuk refused, saying, "That's exactly what the enemy wants us to do, to thin our defenses here and leave this position exposed." Colonel Batyuk – the favorite of the 62nd army, whom we nicknamed "Bulletproof Batyuk" – was right.

After forty-eight hours of attacks on the Tractor Factory, the enemy shifted their attention to our zone. It would have been impossible to calculate the number of bombs they dropped on the Metalworking Factory. What our fellow divisions must have been thinking about the punishment we were absorbing, I have no idea.

By this time each company in our battalion had been reduced to not more than 20 able-bodied soldiers. In the first hour of German bombing alone, twenty seven squadrons of German dive-bombers carried out four passes each. Their bombs kept dropping and dropping…

When their dive-bombers finished, they were followed by an artillery barrage. The repeated concussions left many of our men with their hands and lips trembling uncontrollably.

The German artillery had created a firestorm, and as soon as it slackened the enemy infantry charged us.

We beat back their first attack with the Maxim guns. The second wave succeeded in getting closer, and we had to repel them with grenades and Tommy-guns. The Germans' subsequent attacks began with a massive onslaught of grenadiers, who came from three sides simultaneously. These grenadiers penetrated on our right wing, and shortly afterwards on our center and on our left. All our positions were engulfed in hand-to-hand combat.

I let my attention slip for a moment, and a grenadier managed to stick me in the back with his bayonet. I must have collapsed, because the next thing I knew I was in the med station at battalion headquarters. Our stretcher-bearers had carried me there.

It was midday, and the battle was still raging outside. Several of our nearby bunkers had caved in from direct shell hits, burying wounded men who had been brought there for medical treatment. So now all the wounded that came in were being carried directly to this med station in battalion HQ.

Two older soldiers walked in with a stretcher, bearing a wounded sailor. They set him down on a cot, then they immediately took off again. These same guys may have been the ones who brought me in. I had been one of the lucky ones.

Apparently we were retreating. The Krauts had taken back the factory tool room. The turning shop was still no-man's land, but the Krauts had also taken back the Icehouse. Our fourth infantry rifle company had been pushed behind the trolley lines, and they had to dig in outside an unfinished red brick house nearby.

Two days earlier, the regimental commander, Major Metelev, had paid our company a visit, and he ordered that I be made a sniper. This is how it happened.

There had been a moment's calm, and a couple of us sailors were sitting in a shell crater with Lt. Bolshapov, having a smoke. Then we came under fire from a Kraut heavy machine gun. The machine gun was about 600 yards away, but because of the recent bombing, the gunner had a clear field of fire and was able to keep us pinned down. He was blasting away so we could not even lift up our heads.

Misha Masayev had a trench periscope, and he was looking over the top of the crater. "Vasya, there he is," he said, and handed me the periscope. I took a quick look, then raised my rifle, and practically without aiming, fired a shot. The gunner collapsed. Within seconds, two more gunners appeared, and in rapid order, I plugged each of them with a single bullet.

By chance, Colonel Batyuk had been watching this exchange through his binoculars.

"Who was that?" he asked, and Metelev told him it was me.

"Get him a sniper's rifle," Batyuk ordered.

So Metelev came over to visit us. He ordered me to keep track of all the Nazis I took out.

"Comrade Zaitsev," he said, "you've already got three. Start your tally with them…"

Circumstances did not allow me to begin adding to the tally that day. First of all, no sniper kill could be verified without filling out some forms, which required a description of events, my signature, and the signature of a witness. And I wasn't yet familiar with these procedures.

But what was more important, was that we were nearly surrounded, we had fallen back and lost a lot of our positions, and there was only one way out: by the passage through the Dolgiy Ravine, and then by slipping through the empty pipes of the petrol storage yard, which reached all the way down to crossing #62, on the riverbank. This was part of the same passage that Misha and myself had used to relieve Plaksin.

In the entire battalion only four of us knew about it, being myself, Misha Masayev, Lt. Bolshapov, and Captain Kotov. But we did not want to breathe a word about it. If we were to start withdrawing, it might have led our besieged troops to stampede. The pipes could only accommodate a few men at a time, and a mass retreat would be impossible – it would have been hopeless. So such an idea could not even be whispered about.

It would mean abandoning most of our equipment and all of our wounded. And the Nazis had been executing our wounded by the most hideous means, with flame-throwers, or by setting dogs on them.

Worse, any withdrawal would have been a direct contradiction of the orders from Comrade Stalin.

To get my mind off this idea, I looked around myself. Immediately above me, just beneath the roof, was a big ventilation pipe with an internal exhaust fan. An iron ladder reached up to the fan from the floor. Two days earlier, I had used this space for a sniper's nest. From the elevated vantage point, it was easy to observe the movements of the Germans below.

An artillery observer, Vassili Fyodanov, set up a position next to me. His telephone connection back to HQ was terrible, as his phone constantly buzzed and whined. This made Fyodanov very agitated. In order to be heard, he had to constantly shout into the handset. He was a big distraction, but despite being stuck next to him, I was able to keep cool and go about my business.

I liked being a sniper and having the discretion to pick my prey. With each shot, it seemed as if I could hear the bullet smashing through my enemy's skull, even if my target was 600 yards away. Sometimes a Nazi would look in my direction, seeming to stare right at me, without having the slightest idea that he was living out his final seconds.

A shell hit nearby and the shock wave rocked through the piping and tore the ladder from the wall. Fyodanov and I managed to escape the hail of fragments by diving into the cellar, where our battalion medical station was located, next to our battalion HQ. Nurses Klava Svintsova and Dora Shakhnovich, the very nurse who had sewn up my shirt, were tending to the wounded. It was then I remembered about my leg, and how I ought to have it looked at. The bandage had become torn when I ran into the cellar, and I could feel warm blood trickling down. I waited next to Dora. She was finishing bandaging the head of a wounded soldier.

She raised her gentle brown eyes and spoke with feigned severity:

"You never give up, do you? So the barbed wire stuck you

again?"

"Not this time," I said.

"Why do you keep hanging around and pestering me?" she asked.

"When you're in love," I said, "you're in love."

"You've certainly picked the right time to tell me about it," she said. She continued to bandage the sailor's head, without paying me any attention. Finally she finished with him, dabbed some cotton with alcohol and cleaned off her hands.

"Well, out with it, loverboy, what's up this time?"

She was so beautiful that I flustered for a moment, and almost forgot where I had been hurt. Then I told her about bandage on my leg.

"Don't stand there with your hands in your pockets," she said, "take off your pants and let me see the wound!"

I was embarrassed and was slow to unbuckle my belt.

"Really," said Dora, "do you think you're going to show me something I've never seen before? Hurry up!"

I dropped my pants and gritted my teeth as she applied alcohol to the wound. When I bent over to pull up my trousers blood trickled down my back from beneath my shirt.

"Whoa," said Dora, "hold it."

She had found the bayonet wound in my back. It was a flat cut just under the skin. Luckily the blade had not struck anything vital.

After Dora cleaned it and bandaged it, I left the med station and ran into our Battalion Commander, Captain Kotov. Kotov had just exited his office, and he was accompanied by his adjutant, Logvinenko. We stood at the door as Kotov surveyed the never-ending line of stretchers being carried in with wounded and dying soldiers.

Kotov threw open the door. "Just bring your pistols," he ordered, and we lay down our rifles and Tommy-guns in a corner of the cellar.

"Follow me!" Kotov said, and the captain started racing off

towards Dolgiy Ravine, with Logvinenko and me doing our best to keep up.

My wounds were taking their toll, and all this running, ducking and leaping through the ruins in pursuit of the captain was exhausting. Kotov and Logvinenko halted at a trench and I caught up with them there.

Captain Kotov was tired too. He leaned up against a wall of the trench, gasping. He had turned white as a sheet and beads of sweat covered his face.

I sat down next to him. I had to catch my breath before I could speak.

"Captain," I said, "we've just abandoned the wounded." It was the voice of my conscience, speaking to myself, more than speaking to the captain. But Kotov stared at me, his gasping making him resemble a fish out of water.

It seemed like my words startled him out of a stupor.

"We won't get a medal for this one, will we, Cap?" I asked.

Kotov recovered his composure. He brushed the dirt off his uniform, scanned the horizon, and spat in the direction of the Krauts. Then he took off at a run, heading back for our positions. Logvinenko and myself loped behind him, keeping low to avoid enemy machine gun fire.

By the time we returned to the cellar, the entire room and the floor above were crammed with casualties. The wounded had been laid out in two enormous halls, and our overworked medic Leonid Seleznev was rushing upstairs and downstairs, trying to keep men alive until a doctor could treat them. Wounded soldiers were literally crawling in from all sides. A reserve company of Tommy-gunners was covering all the approaches to the building.

The Captain and Logvinenko and I were too ashamed to look each other in the eye. We had panicked and run towards the Volga, leaving these helpless souls behind…it was shameful.

I was angry with myself and agitated, I smoked cigarette after cigarette to try and calm down. Then I climbed up the broken ladder to the second floor, back to my old sniper's nest.

Bullets were flying in through the windows and doorway, and I had to flatten myself like a worm. I inched my way over to a crack in the brick wall and took cover behind a pile of boards. When I peered out I managed to scan the surrounding area below. I could see that a Kraut heavy machine gunner had targeted our building. Unfortunately this gunner was over five hundred yards away.

I had forgotten my rifle in the medical aid station, and I had to back out inches at a time, so the pile of boards I was using for my protection would remain intact for the future. I was almost out of the position when I heard Logvinenko behind me.

"Vasya, why are you wriggling around like that? Did you get wounded again? Or is that some new dance you've learned?"

Logvinenko had the typical Russian soldier's ability to crack a joke in the worst of circumstances.

I asked Logvinenko to retrieve my sniper rifle from the cellar, and as he had not been wounded, he was able to return in a flash and hand it to me. I crawled back behind the planks.

I adjusted the sights for five hundred-fifty yards and looked to see if the wind would throw off my shot. Most of the smoke from the battle was wafting straight up, a sign that that there was very little wind that day, so I didn't have to compensate for windage.

It always intrigues me to look through good optics at an enemy hundreds of yards away, whom before you could see only as a small and indistinct shape. Suddenly you can see the details of his uniform, and whether he is short or tall, skinny or fat. You can tell whether or not he has shaved that morning. You know if he is young or old, and if he in an officer or an enlisted man. You can see the expression on his face, and sometimes your target will be talking to another soldier, or even singing to himself. And as your man wipes his brow, or lazily moves so that his helmet shifts, you can find the best spot to plant your bullet.

I was lying behind the pile of boards, where I was not exposed to enemy fire. I put a round in the chamber, rolled into a firing position, and sighted on the German machine gunner. Even at this distance it was easy to lay my crosshairs across his face. His helmet was tilted back, so I was able to center my crosshairs between his eyes. I pulled the trigger. The machine gun instantly stopped firing as the gunner collapsed over the barrel. I dropped the gunner's two ammo carriers, neither of whom could react fast enough to take cover. They twitched for a few seconds and then they were still.

All it took were three well-aimed shots, and the threat to our side was eradicated. Our battalion came back to life. Our signalmen, messengers, and ammunition carriers leaped into action.

Although I had been designated as a sniper several days before, it was really only after this incident that the high command began to take me seriously. Subsequently they understood how vital I could be to a rifle company.

Prior to that, the brass would look at my height and say I was useless, and only good to be a clerk! To be honest, there had been many humiliating times like that, when us sailors first joined the ranks of the riflemen.

I remembered back in Krasnoufimsk, when a rail car of army headquarters brass inspected our unit of sailors. We were standing in formation. A couple of hard-looking infantry commanders, their chests covered with medals, were running the inspection. They were men who had clearly seen a lot of action. As they approached, our CO slapped his hand against his briefcase, as if to announce: "What do you think of our sailors, we've spent five years training them for battle on the high seas, you want to test them out on land, try them, they're ready!"

The brass divided us up into different units, and each commander was selecting the men he wanted. I could see that they were all going for the biggest and strongest looking sailors. They were sifting through us like a sieve. The big types like Afonin and Starostin were immediately snatched up by the artillery. They would filter out the small fry and keep the big ones for combat.

Obviously this process did not favor me, a bookkeeper and a

clerk. Front-line commanders had no need for my type, or what they presumed was my type. I even heard one colonel say, "What the hell do I need with your clerk? My unit's got more dead weight than it can handle as it is."

Our formation of sailors got thinned out as each fellow was assigned to his new unit, until I was the last one standing there. I was boiling with shame and resentment. I was prepared to go anywhere, do anything, just let me go where the fighting was, for God's sake! It is agonizing to feel that you are superfluous and unnecessary.

I approached a senior artillery lieutenant. He was wearing the order of the Red Flag on his chest. I discovered later that this was Ilya Shuklin, who was the commander of the anti–tank rocket forces at Stalingrad. He had distinguished himself at the battle of Kastornye. He needed one man to round out a gun crew.

Our CO saw that I had been left with no assignment and he felt bad for me. He also approached Ilya Shuklin.

"Why not take Chief Master Sergeant Zaitsev? He's finished high school, and he's a competent young man. He'll suit you fine."

The CO handed Ilya Shuklin my personnel card, Shuklin took one look at it and snapped, "I need an artillery man, not a bookkeeper!"

This sad day finally ended with my being drafted as a book-keeper for the second battalion.

Before we left Vladivostok, I had been put on temporary assignment with Lieutenant Trofimov's company. Trofimov was one of our instructors in hand-to-hand combat. During the demonstrations, he would scream at his opponent, "Come on, hit me like you really mean it!" No matter what move you tried on him, you could never lay a hand on him. When he saw me, he snickered and commented, "...your arms are a bit short for fist-fighting, aren't they, Comrade Sergeant?"

Trofimov had dumped me at the personnel department of the aviation unit. I reported to the aviation unit as I was ordered: I found the major in command sitting behind his desk. He had gold-rimmed glasses and was wearing a spotless air force uniform with a Sam Browne belt. He was bald as an egg and his baldness exposed a glossy, paper-thin scalp. His bald head, combined with his thick lips, heavy chin, and fleshy nose, gave him a harsh and imposing appearance.

A heap of personnel cards lay on his desk. I saw that my card was sitting on top of the pile, and it noted that I was an excellent marksman. The major stared at me silently, as if he were trying to find some redeeming qualities in me that no other superiors had been able to discover.

By this time, I was so infuriated by the whole process that all I could do was to stare back. The major was the first one to grow tired of our staring contest. He cleared his throat.

"So," he said, "where did you learn how to shoot?"

"In weapons training," I replied, thinking that this guy was just another bureaucratic jackass.

"Well," he said, "now I'm going to teach you the real way to shoot."

I was already in a foul mood and his words made me feel even worse. Sure, this chump was going to teach me how to shoot, and meanwhile the war would be over!

"Excuse me sir, you want to teach me how to shoot? I guarantee that I'm already a better shot than you. For more than a year now I've been begging for a transfer to the front. Let me shoot at fascists, not paper targets!"

The major could have had me court-martialled for this idiotic outburst, but instead something unexpected happened. He got up from behind his desk and shook my hand with a firm grip. He said, "Why, you're a real sailor, not some pansy. Lots of guys will jump at the slightest chance to weasel out of going to the front – cart them off to wherever you want, just don't sent them to war. But you've got some backbone. Fine, I'll work on it. Consider your request granted. You're dismissed."

After he said this, I was ready to hug this bald and goggle-eyed old soldier! I never would have believed that beneath his steely exterior there was an understanding soul.

So that is how my assignments were juggled, and how I missed out on the school for riflemen and radiomen, and ended up in *Starshiy* Lieutenant Bolshapov's machine gun company.

Bolshapov was a severe and demanding officer. He was also extremely intelligent. On one of our train stops en route to Stalingrad, he pointed to a Maxim gun that was stored nearby.

"Know anything about this?" he asked.

"A little," I answered. "Here, put this over my eyes." I handed Bolshapov my kerchief, and had him tie it so I was completely blindfolded. Meanwhile, a small crowd gathered. Then I proceeded to dismantle and re-assemble the weapon. When they took off the blindfold, I could see that Lt. Bolshapov had a big grin on his face.

At the next stop, battalion Captain Kotov approached me.

"Lt. Bolshapov tells me that you're familiar with the machine gun, and your service record says that you're an excellent shot. But tell me, how does a bookkeeper like yourself stay in practice, when you're lucky if you see a target range once a year?"

Kotov's question angered me. Here I had volunteered for the front, but these officers still presumed I was incompetent, because I had been a bookkeeper! It was as though I wasn't a real military man.

"Careful what you say, Comrade Captain. I might be a better shot than you."

Kotov was astonished at my audacity, and the soldiers and sailors nearby who overheard my remark were all taken aback. But since I had tossed down the glove, Kotov had to respond to my challenge.

We stepped off the train.

"Reutov!" he shouted. Sasha Reutov was his orderly. "Reutov, measure me off thirty paces and set down three bottles."

Reutov located some bottles and paced off the range.

Lt. Bolshapov was standing besides Captain Kotov, and

Bolshapov appeared to be nervous about how I was going to perform. After all, he was the one who had recommended me.

The sailors from the nearby train cars had all heard about the contest and had gathered to one side, while the regular soldiers from Kotov's battalion gathered on the other. This was going to be a contest between the Army and the Navy.

Captain Kotov unholstered his Parabellum and started to take aim.

"Now I'll demonstrate how a real marksman shoots," he said.

He took careful aim and pulled the trigger. His first shot kicked up some dust, almost a foot off the mark. The soldiers groaned, while the sailors all chuckled.

"Just warming up," said Captain Kotov. He was embarrassed and was turning a bit red. He shot again, and this time he hit the first bottle. By the time he emptied his clip, only one bottle was still whole, but it had fallen so that it faced us end-on – a much smaller and more difficult target.

The captain loaded a few bullets into the parabellum and handed it to me.

"Alright, chief, let's see if you can live up to your recommendations."

I took the pistol and raised it theatrically, in the style of duelists of the 1800s. When I leveled it, I smoothly pulled the trigger and shot the bottle through and through.

My fellow seamen laughed and said, "There's a sailor for you!"

The soldiers groaned. "Luck, luck!" they chanted.

"One shot doesn't prove anything," huffed Captain Kotov. "I doubt that you could pull that off again. Why don't you try a different target?"

He pulled off his hat and tossed it to Reutov, and Reutov ran back to place it next to the broken bottles.

I had three bullets left.

"But Comrade Captain," I protested, "you'll end up without your hat."

Captain Kotov folded his arms. "Proceed, Zaitsev," he told me.

I quickly put all three shots through the red army emblem on top of the hat's visor. The sailors were cheering, while the army guys were left shrugging their shoulders.

"Not bad," Captain Kotov conceded.

When I tried to return his parabellum, he refused, and he presented me with the belt and holster as well. I was so stunned by the magnitude of his gesture that I was speechless.

"Chief Master Sergeant Zaitsev," he said, "I'm issuing you this pistol and a hundred bullets. Welcome to our battalion." He put his hands on my shoulders. "Now go drill holes in some fascists!"

The other sailors congratulated me on my 'baptism of fire.' One doubter cropped up, claiming "Zaitsev just got lucky," but the others rebuked him, saying: "Have you ever heard about the hunters that come from the Urals? No? Then button up, wise guy."

~~~

Night had fallen, and flares were going off intermittently; so that blinding light alternated with pitch-black darkness. I went downstairs to find Captain Kotov. He was seated lotus-fashion on a tarpaulin, shouting into a telephone. From what I could make out of the conversation, we were being ordered to recapture some positions we had lost. Of course, I should have expected this. Tonight we had to take the offensive.

Kotov gathered us together.

"I need *fyenki* and *dyegtarevki*, with their shirts off," he said. He was calling for grenades, *fyenki* were F-1s, while *dyegtyarevi* were RGDs, without protective covers, or "shirts." The battalion commander repeated General Chuikov's instructions:

"Grab a dozen grenades and burst in on the enemy together, you and the grenades, that is. I want you both dressed lightly, you without your rucksack, and the grenades without their "shirts."

The grenade is an excellent weapon. We loaded up with them and took off. Tonight we were going to kill some Krauts.

The Krauts really caught it from our "pocket" artillery that night. We took them completely by surprise, they must have thought they had us on the run, and they weren't anticipating an attack. By morning we had regained most of the positions we had lost the previous day. We had re-established our positions at the factory's forge. After it was secured, our battalion command was supposed to be transferred to this new location.

The forge was divided in two by a white brick wall. This wall was rooted to the stone foundation, and its brickwork extended up several yards beyond the roof. Everything adjacent to it was in ruins, and the wall stood by itself, separating us from the Nazis. We were so close to the enemy that we could hear them if they farted. You had to constantly be aware of every noise you made, or you could betray your location.

Sasha Reutov was hoping we could tunnel under to the Krauts' side in order to plant some explosives, and he had started digging under the wall's foundation, until his progress was halted by a large rock. No matter how he tried to lever it out, the rock would not budge. So Sasha searched around the forge until he discovered a big sledgehammer. He bent back, the muscles in his arms braiding like a whip, then he struck the rock a tremendous blow. It immediately popped out, like a cork flying from a bottle of champagne. From underneath, someone screamed in German and started firing a Schmeisser at us. The rapid fire beat a tattoo against the brick wall as the bullets whizzed past Sasha's face. If the enemy soldier had pointed his barrel two centimeters to the right, Sasha would have lost his nose and the rest of his face as well.

Sasha collected his wits and dropped a grenade down the hole created by the vacant rock. There was a muffled boom! which was immediately followed by a much larger explosion, which cracked the foundation and threw us off our feet.

Black smoke poured out of the hole. These Krauts had been on their way to mine us, when Sasha's grenade had detonated their explosives prematurely.

Sasha wanted to dig into what was left of the Germans' tunnel, to see if we could make our way over to their side and plant some charges. I was all for the idea, but then another Luftwaffe attack commenced, with the screeching approach of the Stukas. And everything started all over again, the dive-bombing, artillery, and mortars. This time their infantry didn't attack, but three Panzer tanks showed up. Our anti-tank riflemen were able to set the first one ablaze, and the other two could not maneuver around it, and were forced to retreat. Our machine gun fire was too intense for the Germans to follow up the tank assault by unleashing an infantry attack. It seemed that after that day the enemy lost their appetite for frontal assaults. The fighting went on until midday and then quieted down, and as the hours ticked by the German's assault slackened off.

This was October 21st, 1942. From that day on, Paulus's soldiers no longer believed they were supermen, and Stalingrad became more of a battle between two entrenched forces. This is not to say that German frontal assaults totally halted, but they became much rarer and more hesitant.

This was also the day I was officially written into the ranks of the Russian snipers. From here on in, my only assignment was to master the sniper's art.

CHAPTER 9.
FIRST STEPS

Goebbel's propagandists started showing up more and more, opposite our positions. "Russkis, surrender!" they'd shout through their bullhorns, "resistance is futile!" They would keep babbling until they shouted themselves hoarse.

We knew that the enemy had a numerical advantage, and better equipment, we didn't need their propagandists to remind us. This is what had allowed them to cut the city in two, and cut off our supply lines.

But we also knew, that we, the city's defenders, were resisting ferociously, killing Nazis day and night, and inflicting blows that kept them constantly off-balance. We were wearing them down, both physically and psychologically.

The Nazis' propaganda belied the fact that that now the German army was truly suffering. They had stopped believing in easy victory, and the momentum was slipping through their fingers like sand. It wasn't out of kindness to us that they stopped trying their all-out assaults. The reality was that they could no longer afford the high casualties from frontal attacks. Still, it would have been suicidal for us to let our guard down. The serpent's bite is poisonous, after all; and the Germans were like a wounded snake hiding amongst the rubble, and that snake was still capable of making lethal strikes.

~~~

A crowd of soldiers we didn't recognize had gathered in the trench outside our bunker. They were all bristling with weapons. Every one of them had a cigarette in his mouth, and the air was thick with smoke.

"Why are you guys hanging out here? Get lost!" I ordered them, in an imposing tone. All but one complied with my command. This one lingered in front of me, a stocky soldier with his legs set far apart. While he wasn't that tall, he had extremely broad shoulders. You could just feel the power in this soldier, and he knew it, too. The rest of those gathered had obeyed me and moved on, but this soldier continued to stand there, defying me, stiff as a pole. I slapped his shoulder.

Without turning around he bellowed, "What do you want?"

"Into the bunker." I said.

"I got no business there," he said.

"If you've got no business here, then what are you standing around for? You waiting for a grenade to drop in?"

"Look at this – a little rooster like you making all this noise! Maybe I ought to clip your wings to make sure you don't get too excited and fly away!"

Lieutenant Fedosov, the staff commander from the 2nd Batallion, overheard our raised voices. When he spotted me, he immediately said, "I need to speak you," and the two of us stepped inside the bunker.

"Did I miss something? " I asked Fedosov. "Is today some sort of holiday? Why have these guys assembled here? Are they *raspeezdeyi*[24] who've abandoned their positions?"

"Vasya, don't get upset for no reason," said Fedosov. Fedosov was an irritable fellow with a pockmarked face, and a red nose from all the vodka he drank to lift his spirits. "It's a storm group – a reserve one, that is. Whenever there's an assault planned on a fixed position, we send groups like this to the scene."

[24] *raspeezdeyi*: slackers
.

Both of us had to make reports at battalion headquarters. En route, Fedosov explained the make-up of the storm groups to me:

"They draft the strongest and most foolhardy men they can find for these groups…"

"So I noticed," I replied. "Just now, one of them threatened to clip my wings."

"Don't take it personally. He's a heck of a shot with an armor-piercing gun."

~~~

Our division had been assigned to retake Mamayev Hill. Battalions of the 1047th regiment had sunk their teeth deep into the enemy's defenses on Mamayev's eastern slopes. From a distance you could see furious clashes breaking out where our storm groups were carrying out their lightning attacks.

But the enemy was not without new tricks. They had begun to use light machine guns.[25] These could be fired from a standing position, or placed on a bipod. These guns provided a very high rate of fire, utilized a high-velocity round, and were accurate at long range, making the soldiers equipped with them much more of a threat than enemy soldiers equipped with short-barreled sub-machine guns. And these "roving" gunners were a hundred times more mobile than stationary gunners equipped with heavy machine guns. To make matters worse, the mobile Kraut gunners had good radio co-ordination, so when they suspected a Soviet storm group's approach, several enemy light machine gunners would pop up simultaneously and lay down withering co-ordi-nated fire. This prevented our storm groups from reaching their objectives. Even in the pitch dark, the German gunners were able to effectively co-ordinate their moves. The result was that they were robbing us of our ability to operate at night, which had been our time of advantage. These Kraut mobile machine gunners were more of a threat to us than any pillboxes or fortified

[25] Zaitsev is apparently referring to Bren-type guns the Germans seized when they annexed Czechoslovakia. These were issued to the Wehrmacht before the advance on Stalingrad.

emplacements, because they could appear and disappear in a flash. We never knew where they would come from next.

~~~

My bandages were wearing out and exposing my raw skin. I had to return to the med station to get the bandages replaced. While I was there I ran into the battalion's *zampolit*, senior political instructor, Yablochkin. Yablochkin was a man of medium height with a barrel chest, a booming voice, and a double chin. Somehow he managed to always be wearing an elegant fur hat.

"You have new orders," Yablochkin told me. "From now on make eliminating those roving machine gunners your top priority."

"Please be reasonable, comrade," I protested. "You can't expect me to do that by myself."

"I understand," he affirmed, "and that's why I'm giving you this order as a *komsomolyets*: I want you to look around this room and pick out a couple sharpshooters, and then I want you to train them to eliminate those roving gunners. Is that clear?"

I had been ordered to start up a sniper school.[26]

~~~

"Well, brother, how goes it out there in the Dolgiy?" I asked one soldier. He coughed up some blood, looked me over from head to foot, and said dryly, "It ain't pickin' daisies."

If I was going to recruit any snipers, it would have to be from among these walking wounded. This was the clay I had been given work with.

I noticed a young soldier staggering out, his gait unsteady. He was wearing a sweater, and his big feet were clad in water-repellant boots that he must have taken off a dead German. His head was bandaged. His hands were shaking badly and he was trying unsuccessfully to roll a cigarette.

"Let me do that," I said, and took the tobacco and paper from him.

---

[26]This is the only specific reference Zaitsev makes to having received orders to set up a sniper group. Zaitsev was subsequently able to recruit Alexander Gryazev, Okrihm Vasilchenko, and other sailors from the Pacific fleet. Obviously Zaitsev's commanders subsequently gave him more discretion in how he would recruit snipers.

This soldier was obviously shell-shocked. I was silently cursing the political officer. How did he expect me to pull together a unit of snipers from dregs like this?

I introduced myself. "Chief Master Sergeant Vassili Zaitsev," I said, and put out my hand.

"Mikhail Ubozhenko," he said, and we shook. He had a fluid baritone voice, like a singer in a church choir.

"You're Ukrainian?" I asked.

"From Dnepropetrovsschina," he affirmed.

"How'd your head get so banged up?" I asked.

"I'm a sapper," he said, "at least I was a sapper. I was in Lieutenant Kuchin's zone. We were building a bunker, but the last time the Krauts shelled us, some boards collapsed and knocked against my-" and he tapped his head.

"So why didn't they ship you out?" I asked.

"I can still fight," he said. "I told them, I wanted to stay. I can't drag logs around anymore, it makes my head spin, but I'm willing to try my luck with a rifle."

I liked his attitude. His injuries hadn't rendered him useless. Certainly he was no coward. With a concussion like he had, he could easily have opted to be transported across the Volga. Instead he had elected to stay in the city and fight.

I invited Mikhail up to the second floor, to have a go with a sniper's rifle. I explained my assignment to him, and camou-flaged the white bandages on his head with some shreds from a discarded uniform. We enlarged my blind with some construction materials we found, so that it was big enough to provide cover for two people. Mikhail found himself a spot adjacent to a bombed-out wall.

Mamayev Hill was shrouded in smoke from the base to the peak. A Luftwaffe attack was just winding up there. Just before the Luftwaffe flew over, our artillery had been hammering the Nazis for a couple of hours. Despite all this mayhem, the smoke was slowly clearing.

Mikhail had sharp eyes, and he was the first to notice when

German soldiers started running across to the railroad embankment, in order to dig new trenches.

"What do I do now?" he asked me.

"Those Krauts are four hundred yards away." I showed him how to adjust the telescopic sights on the sniper rifle for the correct distance.

"Aim at your target's chest, but don't shoot yet," I said to Mikhail, "wait until he turns to face you."

"Alright, chief," he said, "but why's that?"

"Think of this like a game of billiards," I explained. "You're always trying to set up your next shot. If you shoot him now, while he's turned away from you, both he and his shovel fall into the ditch. But if you wait and get him when he's facing towards you, his shovel stays up on the near side of the embankment. That way, when the next guy grabs the shovel, you can get him, too."

The rifle banged. I jumped; I wasn't used to being a teacher and somehow the discharge sounded louder than if I had been shooting myself. I looked through my binoculars in time to see the Kraut who had been digging, as he sank into the trench. Seconds later, some fool reached up to retrieve the shovel and Mikhail shot again.

"Vasya, Vasya, I nailed two Krauts!" Mikhail Ubozhenko was overjoyed.

"Nice shooting," I congratulated him. I was scouting the battlefield through my binoculars, when I noticed several Kraut rifles swinging over to line up on us.

"You're learning fast," I told Mikhail, "but let's get our asses out of here, or it's us who'll get nailed!"

As if to emphasize my words, some high velocity bullets whizzed past us like angry bees. We slid down the ladder, where we were safe from the Nazis trying to avenge their lost comrades.

And thus began our snipers' training school. I, the professor, had in reality been the school's first student. Up to now my only teacher had been my own mistakes.

~~~

A sniper must be courageous and have an iron will. This description fit Sergeant Nikolai Kulikov to a T. Kulikov later became one of my students, and subsequently my friend, and one of our best snipers.

Kulikov was a sinewy soldier of medium height. He was an intellectual, and whenever he spoke, he chose his words carefully. The day I first met him, I saw him in action, and what follows is a description of the incident that so impressed me.

Two hundred meters south of the water towers, on Mamayev Hill, stood a bombed-out T-34 tank. Five soldiers from Ivan Shetilov's company, under Sergeant Volovatikh, had burrowed under the tank and set up a Maxim gun there. Their position proved to be excellent. They had a wide field of fire, so they could torpedo any Nazi infantry attacks as soon as these attacks were launched. The Krauts tried repeatedly to take the tank, but they had no luck moving against this position. However, after three days of struggle, the Krauts finally managed to sneak up and surround Volovatikh's unit. However the enemy overlooked one factor: the telephone connection we maintained with our stalwarts in the burned–out tank.

A call came in from Volovatikh, who reported that his team were in good spirits "..but we're taking fire from all sides. We need some grenades and rounds for the machine gun."

Ivan Shetilov, the company commander, asked for a volunteer.

I was standing next to the sniper Sergeant Abzalov, and also by a soldier from Yakutsk, Gavrili Protodyanov, who manned a 45 mm gun. Nikolai Kulikov was also there. He was a newest replacement in our company. Each of us was silently contemplating the best way to reach the tank, as we calculated the odds of survival. Reaching the tank would mean passing across open terrain in clear view of the enemy's positions. There was no cover whatsoever, except for a few scattered shell-holes, and the bodies of some dead soldiers.

Before any of could say something, a messenger from regimental command volunteered.

The messenger inched forward relentlessly, nudging a box of ammo in front of himself. It was getting dark, and it looked like the Krauts wouldn't notice him – when suddenly an explosion thundered out next to him, and the German submachine gunners opened fire.

Sergeant Volovatikh rang up again, to report that the messenger was wounded and needed help. Nikolai Kulikov took the call.

"Don't worry," he said.

Volovatikh recognized Kulikov's voice. They had known each other before Kulikov had been assigned to our company.

Volovatikh beseeched him for help: "Kolya, old buddy, can you deliver some hardware for us?" He didn't say a word about food or water, although they must have been close to dying from thirst and hunger.

"I'm already en route," said Nikolai Kulikov. "Fire up the samovar, prepare some hors d'oeuvres, and don't worry. I'll bring the wine."

It was the end of October. A cold autumn drizzle was falling. Kulikov grabbed a tarp, laid it out on the floor, and asked the rest of us to help him pack some food and ammo so it wouldn't get wet, and so that it wouldn't rattle around and draw unwanted attention.

We made up a nice picnic bundle: grenades, bullets, water, some kasha, tobacco, and tinned meat from the "second front." We packed it exactly as Kulikov had ordered, then dragged the load back and forth to make sure it wouldn't unravel. When Kulikov was satisfied, he tied a rope to one end, then took the other end in his teeth, and set off crawling.

Nikolai made his way forward moving like a big lizard. He kept his body flush to the ground, and wriggled from crater to crater. Soon he disappeared into the dark and we could no longer monitor his progress. We didn't hear any firing, so we surmised that he was progressing OK.

After a few minutes, the telephone rang. Volovatikh was on

the line.

"Nikolai made it, we're saved!"

Before the night was over, Nikolai Kulikov completed three more runs, so the men in the burned-out tank were prepared to withstand a siege. After Nikolai made his last run, Volovatikh called to inform us that Nikolai was on his way back. We waited and waited, but Kulikov didn't show up.

We were afraid that he had been captured, but the morning light revealed him sleeping, just outside our position. He had crawled back to safety and collapsed with fatigue. When we woke him up, he was ready to make another run.

That was how I was introduced to Nikolai Kulikov. And in general, fate smiled on me with the whole group of snipers.

Take Alexander Gryazev, for example. He was a giant of a man, a farmer with straw-colored hair. Before he joined the navy he had spent his days plowing fields. He was big as an ox and could have been yoked to a plow himself.

When we camped out in the Metalworking Factory, sometimes we would tease Gryazev. We would be stuck in workshops cluttered with trolley wheels and broken lathes, so that there would be no place to lie down, no place where we could sleep comfortably. We would all be exhausted, so we would summon Gryazev and ask him to move this industrial clutter out of the way.

"But why me?" he would ask, and we would explain to him that if anybody else tried to pick these things up, we would get a hernia.

And so Sasha would calmly pick up an entire axle, or a big machine lathe, weighing several hundred pounds, and not even break into a sweat. He would move these awkward loads as delicately as if they were fine china, and when he put them down, he set them down silently, without dropping them – so as not to wake up any of the rest of us. In a few minutes the room would be clean and bare, and we had room to stretch out full length and sleep.

In battle, Sasha often used an anti-tank rifle to take out enemy pillboxes or blast other fixed positions. Our anti-tank rifles were two feet taller than I am, and very heavy, weighing more than forty pounds. But the anti-tank rifle was like a toy in Sasha's big mitts, and he could tote one around all day without getting tired. And in battle, he knew how to select the perfect position and level shots from the anti-tank rifle directly into the embrasures of the enemy's strong points. In his hands, it worked perfectly as a one–man portable cannon.

Once Sasha Reutov - the tiger hunter from Usirisk, as his friends called him – decided to play a prank on his namesake, Sasha Gryazev. Reutov brought out a sixty-millimeter iron rod, ran it through the safety lock on the anti-tank gun's trigger, bent the rod around one of the factory's column, and wound up both ends. As I watched Reutov, I thought, "Bending iron is easier than unbending it. Who's going to be able to undo that?"

The sun was sinking quickly and had already started to dip below the horizon of Mamayev Hill, when, like a bear from his den, Alexander Gryazev emerged from the rubble. He had been on guard duty that day. He strolled in, took a look around, and like a child reaching for his favorite toy, he walked over to his anti-tank gun. And there it was tied to the column! He immediately saw it was a prank, but he acted like he didn't know anyone was watching. He only muttered, "Two can play at this game.."

He calmly leaned over and grabbed the rod by its twisted ends. His neck grew beet-red, his veins bulged and filled with blood. The metal resisted, then started to creak and finally gave way! He flung the rod to the side where it landed with a clang.

Dinner was brought to us. The snipers were gathered in the factory's forge.

Reutov and Gryazev – the two Alexanders – sat next to each other and ate in silence. They had quickly become good friends and could sit next to each other for hours at a time without either of them saying a word. Dinner wound to a close. We stashed our spoons back into our bootlegs, and the bowls were collected for washing in the Volga. It was the closest water available.

"Well sailors, I don't suppose anyone would object to an after-dinner smoke?" offered Okhrim Vasilchenko.

"Leave Gryazev and me out," said Reutov. "Your *makhorka* never helped anyone."

This for some reason rubbed Gryazev the wrong way, and he turned to Reutov. "Thanks for the concern, now just how were you trying to help me when you tied my gun to that column?"

"Well now that's different. There was a reason for that."

They had both got up and were standing in each other's face. They were both enormous men – over two hundred-fifty pounds apiece.

"What kind of reason?"

"I'll explain. Let's say some Krauts burst in on us and we, according to pre-arranged plan that is, all take off to hide. The Krauts meanwhile go straight for your armor-piercer, but it's locked up! No matter how hard they try, they just can't break it free. You see? I would have saved your weapon for you!"

Gryazev backed up a step, smiled and decided to play his own joke on Reutov.

"Thank you. Allow me to shake the hand of the kind man who's rendered such a thoughtful service to me."

Sasha Reutov knew what to expect. He took a wider stance and offered Gryazev his broad and calloused palm with its thick, knotty fingers. They locked hands, squeezing tighter and tighter. It seemed someone's fingers were bound to crunch at any moment, but neither man would consider easing up.

Two minutes passed, three…five – still neither would give in. They were flushed and their breathing was ragged; but finally both mens' powerful shoulders started shuddering. Sasha Reutov was the first to give in.

"Enough – or my hand will wither away."

Gryazev released his grip, and we could see that tiny drops of blood were oozing from under Reutov's nails.

"Damn gorilla!" said Reutov, "could've crushed my hand!"

Gryazev smiled.

"A hydraulic press couldn't crush that shovel of a palm you've got." said Reutov.

Then they gave each other a hug and walked off together. With their broad and powerful hands, Reutov and Gryazev could each comfortably handle a sniper's rifle.

~~~

The following night Misha Masayev and I were returning to our company. We followed barely discernable trails through the rubble, all the time worried that we would run into a minefield. In front of the Metalworking Factory, both our side and the Krauts had planted mines thicker than potatoes in a garden.

We caught sight of Lt. Bolshapov. The lieutenant was a dapper fellow, and as he stood next to our Maxim gun, he was trimming his moustache. He was holding a mirror in one hand and a small pair of scissors in the other. Whenever a parachute flare lit up the sky, the lieutenant took advantage of the illumination to make a few cuts with the scissors.

In the adjacent workshop we could hear Kraut soldiers talking and singing. They were celebrating having captured this particular workshop, which had already changed hands more times than I could count.

It sounded like there were quite a few of them on the other side of the wall, definitely more than the three of us could take on. Masayev and I wondered if we should roust some more of our company for an assault, and we started to ask the lieutenant about this, when he silenced us by raising a finger to his lips.

"Everyone's asleep," he whispered. "They've been at it for three days straight, and it's useless to try and wake them. I was on guard duty, but now you guys are going to relieve me."

The lieutenant smiled. He was in a cheery mood. Clearly he didn't think there was anything especially dangerous going on in our zone that evening.

Misha tried to protest, saying that we hadn't had any sleep either, but Bolshapov cut him off.

"Someone's got to do this," he said, "and now it's your turn.

Zaitsev, you're in command. Whatever you do, don't nod off, because you have to sound the alarm if these Krauts," and here the lieutenant tapped on the wall, "..decide to go on the warpath."

The lieutenant vanished to join the other sleepers.

Misha and I wanted to sleep too; our eyes closed by themselves. I started dozing, and everything that was going on around me took on the haze and incoherence of a dream. I asked myself, "…why is the sound of that grenade going off so much softer than usual?" and "..why does that grenade's explosion look like a rainbow colored bouquet of flowers?" As you can only see something like this in a dream, I realized I was falling in and out of sleep, and my mind began to fill with troubling thoughts: maybe the Nazis had already slipped past us. I imagined a bunch of Krauts, their faces smeared with camouflage paint, sneaking past me with their knives held between their teeth.

"What have I done?" I admonished myself in my sleep, "I haven't lived up to the faith the Lieutenant put in me, I haven't protected my friends, how can I look anyone in the eye after this?"

That night I cursed our medical system for not having issued us Benzedrine pills to stay awake in emergencies. I am convinced that there is no torture worse than depriving a man of sleep.

I bit my tongue so hard that the sharp pain woke me up like being drenched by a bucket of cold water. I could taste a salty liquid in my mouth, and realized it was blood. I spit, and Masayev turned to me.

"Hey chief," he said, "you spit just like a camel."

"It's nothing," I said.

Then Masayev confessed: "I took my knife to my arm."

"Did it work?" I asked.

"It kept me alert," he said. Masayev held up his arm to show me several small slices he had cut into it. "I sharpened my trusty Finnish knife, just for this purpose."

We staggered back towards the crack in the tool workshop's

wall, where he had first listened to our Kraut neighbors. We approached slowly, inching along through shell craters blown in the factory floor. It appeared that the Krauts had moved on – there was no noise from the other side of the wall, and we could not discern any movement.

We lowered ourselves into a deep crater, pressed close to the ground, and inched upward, in order to peer through the crack at whatever the enemy was up to.

At first, we couldn't see anyone, and we were ready to enter the tool room, but just as I started to wriggle through, Masayev spotted the boots of German soldier. Masayev seized me by the arm and we both froze.

We could hear the measured pace of the Kraut's boots. He was pacing the length of the wall like a caged animal. Metal caps shined on his heels. He would come right up to the hole we were hiding in, so we could make out the thick soles on his enormous boots. He must have been a size 12. While this Nazi was strolling about, Masayev and I figured out a way to catch him. We were going to lure him with bait, and land him like a fish.

Masayev had looted a gold pocket watch from a dead German officer. The watch was a real treasure, with a solid gold case, and it had a long chain.

When the Kraut paced away to the far side of the room, Masayev placed the watch in a crevice between two bricks, and ran the chain back so he had a good grip on it. This way, if the Kraut tried to reach it, Masayev could yank the chain and jerk the watch backwards.

We could observe the success or failure of our trick through other peepholes at ankle level.

The German's heavy boots approached once more. He stopped about a few yards shy of the watch, and stood there, silent. We knew he must have seen the watch, and that he had to be figuring out the best way to snatch it. The Kraut stood there for a minute, and then – much to our surprise - his feet turned and he walked away.

Masayev was getting cold feet. "He must have gone for help," Masayev whispered, agitated, "let's get out of here, otherwise him and his buddies will catch us when they come back!"

"Relax," I told Masayev. "He won't want to share it with anybody. He'll come back soon – alone."

We heard the knock - knock - knock of heavy boots approaching. The soldier reappeared, by himself, as I had predicted. He had a long thin board in his hands, with a nail protruding from one end, the perfect pry tool. Pretty clever, I thought.

I was watching Masayev's face. Obviously he was sorry to part with the watch, but there was nothing he could do. We had started this game, and now we had to see it through.

The Kraut tried and tried, but he couldn't knock the watch free with his board. He nudged the watch around, but it only got wedged deeper between the bricks.

Masayev and I had to bite our tongues to keep from laughing. The Kraut was getting more and more worked up, like a real gold miner. He threw the stick aside, got down on his knees, then stuck one arm deep into the crevice, to try and get a grip on his plunder. His fingers fumbled near the watch's slippery cover, but whenever he came close to getting a grip, Masayev would yank the watch a few inches back.

The Kraut was really frustrated now. He muttered some obscenity. Then the Kraut took his rifle off his shoulder, lay down, got down on all fours and crawled right into the crevice….

~~~

We frog-marched our dazed prisoner back to the liberated zone of the factory. The prisoner wore lance corporal emblems on his epaulets.

Lieutenant Bolshapov grinned from ear to ear when he saw who we were delivering.

"Nice catch, sailors," he congratulated us.

Nurse Klava Svintsova appeared. With her usual indifference, she took some iodine and began to treat the cuts in the German lance corporal's scalp.

One of the sailors watching this scene was bitter: "They set dogs on our wounded, while Klava swaddles this Kraut with sterile bandages!"

Our prisoner was only half-conscious. I had tapped the base of his skull with my rifle in order to make him more tractable. We were starting to wonder if I had hit him too hard – maybe he would never come back to his senses. Klava took an ammonia swab and dipped it under his nose.

The Kraut sneezed and blinked as if he had been thrown under a spotlight. Meanwhile, Masayev was relating how we had snared this German soldier.

Lieutenant Fedosov decided to have a laugh on us.

"Friends, this story sounds like hogwash to me," said Fedosov. He took a long pull from one of the flasks he always had with him. His eyes were red and nose was bulbous. "Everybody knows that Zaitsev and Masayev are as useless as trying to make bullets out of dogshit," continued Fedosov. "This factory's got tons of wounded Krauts lying around. They probably picked this guy up on their way back, then invented this story to make themselves look good."

Meanwhile our prisoner still hadn't quite come around.

Masayev looked at me, his eyes burning. Masayev's accusing look said, "you were the one who hit him in the head!"

Precisely at this moment, the German lance corporal came to. He dashed for the door like a cheetah from the jungle. Lt. Fedosov was sitting on a nearby stool, and the German corporal sent Fedosov and his papers flying.

The Kraut would have made it out the door, except that Reutov snared him and spun him around by the elbow, then tripped him up and sat on him, pinning the Kraut to the ground.

The lance corporal's eyes became bloodshot, and his nostrils flared like those of an enraged beast. We had caught a truly hot-blooded fighter.

When a translator showed up, the Kraut corporal kept repeating the same statement: "I never surrendered. Russian soldiers don't fight fair!"

It was only nine o'clock in the morning, and during daylight hours it was impossible for us to send a prisoner back across to the other side of the Volga. Since we had a long wait until sundown, and we had many other more pressing things to worry about, we tied up our captive and put him in Klava's care, at the field hospital. We wrapped him up like an Egyptian mummy and left him leaning against a radiator.

Masayev and I then had a real sumptuous breakfast. I can still remember how good it tasted. But it made us sleepy, as if we hadn't been tired enough already. Sleepless nights and exhaustion were gaining the upper hand on us, and our strength was waning. Lt. Bolshapov granted us a 3-hour break, and Masayev descended to the cellar, opened the iron door, grabbed a place among the wounded soldiers, and immediately was snoring.

Nikolai Logvinenko showed up, looking for me. He had come to take me to Captain Kotov for a debriefing. Logvinenko gathered up his papers and he, Lt. Bolshapov and myself clambered through the rubble until we reached the factory office. Since the last time we had recaptured the building, the battalion HQ office had been moved into another section of the cellar. This room was large and had double steel doors set in the wall. Captain Kotov had inherited a beautifully carved wooden writing desk and a plush black sofa. They had been used by the factory's management before the Germans invaded. Field telephone equipment sat in leather military issue cases on top of the carved desk. It was an odd jumble of civilian elegance and military necessity.

From the cellar's window, a tall tower was visible. Somewhere on top of it, the artillery observer Feofanov was sending instructions back to the artillery commander, Ilya Shuklin. Shuklin was sitting by Captain Kotov.

Shuklin had a smile on his face, but Kotov appeared to be very upset. He was pale, white as a sheet, and his hands were shaking. I could tell that the burden of command while we were taking so many casualties was eating away at him.

My legs were giving out and I was swaying from side to side.

When the adjutant informed Kotov that I had arrived, the incensed battalion commander looked me up and down, saw how far gone I was, and snapped at Logvinenko: "Take him out of here and get him some sleep!"

I staggered up out of the cellar, barely able to keep my eyes open. It was approaching noon, and it was getting warm. As usual, German planes were buzzing overhead and the odor of smoke and cordite from their bombs hung in the air. By this time I was so accustomed to them, I would have felt like something was wrong if no Kraut planes were around.

Two anti-tank rifles had been set up on a crumbling wall, which was all that remained of a factory building. A big cheerful soldier was sitting next to them.

"Nice to meet you," he said in broken Russian. "I—Gavrili Dimitrievich Protodyakonov, from Yakutsk.[27] Commander say me to "shoot German tanks here." Who are you?"

I introduced myself.

"Good to know you, yes, good. You need much sleep. Go to my room. Blanket and pillow there. Have good sleep!"

Gavrili took me to his bunker and I collapsed on his bed. It was made from boards and old ammo boxes, but at that point it seemed like the most luxurious feather bed I had ever seen.

~~~

On the 24th of October, our sniper group – Gryazev, Morozov, Shaikin, Kulikov, Dvoyashkin, Kostrikov and myself – was transferred to the territory of a neighboring regiment on the eastern slope of Mamayev Hill. We were assigned a position at elevation 102 meters – a very awkward and dangerous location. Our trenches had been dug into the hillside at an angle; and we were about 150 yards from the Nazi front lines.

Before we got this assignment, the zone had been defended by a company of our anti-tank gunners, but during the preceding

---

[27] Yakutsk is the major city of the Sakha Republic in NE Siberia. Much of the population speaks a Turkik language, and Russian is a second language for them.

week, their commander had been wounded and sent to the field hospital. His soldiers remained, but without their commander they were suffering tremendous casualties. Their dead were buried right there, in the trenches. Only a small number of soldiers in the unit had survived. They would crawl from one gun to another, giving the enemy the impression that more men were still alive, and that they could still present a formidable defense.

A small spring trickled through the area. Its clear waters were a magnet for the Nazis, luring them to its banks.

Our guide was a corporal who had been part of the anti-tank unit. He told us, that despite the danger of attack, the Krauts made trips to the spring early each morning, bringing jerry cans and canteens. They were even building a bathhouse there.

"It's a perfect stakeout for a sniper," the guide commented.

Early that morning, I asked our guide to lead Gryazev and me to the spring, but the guide wasn't interested.

"The place will be swarming with Germans," he said. "And when they approach, they do a recon by fire. They'll hit every shellhole with grenades, and they'll machine-gun any bush big enough to use for cover."

It was about four AM.

"They haven't started shooting yet," commented Alexander Gryazev. Gryazev was a perpetual optimist. He persuaded the corporal to take us on up.

It was quiet, really silent. There weren't even any flares going off. We dropped to the ground and crawled, as if we were hunting for wolves. We kept moving, searching for a foxhole or a vacant trench.

Crawling is difficult when you're a sniper. The long rifle on your back is constantly shifting from side to side, forcing you to stop and adjust its position. Simultaneously, your Tommy-gun always ends up dragging in the dirt, and if dirt gets into the gun's action, the Tommy-gun will surely jam on you when you need it most.

We hid at the base of the ravine and listened as the Kraut above emptied his machine gun, blasting at shadows.

They never hesitated to burn ammo. The Kraut machine guns

had a higher rate of fire than our guns, so it was easy to differ-entiate the sounds.

Then some bullets stitched a pattern over my head, on the far wall of the ravine. Dirt tumbled onto my face.

"Damn it," I said, "he's made us!"

"Don't worry," said the corporal. "He's firing around himself in a circular pattern, he wasn't shooting at us."

Sure enough, the machine gun moved on, riddling the eastern wall with fire.

"When he quits," said the corporal, "we can hide behind that ledge." He pointed out a barely visible ridge. "My company should be there."

We waited, and soon as the gunner completed his circuit, he stopped to re-load. We ran behind the ridge and hid. But our anti-tank company wasn't there. This new spot was completely deserted.

We were all breathing hard from the run. Sasha turned to the corporal.

"So where's your guys?" Sasha asked.

"Damned if I know," said the corporal. "Listen. They're around somewhere. I'm going to walk along and talk out loud. I have to do something to signal my men, so they don't shoot me thinking I'm a Nazi. I'll shout out if the Krauts grab me, but if the coast is clear, I'll come back and retrieve you guys. Don't come out until I give you the all clear, OK?"

Gryazev and I told him we agreed, and the corporal started off, then he remembered one last thing.

"If the Krauts nab me, it's up to you hit their trenches. Our Maxim guns are over there." He pointed to the south. "From the near side you can fire on the railroad bridge and the slopes of Mamayev Hill. From the other side you can hit the water tanks. And there's two Tommy-guns buried with some ammo by the north end of the trench. The spot is marked by a German helmet."

The corporal trotted off through the dark, while Gryazev and I hid and waited. Soon we heard his voice calling out, "*doroga, doroga.*"[28]

---

[28] *Doroga:* make way..

'*Doroga*' is a good Russian word. By having people say it, you know immediately if you've got a Russian or a German heading your way. Germans can't pronounce it properly, when they say it, it always comes out sounding like 'taroka.' That word would trip up even a German scout dressed like a Russian. As soon as he said 'taroka,' we would nail him.

The corporal's voice disappeared. Where the hell was he? We waited, afraid even to smoke cigarettes, because they might give us away. We thought the Krauts might have slit the corporal's throat before he had a chance to yell. We were getting more nervous by the minute. Finally the corporal showed up, out of breath. I asked him if he had found anybody.

"Only two of our guys are left," he said. The corporal was so upset he could barely speak. "They're waiting for you," he muttered. "A company of Krauts has been trying to surround them since last night."

"So what are we sitting here for?" snarled Gryazev. "Let's go!"

"Slow down," I warned Gryazev. "First we have to collect the ammo the corporal told us about."

We crawled to the hidden stockpile and picked up as much ammo and as many grenades as we could carry. Then we followed the corporal, to join the survivors of his company.

We could smell them before we saw them. They had been glued to the same positions for several days, never leaving even to relieve themselves.

The first survivor we saw had his bony hands tightly gripping a Maxim gun. He was emaciated and unshaven. His eyes were wild and his clothing was ragged. Without turning his head, he said: "The enemy...look, you see there?"

He pointed to some silhouettes on the horizon.

"They're getting ready to make a move for another trench," said the wild-eyed gunner. "If we allow them to take it, they'll be within mortar range of our docks on the Volga. They'll be able to hit every boat we send across!"

Gryazev was enraged. "I can see them fine," he said. "I'll send them a few pineapples,[29] to have a party with."

In the moonlight, Sasha and I looked at the massacred bodies of the Red Army soldiers around us. The survivors had no opportunity to bury them. The bodies were those of young men. Some of them looked no more than eighteen years old. Sasha shut one young soldier's eyes.

"Vasya," he growled, "I'm going to make the Krauts pay. For all of them."

The odds were badly stacked against us. I had to cool Sasha down a bit. I grabbed one of his bear-sized paws and said to him: "So you hit them with a few grenades, then what? They must outnumber us thirty to one. And you don't even know the terrain."

"Chief, have you got a better idea?"

"First," I said, "we learn the lay of the land and figure out how to set up an ambush, so we can pin them in their trenches."

"Why bother with all that?" Gryazev was pulling away from me and I could not keep my hold on him much longer. "Give me a pair of grenades," he said.

"Listen, you dumb ox," I told him, "in the trench their field of vision is limited, they won't be able to see where we're shooting from. That trench can be the perfect trap, like a firing corridor …and we can block their escape with grenades. Now do you get it?"

Gryazev reluctantly agreed that he understood.

~~~

Instead of singing birds, morning was announced by the spitting of machine guns and the whistle of rounds flying overhead. We had set up our sniping position at the very front edge of our lines.

Our orders were to take out the Kraut officers, then their non-coms, and finally, to use grenades on their equipment.

During the night five more snipers from our group joined us.

Sasha had spent the night brooding, and in the morning his temper overwhelmed him. He waited for a moment when I was

---

[29] Pineapples: American grenades were reaching the defenders of Stalingrad via Atlantic convoys sent to Murmansk

distracted, then filled an empty gas mask bag with grenades and set off crawling towards the machine gun that was covering the Germans' advance to their new position. Sasha reached it without being spotted and flung two grenades. The Kraut gunner and his loader were killed instantly, and their gun was rendered useless.

As you would expect, a lopsided fire-fight broke out. Our only possible escape routes were cut off, and retreat was impossible. We dug in for a siege.

Twenty-four hours passed, then another twenty-four. We managed to hold out. With our sniper rifles we could control the access to the spring, and pretty soon the Krauts were getting parched. We made sure to expedite this by shooting holes in all their jerrycans. We thought it was an excellent joke, and we listened to the Krauts cursing and whining as their water drained away.

"Pretty soon they'll be drinking their own piss," said Nikolai Kulikov.

I was fuming over the revolting life in the trenches the Germans had imposed on us. Lice had colonized my body. I was scratching constantly, as we all were. I hated the Germans more than ever.

"We have to keep them from reaching clean water," I instructed the other snipers. "We want to make their guts run."

So our sniper group forced the Krauts to give up their excursions to the spring, and we were also able to turn most of their mortar crew into casualties. This way we kept them from being able to lob a single mortar shell at the Red Army positions on the docks.

The second night, a messenger from battalion HQ reached us. The orders he brought were: "Do everything possible to hold your positions." What that meant was, do not to even think about retreat.

It was late October and fall had arrived. The weather changed constantly. One minute the sun was hot, and the next we would be at the receiving end of a cold drizzle. This was the weather of the steppe. We sat through four days of this, awake and asleep, our guns always clenched in our hands. Some nights we had rain and cold winds. We would huddle in the corner of a trench, shivering, as freezing drizzle fell. The water pooled at the bottom of the trenches. This constant damp would lead to various forms of misery. In the mornings there was always a chill, and we would wake up to discover our asses had frozen to the ground.

The fascists never gave up. They kept slithering down the hill towards our trenches, but when they came too close, we were always able to repel them with grenades. Because the Krauts were coming down a steep grade, we had to make sure to throw our grenades far enough, so they did not roll back down into our own positions.

Gryazev's long arms were well suited to this job. He was like a watchman on a ranch, patrolling a fence. If an enemy came within throwing distance, he would heave a grenade at them. He never missed. His aim was remarkable. When the grenades went off, all you could see was dust and smoke, but once the air cleared, the Krauts' limbs would be scattered in various places, along with shreds of their uniforms and their weapons. Gryazev could drop an enemy at a hundred paces, throwing uphill! He truly had a magic arm.

One time I picked up a few grenades and he took them from me, admonishing me: "Vasya, your arms are too short! We can't afford to waste any of these!"

As our third night on Mamayev Hill was winding to a close, not a single star was visible. Heavy clouds obscured everything.

The German positions were less than a hundred feet away. We could hear the metallic clink of pots and pans, and heels knocking against each other as the Germans scraped the mud off their boots. We could overhear entire conversations, but neither myself nor Gryazev could figure out a word. As it happened, both of us had enrolled for German courses in high school, but we had spent the days skipping class. Now we were cursing ourselves for it.

We were always shaking with fatigue. At night we had to observe the enemy's activities – no one could really sleep. Sometimes we would catch a glimpse of the Volga and watch the wind ripple across the water's black surface. The frigid sky overhead only made us more weary. We watched as clouds hovered over the city's ruins, and the biting wind grew colder and colder.

The Krauts apparently had not had any fresh water since we arrived, and they were getting desperate. Our plans at keeping them pinned down were working perfectly. On the 4th morning, their soldiers boiled out of their trenches, and small groups began inching forward towards us

Even with their bodies pressed close to the ground, the descending Germans had no cover. They were approaching us on a down-grade, so that the entire length of their bodies was exposed. We didn't even need our telescopic sights. It was like shooting fish in a barrel. The element of surprise, if that was what they were after, was lost.

This was their final attempt on us, while we were posted at position 102. Our sharp-shooting and supply of grenades helped us carry out the division commander's orders; the position at elevation 102 meters remained in our hands. And judging by the looks of things, we wouldn't be leaving it any time soon. None of us were even thinking about retreat.

CHAPTER 10.
A DIFFICULT POSITION

It was day four. We were waiting for nightfall to take up our new posts. At last the sun began to set. It painted the cirrus clouds a bright pink. The droning motors from Nazi aircraft died away. The sky over the city grew dark, but it still took a long time for the sun's light to completely disappear from the horizon.

By midnight we had finished setting up our snipers' posts. Exhaustion and thirst were setting in. The vengeful Germans had cut off our path to the spring with a string of mines, but thanks to our machine guns and snipers, the spring was off-limits to them, too. We had been reduced to a stalemate.

This was another evening with no dinner. We were tortured by hunger and even more so by thirst. Our mouths were like cotton and our tongues were swollen.

We worked in silence. We all understood each other's misery. No words were necessary. I could tell everyone was dying for some sleep, if only to lie down a few moments and regain some strength, so I granted the others a break while Kostrikov and I stayed on watch.

Kostrikov and I agreed on a distress signal to use with our flare pistols, then we split up. I distinctly remember the whisper of the evening breeze, the flickering embers of cigarettes in the enemy's camp, and the barely perceptible aroma of tobacco smoke. That made my desire to smoke even stronger, but none of us had any cigarettes.

~~~

The muffled clang of metal against metal and random excerpts of German conversations I kept overhearing were driving me crazy…I had to have a smoke.

As if he'd read my mind, Kostrikov started rifling through some dead Krauts' pockets. In no time, he hit pay dirt. We lit up and the tobacco took away our fatigue.

We suspected that the Krauts were preparing a trap. We were setting up decoy positions, and we knew they had to be doing the same. Outsmarting them was going to demand all our cunning and vigilance.

I drove a shovel deep into the earth, placed my ear against the handle, and listened to it, as if it were a stethoscope. A shovel in the ground, like a stethoscope against someone's chest, conducts vibrations. But with my shovel, the vibrations came from the summit of Mamayev Hill, instead of from someone's beating heart.

Somewhere nearby the Germans were chiseling out rock or driving in a stake. A little farther away – they were dropping something heavy onto the ground, maybe boxes of supplies, or sandbags. I didn't hear any digging. But very close by I heard steps. Nazi jackboots were marching up and down in their trench, thumping loudly against the earth. They were changing their guards.

I woke Nikolai Kulikov, who had been sleeping nearby. He jerked up like someone had scalded him with hot water, his rifle in his fist.

"Where are they?"

"Nowhere," I said, "relax. It's your turn to keep watch."

While Nikolai rubbed his eyes, the Krauts continued changing their guards. A new enemy machine gunner above took up sentry duty. He was obviously a greenhorn. Despite the darkness, I easily lined him up and picked him off. Nobody came to replace him, as the enemy realized that the machine gun position was too exposed.

I was in command of our little detachment, and therefore was obligated to check that everything was OK before I sacked out. So I made the rounds of our positions and found that the snipers had all switched off, and that those who had been relieved were huddled up and resting.

I returned to Kulikov's position. In our trench's shelter, soldiers' greatcoats lay on the ground. These were the final gifts from comrades long dead and buried. I burrowed underneath a coat and drifted off to sleep.

Kulikov stayed standing at his machine gun, because he was afraid that if he sat down, sleep would overwhelm him. He said it was better to fight it off by standing up, never mind that he presented a bigger target.

Kulikov woke me just before dawn, as we had agreed.

The first thing he said was, "Chief, this thirst is driving me nuts." He could barely talk, as his throat was so parched. "I thought that getting through the night would be easier than the day," he said, "but I was wrong."

Every minute it grew lighter. One after the other, the snipers approached me, all asking about water.

"We'll get by, relax," I assured them. Their lips were cracked and their faces drawn. Then a spark of inspiration flared up in Kostrikov's eyes. He flopped down on the ground, wiggled his legs like a happy dog, tossed his head back and cried out, "Boys, we've got water!"

Then he was silent, smiling to himself contentedly. We looked around him but none of us saw anything. It appeared that the prolonged hardship had caused Kostrikov to become unhinged. Finally Gryazev spoke up.

"Well, come on, where's this water you're so pleased about?"

Kostrikov was a Georgian, with hooded black eyes.

"Where's the water, you ask? Out there, you know how many

dead Germans are lying around?"

"So what?" said the now irritated Gryazev.

"They've all got water in their canteens." Kostrikov laughed like a madman. "We just have to round them up!"

"I should have thought of that," croaked Kulikov. He was suffering the worst of us all. "But you'll need cover to retrieve them."

Kulikov, Dvoyashkin and I set out for our positions. I barely managed to shoulder my rifle, before the Krauts moved up a machine gun on their side of the embankment and opened fire. But this new gunner of theirs had no cover whatsoever. I took aim and shot, and the machine gun fell silent. Then I realized that the enemy was watching me. Perhaps this gunner had been used as a pawn, to discover where I was.

I knew I had to change my location. I left behind my helmet, using it for a decoy, then I grabbed my periscope and scurried through the trench in search of another position.

Meanwhile, Gryazev and Kostrikov completed their canteen "roundup." They had returned to a site near our mustering point. Whenever we had to meet, I would go there and raise my cap in the air. But this time, it was Kostrikov who gave the signal to assemble.

I couldn't believe they had finished their run so quickly, but when I got to the mustering point I saw five canteens, laid out on a tarp at Kostrikov's feet. The canteens contained some sort of rusty, bitter liquid we would normally never have touched, but in our present circumstances, we drank it down greedily. We were all re-energized immediately.

~~~

At about ten AM, large movements of fascist troops began on the southern slopes of Mamayev Hill, to our left. They were shifting men from a deep trench that went down the hill towards an anti-tank emplacement that could fire on the railroad bridge. Their designs were easy enough to figure out: they wanted to set up an ambush against our tanks, should we try to bring them over the bridge for an attack.

If our forces inside the city had tried such an advance, this battery could have inflicted crippling damage, but we had too few tanks to even dream about mounting an armored attack. So I only assigned two snipers to watch over the emplacement – Volovatikh and Podkolov. Volovatikh and Podlokov were our only reinforcements so far – they had just moved up to join us, led to our position by a regimental messenger.

These two took up excellent positions, camouflaged themselves, and started picking off members of the battery's gun crew. For this reason, the enemy battery was usually dead quiet during the day. From our elevation on the upper slopes, we had an unobstructed view of their weapons below; they stuck to the southern base like frozen snakes, and their artillery positions appeared to be silent and abandoned.

Soon we stopped paying them much attention, and this was our mistake. More German troops had slipped in to those positions, but they stayed clear of the emplacements we could target, and diligently kept themselves hidden. They were obviously plotting something – but what?

I took a good hard look. I was surprised to see that the German line had sprouted antennae, that is – they had built narrow, shallow trenches at right angles, with circular foxholes dug on the ends. How the hell could we have missed this? When had they managed to construct them? Last night? It did not seem possible. Had my "shovel-stethoscope" deceived me? I could not believe it.

At that moment Volovatikh spotted a new group of enemy soldiers assembling near our landmark #5. 'Landmark #5' was a wrecked antiaircraft gun on the hillside. It was no more than eighty yards away.

Before I managed to say a word, Sasha Gryazev had picked up two grenades and darted off down the trench.

"Stop, get back here!" I yelled.

Sasha halted and turned to me with a real hang-dog look.

"Chief, permission requested to kill the enemy. I'll take out the entire position with one go," he said with a chuckle. Then he continued, in a more serious vein. "Chief, they're not all for you to kill. Let the rest of us chalk up a few."

This rebuke caught me by surprise, but I should have anticipated it. The rest of the guys had been keeping track of their kills - I wasn't the only one. We'd set up daily "personal head counts." Each sniper had to confirm his kill, with an eye-witness's signature. And it was true, I had quite a few more than anyone else. Sasha Gryazev's own signature attested to this. So, what could I say to him? He stood there waiting for an answer, while the rest of the snipers watched us.

I was hurt by what Sasha had said, and didn't have an adequate reply. So I waved my hand, to signal my accord. He smiled triumphantly and quipped, "About time!"

But my conscience was tearing me up. I tried to recall an incident where I'd abused my command, or used one of my sniper partners as bait, to lure targets for myself. I couldn't think of any, and I hoped I was correct.

My crew was standing around in silence, smoking. They could all see me struggling with what had just happened.

Then I started thinking about the Krauts by landmark #5, and how they were deployed, and how they had so carelessly allowed us to spot them, and then it hit me, all in rush.

"Guys – it's a trap! Nikolai Ostapovich," I said to Kulikov, "…go catch Sasha and tell him it's a setup!"

Unfortunately, Kulikov couldn't reach Sasha in time. Sasha had to break cover to heave his first grenade - and he hesitated a second too long before ducking down again. An explosive bullet hit him in the right side of his chest and spun him around like a top.

I ran over to him. Sasha knew he was going. His eyes were already glazing over. He appeared resigned to meeting his fate. Sasha calmly pulled out his *Komsomol* card and said, "Take this, Vasya…you were right; it was a trap…tell my comrades that I died a communist…"

We took off his shirt, to try and cover up his gaping wound. It was hopeless. His right arm hung limp and blood was rushing from his torso. We had nothing to dress the wound with, so we cut off his *telnyashka* to use for a bandage.

Sasha's eyes came alive one last time. He pulled the blood-soaked *telnyashka* from my hands, stuck it on the end of his rifle, staggered to his feet, and brandished his gun in the face of the enemy.

"Hold me up," he muttered, and we did, so he was facing the enemy's position.

"We're going to win!" he shouted, and then he collapsed into our arms.

The Nazi position was about eighty yards away. Sasha's grenade hadn't come close to it, and with a single bullet the Krauts had robbed us of this great man…I cursed myself for not having stopped him.

On his *Komsomol* card, Gryazev had scrawled a message for his son: "A patriot is not the man who talks about his love for his country, but the one who's ready to give his life for it. In the name of my country and in your name, my son, I am prepared to sacrifice everything. Grow, my son, and learn to love your country not only in word but in deed."

When we buried Sasha Gryazev, we swore to take our revenge on the Nazis.

That was a difficult day for us, despite the fact that the Krauts did not launch any significant attacks. Nor was there any aerial bombardment. Two separate waves of Nazis probed our positions near the water tanks, but we repelled each of them with our machine guns.

The sun was getting low. The horizon turned crimson. A light breeze started blowing. It was only by the drift of smoke through the air that could you tell the wind's direction. Brown dust was settling on the earth and on our shoulders.

Night finally lay down its curtain. The eastern sky was painted in a gray and black velvet while to the west a band of bright light glowed. I looked off to the horizon, in a stupor. Gryazev's death was weighing heavily on me, and I had no desire to eat or drink. My sorrow was only occasionally perturbed by the goings-on in the enemy's camp.

Down the hillside, near the railroad tracks, which was by one of our medical stations, I could hear a metallic clanging. I could also hear distant shouting from our officers.

One of the German machine guns opened fire; and as far as I knew, they didn't have any targets. It wasn't like they'd be shooting at stray dogs - every dog in Stalingrad had already swum to the other side of the Volga. I figured the Kraut gunner must be shooting into the air for the hell of it.

Suddenly a thick fog set in, which made it hard to see your hand in front of your face. The pitch-black darkness jolted me back to reality. An enemy scout would love weather like this; he could easily crawl up and take a captive…

But in a thousand years, we would never have dreamed about what happened next. Under the cover of the fog, soldiers of our third battalion broke through to us. They were led by Lieutenant Fedosov, the former staff commander of the second battalion.

As always, Fedosov smelled like a brewery. When he saw me he slapped me on the back.

"Congratulations, Zaitsev," he said. "You fellows are to pack up and head to the rear, on the orders of Major Metelev."

Of course, I was relieved - but curious. "What's the rush?" I asked.

Fedosov lit up a cigarette and offered me one, then looked straight at me with a frown.

"*Ti ne podmakhiva*,"[30] he replied, his voice hoarse. Apparently Fedosov was feeling sorry for himself, for having been ordered to this meat-grinder position.

The college boy *politruk*[31] Stepan Kryakhov walked over to us. We shook hands. Meanwhile Fedosov ambled off, taking long

---

[30] *Ti ne podmakhiva*: "None of your God-damned business," or a more literal translation: "you're not the one being screwed, so don't wiggle your ass!"
[31] *Politruk:* short for *politicheskiy rukovoditel*, political instructor

pulls from a bottle he had been keeping under his coat.

Once we were alone, Kryakhov told me that Fedosov's *Komsomol* card had been revoked, as a punishment for his chronic drunkenness. Fedosov had been put in charge of a penal company, and sent here, to the most dangerous front. To quote Comrade Stalin, he was here "to redeem his sins by blood."

"Are the rest of these men serving out punishments, as well?" I asked.

"Yes," said Kryakhov.

"Then answer me this: what have they sent you here for?"

Kryakhov paused to think for a moment and then spoke in a quiet voice.

"I'm a *politrabotnik*, and I answer for everything that goes on here, including the character of our troops and their misdeeds. We haven't written these men off completely yet; I want to help them atone for the mistakes they've made…"

We got to talking – openly and honestly – and at the end of our conversation I asked Kryakhov to put in a request to the regimental commander, Major Metelev. I explained that my sniper group should not be withdrawn just yet, because we were obligated to avenge the death of Sasha Gryazev. I also asked that my men and I first be granted twenty-four hours of rest.

~~~

I recalled the game "mystery cards" that we played as children. Each card bore an intricate web of brush strokes and lines, and the object was to "find the boy" amid the confusing tangle. It was an amusing game to play when we were little.

The "game" we played in the ruins of Stalingrad was similar. For innumerable hours we peered amid the chaos of rubble, looking for some sign of the enemy. Only in this game, the stakes were much higher.

~~~

At this point, us snipers on Mamayev Hill had gone for days without rest. Our spirits had been drained, and our sense of initiative was waning.

We knew that danger was hiding behind every corner, but lying in a dirt shell hole all day and staring at an unchanging panorama of rubble led to exhaustion. The consequences, hesitation and indifference, kept threatening to overtake us.

While it may only take a couple of seconds for a sniper to aim and fire, the preparation for this task often requires hours and hours of close observation. But what kind of observing can a sniper do when he's fatigued? He's useless. What's more, he may endanger himself or others, because he's stopped paying attention. And a sniper in this state of mind does not have the correct mental focus for combat.

Therefore, the regimental commander allowed us twenty-four hours rest. Since our line had been reinforced by the penal company under Lieutenant Fedosov, the threat of our being surrounded had abated. It was safe for us to sleep for a few hours.

Before we crawled off to our "bedrooms" (in reality, small shelves hacked into the walls of the ravine), we pointed out the most dangerous parts of the enemy's trenches to Fedosov's men. They probably assumed the Nazi trenches were deserted. Of course, we knew better.

For the first time since my last leave from the naval base at Vladivostok, I had the privilege of sleeping for an entire day. I was awakened by the clang of a kettle next to my ear. It was dinnertime.

After a meal of kasha, meat and hot tea, I wanted to go back to sleep again. We still had some time left, so we burrowed back in our holes and took a few more hours of shut-eye. We awoke to the sound of shelling in the ravine. We had been delivered with some new, dry uniforms, and I put one on. What a feeling, to put on dry clothes, after days of wallowing in soaking rags!

A Nazi machine gun was rattling somewhere nearby. I picked up a trench periscope and used it to scan the horizon. These periscopes had excellent optics and were good for observing from fixed positions.

I could make out tracer bullets sinking into the cliffs above, with a muffled pounding. I was more than curious about where these bullets were coming from. I had to find their source and take it out of commission – if not now while it was dark, then at the crack of dawn. I should have been able to find the shooter by following the brightly lit tracer bullets, but the machine gun had quickly fallen silent, as if the gunner suspected someone was looking for him.

Dvoyashkin approached and sat down next to me. A noise came from within the ravine – the knocking of empty jars or pots. A German machine gun opened fire. Then I realized this was the same gunner I had noticed before.

"What's he shooting at," I asked, "who dropped the bowl down there?"

"Our wounded are being brought in to the medical station in the ravine, and that's the clatter of their mess kits falling, when that s.o.b. hits them," answered Dvoyashkin.

I was enraged. "He's hunting our wounded, is he?" And I was angry with myself for not having eliminated this criminal earlier. I decided there and then to find him and put a halt to his activities.

The fighting started up again at dawn. I changed my position amid the smoke and noise.

This particular enemy gunner had been granted a day's reprieve to keep working his malicious deeds, because our snipers in the sector had all been granted 24-hour leave. So now he had the mistaken impression that he could operate with impunity, and he was getting careless. He should never have kept using tracers. They led me straight back to him.

I found the scavenger and put him in my crosshairs, and his gun fell silent.

БЕЙ НАСМЕРТЬ!

"Fight Them Until They Are Dead."

Soviet poster issued during the battle of Stalingrad. The poster
on the wall above the machine gunners reads, "Save us!"

ОТСТОИМ
ВОЛГУ-МАТУШКУ

We Will Defend the Volga, Mother-River!

Civilian Volunteers. Workers from from the Tractor factory
are mobilized to confront the Nazis

ДОРОГИЕ ТОВАРИЩИ!
РОДНЫЕ СТАЛИНГРАДЦЫ!

Остервенелые банды врага подкатились к стенам нашего родного города.

Снова, как и 24 года тому назад, наш город переживает тяжелые дни.

Кровавые гитлеровцы рвутся в солнечный Сталинград к великой русской реке-Волге.

Воины Красной Армии самоотверженно защищают Сталинград. Все подступы к городу усеяны труппами немецко-фашистских захватчиков.

Обер-бандит Гитлер, бросает в бой все новые и новые банды своих головорезов, стремясь любой ценой захватить Сталинград.

Товарищи сталинградцы!

Не отдадим родного города на поругание немцам. Встанем все как один, на защиту любимого города, родного дома, родной семьи.

Покроем все улицы города непроходимыми баррикадами.

Сделаем каждый дом, каждый квартал, каждую улицу неприступной крепостью.

Выходите все на строительство баррикад. Организуйте бригады. Баррикадируйте каждую улицу. Для строительства баррикад используйте все что имеется под руками—камень, бревно, железо, вагоны трамвая и т. д.

Построим баррикады быстро и так, чтобы боец-защитник Сталинграда беспощадно громил врага с баррикад построенных Нами.

Бойцы Красной Армии! Защитники Сталинграда!

Мы, сделаем для вас все чтобы отстоять город.

Ни шагу назад!

Бейте беспощадно врага. Отомстите немцам за все учиненные им зверства, за разрушенные очаги, за пролитые слезы и кровь наших детей, матерей и жен.

Защитники Сталинграда! В грозный 1918 год наши отцы отстояли Красный Царицын от банд немецких наемников.

Отстоим и мы в 1942 году Краснознаменный Сталинград.

Отстоим, чтобы отбросить, а затем разгромить кровавую банду немецких захватчиков.

Все на строительство баррикад!

Все, кто способен носить оружие на баррикады, на защиту родного города, родного дома.

Сталинградский
Городской Комитет Обороны

STALINGRAD CITY COMMITTEE FOR DEFENSE

Dear Comrades, Fellow Stalingraders!

Frenzied bands of the enemy have come to the walls our native city. Things are once more like 24 years ago, and our city is living through difficult days. The Bloody Hitlerite Fascists are forcing themselves into our sunny Stalingrad, towards the great Russian River Volga.

Soldiers of the Russian Army, defend Stalingrad selflessly!

All approaches to the city will be covered with the bodies of our German fascist enemies.

The super-bandit Hitler brings new bands of his head-choppers to the fight, to try and take Stalingrad by any means.

Dear fellow Stalingraders, we won't give our dear city to the German desecrators.

Let us all stand like one for the defense our dear family. Let us cover all the streets of the city with impregnable barricades.

Let us make each house, each quarter of the city, into a fortress.

Go out everyone, and help build barricades, organize brigades, to barricade each street. Use everything you can find – stone, logs, steel tracks, tram cars…

Build the barricades quickly, in such a way that the soldier defending Stalingrad can mercilessly smash our enemies from the barricades we build.

Soldiers of the Red Army, defenders of Stalingrad, we will do everything for you, so you can defend our city, not a step back !

Fight the enemy mercilessly! Take Revenge on the Germans for their brutality, for the destruction of our homes, for the blood and tears of our children, mothers, and wives.

Defenders of Stalingrad, in 1918 our fathers defended Red Tsaritsyn[1] from the bands of German mercenaries. So we will defend our city in 1942. The red flag and red medal went to Stalingrad……

Defend in order to throw back and then destroy the bloody band of German invaders.

So everyone, go to build barricades.

Everyone capable of bearing arms, go to the barricades for the defense of our homes.

---

[1] Tsaritsyn, the pre-civil war Russian name for Stalingrad. After Stalin's death and the exposure of his crimes, Stalingrad was re-named Volgograd.

Red Army Tommy-gunners prepare to cross the Volga.
The round magazine of the Soviet PPsh-41 submachine
gun carried 71 bullets.

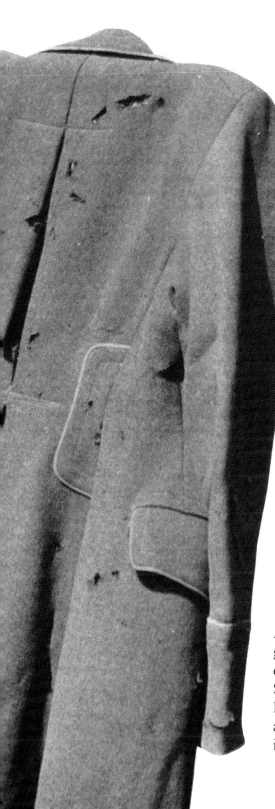

A Russian soldier's
greatcoat, now on
display at the
Stalingrad War
Museum. There
are 22 bullet holes
in the coat

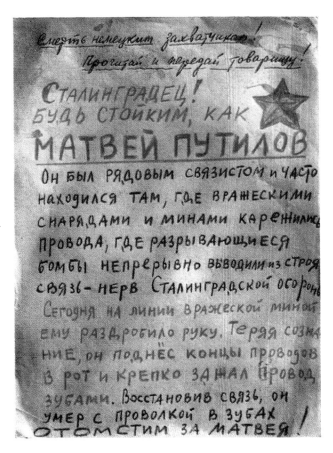

Death to the German invaders!
Read this and pass it around your mates!

Defenders of Stalingrad , be resolute, like Matvey Putilov. He was an ordinary signalman and he always found himself in places where enemy shells and mines shredded cables, in places where exploding bombs would constantly disable our communications systems – the nerve centre of Stalingrad's defences. Today, while serving on the front line, his arm was ripped to pieces by a mine. Just before losing consciousness he managed to put both ends of the cable into his mouth and bite down on them. He restored the line, dying, gripping the cable with his teeth.

WE HAVE TO AVENGE MATVEY'S DEATH!!!

A Political Commissar, Chuikov and Zaitzev, during the battle

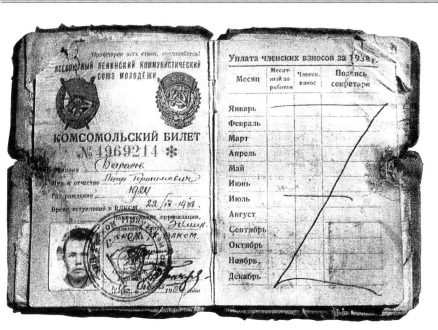

Bullet-riddled Komsomol card of
Pavielienko Alexander Yakovlevich

This sculpture of children playing 'ring around the rosie' is near Stalingrad's city center. This photo was taken at the height of the battle.

Zaitsev (far left) and three other snipers from his group. The sniper standing next to Zaitsev is Galifan Abzalov.

Zaitsev and General Chuikov on a visit to Stalingrad,
20 years after the battle.

Zaitsev and fellow Russian sniper Anatoly Chekhov meet at a
party in the early 1960s. The reunion was a surprise for Zaitsev,
as he believed Chekhov had been killed in action.

In the name of the people of the
United States of America,
I present this scroll to the
City of Stalingrad
to commemorate our admiration for
its gallant defenders whose courage
fortitude, and devotion during the siege
of September 13, 1942 to January 31, 1943
will inspire forever the hearts of all
free people. Their glorious victory
stemmed the tide of invasion and
marked the turning point in the
war of the Allied Nations against
the forces of aggression.

May 7" 1944

Franklin D. Roosevelt

Washington D.C.

President Roosevelt's letter of congratulations
to the victorious defenders of Stalingrad.

CHAPTER 11.
FIND THE SNIPER

I cleaned myself up as best as I could. I was too enervated to sleep. I descended into the ravine to talk to the wounded soldiers who had arrived the preceding night. In order to locate the sniper who had hit Sasha Gryazev, it was crucial for me to find out where and under what conditions these other soldiers had been wounded. I was especially interested in bullet wounds. After all, every wound is different, and each one contains clues about the enemy's fire-power at a particular site.

Near the entrance of the med station sat a heavyset soldier. His black eyes were bright with that bitter soldier's humor that stays with us up to the moment of death. His mouth was bandaged shut. The bandage over his chin was caked brown with dried blood. The soldier's large, dirty hands and shirt were both stained with splotches of blood.

The staff at the Medical Station told me that he had been wounded the previous morning. His ID papers indicated that his name was Stefan Safonov. Next to him lay a torn section of a book with no cover, with a broken-off piece of a pencil stuck between its pages.

"How did a the Krauts manage to locate you?" I asked him.

The soldier gave me a glance full of reproach. His look said:

get lost; but I endured his withering gaze and waited for an answer. Finally he picked up the pencil and scribbled a reply onto a page of the book.

"You haven't had a chance to smell my breath, have you? If you'd like…"

"That's alright," I answered, "just relax. I'm not trying to upset you, I just need to find out where and how you were wounded. It's very important."

With his next response, I learned that Safonov had been shot while lighting up from a companion's cigarette.

"And where's your friend that gave you the light?"

"My friend, Chursin, is still at the front." Safonov was writing furiously with the pencil. "He's just waiting his turn …they'll put a bullet through him, too, soon enough."

"Idiots!" I blurted out angrily. "We spent a whole week up on the hill, and managed to keep our heads away from Kraut fire, while in a single night you greenhorns manage to lose half your unit! What's your problem?"

Safonov scribble some obscenities in response, and I got up and stormed out of the aid station, and back to my position.

I crawled through the trenches, to the grave of Sasha Gryazev, and then descended into a bunker, where after what seemed like a whole day of crawling on my knees, I was finally able to stand up straight. I had to figure out what to do about the enemy snipers in our area. I knew they were out there, but they were operating with a great deal of caution.

As a rule, Nazi snipers would take up positions deep within their own line of defense, whereas ours would crawl up to the very edge of our front lines. The Krauts also set up many decoy positions, making it even tougher to pick out your real target. After I had a little experience, I learned that two things were essential: keen observation and a good dose of restraint.

Let's say you spot what appears to be the reflection of a lighter in the sun, and you presume it's a sniper lighting a cigarette. Maybe yes, maybe no. Mark the spot and wait; a stream of smoke should appear. A little time will pass, or maybe even a whole day, and for a fraction of a second a helmet appears. But don't fire! Even if you can get him this time, you don't know yet, where among the decoy positions you'll find your real enemy sniper. And if you shoot and hit a decoy, you've revealed your position, but gained nothing.

This line of thinking convinced me I had to monitor the area from which the bullet that hit Sasha Gryazev had been fired.

I crawled into the sniper Podkopov's position and began my observation. One hour passed, then two. My eyes ached and my neck grew tired from the strain of holding my head still, but I did not move. Podkopov had assured me that there were no snipers' nests where I was looking, and that he had checked this area at least a dozen times. Then he crawled away. I trusted him, but I had a hunch that there was somebody out there. This feeling, combined with the desire to avenge Sasha's death, kept me rooted to the spot, despite the discomfort.

In an hour, Podkopov and Morozov returned with trench periscopes. All three of us began combing the same landscape I had been monitoring for hours. Heavy shells from Nazi six-barrel mortars soared over our heads. They exploded deep within our lines, shooting up columns of earth. You could actually see these huge shells in flight. They hurtled through the air with a screech. They wobbled from side to side like a piglet in the mud. We started calling the Germans' six-barrel mortars "donkeys" for another reason as well: their screams would be heard three times a day – once at sunup, around five AM; another time at midday, and a final round at the onset of darkness. The German mortar crew knew exactly when our stretcher-bearers transported our wounded to the Volga.

We lay in silence, observing. The rays of the setting sun were lighting up the hill. They illuminated all the dark recesses and bathed every outcropping in bright relief. A bit further down the hill some German artillery shell casings lay scattered. I had nothing to do, so I counted them. There were twenty-three. Then I did a double-take. One was missing a bottom! Through a shell casing like that, just like through a telescope, someone could see a long ways into the distance. I raised myself up a little.

Suddenly there in the casing – it was like a flint struck a spark! An explosive bullet ripped into the embankment behind me.

Nikolai Kulikov was sitting next to me in the trench.

"Chief, are you still alive?" he asked.

I was a bit shaken, but damned if I was going to admit that to Kulikov.

"I'm rolling a cigarette, aren't I?"

"What happened?" Kulikov asked. "Did you get wounded again?"

"I'm alive and well," I replied.

"Then why'd you jump like that?"

"We've been doing a poor job of following the enemy's movements," I replied. Then I explained to Kulikov what had happened. The German sniper, through his hard work and cold calculation, had earned the right to a first shot – and he took it. He had shot for the Russian sniper....

Over dinner we debated a plan of action. Nikolai Kulikov and Podkopov voted to advance on the pile of shells after nightfall. Shaikin and Kostrikov disagreed, insisting that the sniper wouldn't be so stupid as to maintain this position. Morozov and Kuz'min suggested waiting until the Germans launched a general assault, then beneath the cloak of chaos, we could launch our counter-attack, directed at sniper's position. "For us to do our work, a little background noise is best," said Morozov.

To tell the truth, this type of vendetta, where we had committed so many resources, and so much time, to locating and eliminating one Kraut sniper – this was against established procedures. But we were all burning to avenge Sasha Gryazev.

I was too beat to decide on anything. "Let's sleep on it," I suggested.

My friends knew that I preferred to sleep in the evenings because I had trouble getting any shut-eye during the early morning hours. So we deferred the decision while I crawled off into a corner and sacked out.

I awoke at one in the morning. Nikolai Kulikov was busy cleaning his rifle; the rest of our crew was still asleep.

When Kulikov saw that I was awake, he grabbed his rifle and took off into the darkness. I picked up my submachine gun and a pack full of grenades and followed.

The night was uncommonly quiet. The calm before the storm: we presumed the enemy was preparing a new assault.

I took a position not far from my sleeping comrades, and tuned my ears to the silence around me.

~~~

I remember my encounter with our army commander, General Vassili Chuikov. This happened immediately before a battle launched by the enemy, on the morning of October 16th. The commander had invited several of us to his bunker to receive awards.

Chuikov regarded us. He was a short dark man with wavy hair and a very intense gaze. He spoke that morning with a surprising calm.

"By defending Stalingrad, we're tying the enemy hand and foot. The outcome of this war and the fate of millions of Soviet citizens – our fathers, mothers, wives and children – depends upon our determination to fight here to the bitter end. This does not mean, however, that we should let ourselves be guided by foolish bravery."

He placed in my palm a medal that read, "For Valor."

"Our resolve to fight amid the ruins of Stalingrad under the policy 'Not a step back' is fulfilling a mandate of the people," the commander continued. "How could we ever look our fellow countrymen in the eyes, if we retreat?"

I felt the general was directing his question to me. He knew that I had been born in the Urals, that my family – grandfather, father and mother – as well as many of my comrades - were there now. No, there was no way I could face them, my eyes filled with shame and disgrace, if we were to give up Stalingrad. I answered the general, "We have nowhere to retreat; for us there is no land beyond the Volga."

For some reason, these words appealed to Chuikov, and to his assistant from the Komsomol, Ivan Maksimovich Vidyuka. Vidyuka was a tall cadaverous-looking fellow with bushy eyebrows. He clasped my hand and held it for a long time, repeating, "That's the spirit, that's a Komsomolyets for you!"

The night I was hunting for Gryazev's killer, Vidyuka came around to visit my positions. But now, how would this night end, and what would morning bring? I hoped my plan would work. I realized that I should have called Nikolai Medvedev to help me.

Medvedev was a good man. He liked to critique the more sluggish snipers. Recently, he had discussed some of his experiences with a group of new trainees. He walked up to them and, without saying a word, unrolled his tobacco pouch. It was made of red silk and decorated with embroidery. He showed it off, as if to say "just imagine the time and love my girl put into making this!" Two empty shell casings rolled out of the pouch.

"This is all I wanted to say to you," he declared. "Let's head into the field. I think we'll come to understand each other better there."

That was right, Viktor. A soldier learns the sniper's art through practice, rather than through talking about it. I recalled some words of General Chuikov: "The work of a sniper is not to wait for the enemy to stick his head up, but to force the enemy to show himself, and then without delay, to put a bullet in his head."

With these thoughts I whiled away that night's long, solitary hours. The silence was relentless, like a noose around my neck.

Finally I saw a band of light was growing on the horizon. I was ready to go and wake up my comrades, but they were already crawling towards me. They had brought breakfast and more ammunition. One of them announced, "The regimental scouts caught a Nazi and made him talk. There'll be an artillery attack on our front lines at six this morning."

We didn't bother opening the thermoses of kasha. We left it all for dinner, grabbed some zwieback, and took off for our posts. Not far from my position I ran into the red-nosed Lieutenant Fedosov. He had posted his soldiers and was now awaiting the attack.

"Six o'clock's come and gone, and the Germans haven't made a noise," he said.

Nikolai Kulikov was waiting for me, at our position opposite the pile of German shell casings. We had stashed an artillery periscope there, to aid us in surveillance. What we saw when we looked through it didn't surprise us: twenty-two shell casings lay where they were the day before. The twenty-third, with the missing bottom, had disappeared. But where had it gone to?

An artillery periscope has excellent optics. Small details of the terrain, or of a soldier's uniform, will be clearly visible from several hundred yards away. I ran my eyes over bush after bush, foxhole after foxhole, using the magnifying optics to penetrate deep into the enemy's lines. I scanned to the very summit of the hill. Next to the summit was a small depression, and there it was – the artillery shell with the missing bottom! It was camouflaged by an embankment, near the hollow. Through the shell casing, I could see the German's scope. The shell shaded his scope from sunlight, hiding its reflection, and helping its operator see his targets. It even seemed that he had some camera apparatus on his rifle, and was photographing each target, at the moment he fired his shots.

"There you are..." I whispered, as if he would hear me and depart on his own.

I was shaking with rage. In order to calm down, I passed the periscope to Nikolai Kulikov and told him where to find the sniper. I walked his gaze there, guiding him by easily recognizable landmarks.

"Got him! There he is!" Nikolai exclaimed. "Chief, we've got to nail him now. Otherwise, he may get away."

Somebody walked up behind me. I could smell vodka on his breath. This person whispered behind my back: "Just a minute, boys. Let me get a look at a real live Nazi sniper!"

It was Lieutenant Fedosov. We hadn't even noticed his approach. Fedosov was anxious over the delayed enemy attack and was so fidgety that he was drinking twice his normal ration.

Now I had held the Kraut sniper in my sights for over an hour. I was tired and losing my mental focus. I forced myself to banish this exhaustion.

Meanwhile the Kraut kept peering through his scope. It was only a matter of time before he discovered us. I asked Kulikov, "Nikolai, what do you think – does he see us?"

"We'll find out."

Nikolai backed up and used a stick to raise a helmet a few inches above the embankment. The German fired a shot that ripped through the helmet. I was surprised that he went for this bait. Perhaps the tedium of waiting for a target had made him forget the risk he was taking.

I watched as the German sniper placed one hand on the breech and reached forward to pick up the empty shell casing. Collecting shell casings was standard operating procedure after making a victorious shot. As he did so, he raised his head slightly from his scope. It gave me the few inches of scalp I needed to zero in on... and at that second my own shot rang out. The bullet struck him at the hairline. Then his helmet fell forward over his brow and his rifle lay motionless, the barrel still inside the artillery shell.

Lieutenant Fedosov dropped to the trench floor and found my the little note pad that held my "personal headcount." Fedosov licked the lead of his pencil and inscribed in large letters: 'I have witnessed a duel. Before my eyes, Vassili Zaitsev killed a Nazi sniper. – A. Fedosov.'

That was how we took revenge for the murder of Sasha Gryazev. In the days that followed, my student, sniper Nikolai Kulikov – operating with more confidence – used this same position to eliminate two enemy artillery observers working the slopes of the hill.

Meanwhile, the impending artillery attack that our intelligence had reported never materialized. The Krauts must have realized that we had a captive who had spilled the beans, and that we would have our big guns across the Volga targeted and waiting for them. The enemy probably guessed as much and decided not to go asking for trouble. Day by day, they were growing more cautious and more cunning.

CHAPTER 12.
WHEN PATIENCE IS ESSENTIAL

Mamayev Hill occupied an imposing height over the city. Its southern arm was indicated on the map at an elevation marker of 102.0 meters. From its peak, it commanded an excellent view of the city, which by now was almost completely in the hands of the enemy. Therefore it was easy to understand our desire to hold at least the southern slopes of Mamayev Hill, if not the summit itself, and to use this position to attack our enemy's flanks and rear. You couldn't find a better position than this in all of Stalingrad. We could literally peer through our sights and see the backs of the heads of the Nazi soldiers who were mired down in the center of the city.

But before we could go on the offensive, we had first to secure the area and protect ourselves from attacks from the rear. Nazi machine guns and snipers higher up the hill fired on us from time to time. The Germans had stationed various long range spotters for artillery and mortar fire on top of the hill. Therefore, we were forced to monitor and fire on two different fronts simultaneously. That, by the way, was a common occurrence in Stalingrad. It was often difficult to distinguish your front line from your rear guard. Everything was always mixed up.

Once we had secured ourselves from German fire from above,

we turned our gaze in the opposite direction – down the hill, towards the approach to the southern slope. This approach was broken up by little gullies and covered over with thick patches of burs, thistles, wormwood and elderberry.

Our numbers had diminished, as the services of the snipers had come in great demand. Viktor Medvedev and his partner had been called to the area surrounding the Meatpacking Plant. Shaikin and Morozov were working the territory near the Icehouse, while Abzalov and Nasirov were stationed at the "shooting range" in the Metalworking Factory, instructing new snipers and making the Germans in that area keep their heads down.

As a rendezvous point for the snipers in my group, we selected a low, cramped trench near the source of the twisting stream that led to the Tsaritsa River, and then on to the city center.

"Last night," I said to my comrades, "we heard the jingle of pots at the bottom of the ravine. There's a reservoir there, surrounded by thorny bushes …"

"Yes, there are bushes down there," confirmed Nikolai Kulikov, "but so what?"

"I think the Krauts are using the reservoir," I said, "to infiltrate our positions."

After talking it over, we decided to set up a twenty-four-hour stakeout of the reservoir. We planned to split up and observe it from two sides.

Night came, and high overhead, illumination flares went off. For a few seconds each flare would exhume random objects below from the darkness.

Shaikin and Ubozhenko had taken up positions along the ravine's eastern wall – Kulikov and myself, the western one. We climbed towards the precipice, directly in front of the thickest bushes, and huddled near the bottom of a deep crater. A hundred yards below us was a Nazi trench. One of their machine guns was visible. In the light of a flare, we also noticed the bodies of two dead Italians, lying near the edge of our crater. These two bodies were in a state of advanced decomposition.

"The Aryans bury their own kind, but they leave the wops to feed the vultures," whispered Nikolai.

"Vultures deserted this hell-hole a long time ago," I replied.

Sitting in the bottom of a shellhole and counting gunshots was, to put it mildly, a tiresome assignment. We had to do something to occupy ourselves, so we outfitted our foxholes for action. We raked in the soil from the edges of the crater and trampled it down beneath ourselves. With each hour, the crater became shallower and shallower and our positions higher and higher. Both of us wanted to smoke, but because the smoke would have been a dead giveaway, we had to resist. As they say, "Endure, Cossack."[32]

My exhaustion became harder to ignore. My back was aching from the intense strain of such an uncomfortable position. But at last our work was coming to a conclusion. I had built myself a fine foxhole and could finally sit comfortably, observe and shoot. To my right, Nikolai was having a harder time. His position wasn't quite as accommodating, but he wasn't complaining. He was already conducting surveillance. Meanwhile, as it began to grow light, I was wondering how our comrades on the other side of the ravine were faring.

Just then, in the clearing in front of the thicket, a German soldier emerged with a bucket in his hand and a submachine gun around his neck. He halted and looked around as if he was waiting for someone. Moments like this one were so common in war; a man stands there, not knowing that his life is hanging by a thread. I held the soldier's head in the cross hairs of my scope; I could clearly see his trembling lips, his white, even teeth, his straight and slightly protuberant nose and his pale, clean-shaven face. Two more soldiers showed up, also carrying buckets, and then they all disappeared into the bushes.

Five minutes went by. The soldiers emerged again, but now they were straining under the weight of the full buckets. We could see that hiking up the rise was a challenge to them. The

[32] The Russian saying is: "Endure, Cossak, and you'll get to be an Ataman."

water sloshed around inside their pails, but the soldiers never spilled a drop. Water was dear to them. And indeed, it was going to cost them dearly.

Kulikov hissed at me like an angry goose: but I wasn't ready to shoot yet, and I forbade him to shoot as well.

"Strong is the fighter who is able to master himself," I said in a whisper.

I had resolved not to open fire that day. First I had to find out if there were any Nazi officers at this site, and if so, of what rank. I also wanted to pin down their approaches to the spring.

My nerves were stretched to the limit, so I decided to have a smoke and try to relax. I lowered myself to the bottom of the hole – that way the smoke would dissipate before it wafted overhead - and had just lit up when Kulikov called to me, "Just look at what these swine are doing!"

I put down my cigarette and picked up the artillery periscope. What I saw was tempting.

On the same spot where the lone soldier had stood with bucket in hand, several Nazi officers were now washing themselves. They had undressed to the waist, and a private was pouring water over their backs from an aluminum cup. On the ground nearby lay three caps, bearing officer's emblems.

"Look at how these *mudaki*[33] are living it up!" Kulikov was furious. He was gripping his rifle so tightly his hands were turning white. "These intruders act so carefree while we're filthy, stuck with these stinking corpses. Let's show them how to have some fun, eh? Let's see how they dance to our music!"

"Not a chance," I said. "We're giving them a one-day pass. And quit your talking. Chit-chat interferes with our work."

I had offended Nikolai Kulikov. He slid down to the bottom of his foxhole and lit up a smoke.

"A soldier who's afraid to pull the trigger doesn't belong in battle," he hissed.

"Kolya," I said, "I know it's our job is to go after the officers.

[33] *Mudaki* : bastards

"...But those guys are lieutenants. If we waste bullets on junior officers, the big shots will never show their faces."

"We should take the opportunities that present themselves," protested Nikolai Kulikov.

Up on the summit shooting broke out. I could hear the rumble of tank engines from behind the water towers. I could see the Germans running from the spring. From the clearing, they descended into a trench and disappeared beneath the bank of the ravine, into deeply dug trenches. From there they could withstand bombardments and gunfire without any problems.

The Germans were certainly efficient. They had turned that part of the ravine into a fortress. The approaches to their entrenchments were covered by a pillbox that held two machine guns. They could slide shut the embrasures in the pillbox with steel plates. Their trenches and the pillbox were connected by a shallow trench, and we could see their soldiers running back and forth.

It was already midday. Our thirst, combined with the stench from the corpses nearby, was torturing us. When we were setting out the night before, we hadn't counted on getting hung up in this spot, so we had failed to pack any extra food or water.

Just then the Germans' machine gun opened fire. We could see it perfectly. Bullets whistled past our helmets.

Kulikov and I both and I set our telescopic sites for three hundred meters, and we fired simultaneously. But the Kraut machine gunner kept on blasting away at us, as if we had fired blanks.

The shooting in our sector ceased as quickly as it had started. Nikolai and I sat in silence. We were both ashamed because we had missed. Kulikov's head was down, and he was wheezing.

I encouraged him to take a break. We began fishing for reasons why we could have missed. Maybe the strain was affecting our vision, or our scopes had gone bad, or perhaps our breathing was unsteady, or maybe we had simply forgotten how to press the trigger without jostling the rifle? I looked over at Kulikov. He had dropped his head into his hands, wondering, like me, what had gone wrong.

"Forget about it, Kolya," I told him, "get some rest."

Meanwhile I was kicking myself. Then I remembered, we had been shooting down at our target. Under those conditions, it's always awkward to measure distance. You can never believe your first estimate – you always have to add on at least ten per cent of the measured distance, to be safe. And something else – when you've got all kinds of guns firing nearby, the air around heats up and seems to ripple before your eyes. It's a heat mirage, and it makes your target appear closer than it really is. You have to take this into account and either tack on a few yards, or fire a test shot at something close to your target, in order to correctly gauge your distance and zero in.

Down in the ravine the Nazi's machine gun opened fire again. Kulikov pressed his eye to his scope.

"Listen," I said, "I've got him set at three hundred fifty; you shoot for four hundred." We aimed again, and fired simultaneously. The machine gun fell silent. Nikolai had killed the gunner, while my bullet had fallen short.

When dusk came, Nikolai and I returned to the rendezvous point, where things were business as usual. The other snipers were swapping stories of their kills. Every dead Nazi made for an elaborate tale. Okhrim Vasilchenko was keeping score. He was writing on a chunk of plywood with a pencil stub.

"I'll be rating you all on a scale of 1 to 5," he announced. Then next to each of our names he scrawled 1, 2, 3… Next to my name, Vasilchenko wrote a zero.

"You need to get yourself in order, chief!" he said. "You keep this up and you'll end up blacklisted."

A soldier from the third battalion delivered dinner to us. He placed a sack filled with bullets and grenades next to the thermos of kasha and quickly ran off.

Not long before daybreak, we left our rendezvous and took up different positions. I had decided to blockade the enemy's pillbox and their officers' bathing area. My plan was to use three pairs of snipers, stationed at various points. For Kulikov and myself, I selected a new position, not far from that of the day before.

Although I had a periscope with me, at first I couldn't see the pillbox. Some sharp edged shell fragments from a recent barrage were obstructing my view. I had to shove them aside. I had a clear view and then could make out the entrance to the enemy's bunker.

A red-haired Nazi in an officer's cap peeked out of the entrance for a moment and disappeared. I announced this to my comrades, and our teams spread into a formation that allowed us to talk back and forth. All the snipers were suddenly wide awake at the prospect of having targets. We lay waiting in nervous expectation.

The tip of an officer's cap appeared in a trench next to the dugout. You could see the edges of its swastika emblem. The cap rose higher and higher above the rim of the trench, until the visor itself was visible.

"What do you think?" I asked Kulikov.

"It's one of their snipers setting a trap – he wants us to take a shot." The cap disappeared. "Not very subtle," he said.

"What's one of their snipers doing down here?" I asked.

Nikolai shrugged his shoulders. "The devil knows. I guess he's got a death wish."

"That's for sure," I said. "Yesterday, when you took out their machine gunner, where did your bullet hit him?"

"In the mouth," answered Kulikov. "It must have blown off the back of his head."

"With a shot like that," I said, "you've thrown their snipers a challenge, and now they've accepted. They're gunning for you, Nikolai. You've got to set up a decoy that looks like you."

The soft sunlight gently warmed our shoulders while a refreshing breeze blew across our faces. These were the last mild autumn days of 1942.

Lunchtime rolled around. A hunched-over German soldier approached the enemy trenches. He was unarmed, and only carried a bucket in his hand. We decided to leave him be, since he looked so shabby and pitiful.

Another ten minutes went by, when suddenly a heavyset, polished Nazi officer turned the corner of one of the trenches. He had a colonel's insignia on his jacket. A sniper followed behind him, carrying a beautiful hunting rifle with a huge scope. Two additional officers emerged from behind the same corner of the shallow trench. One of them was a major wearing a knight's cross with oak leaf clusters. Following behind the major was another colonel, who was smoking a cigarette in a long holder.

Nikolai and I exchanged a glance. This was what we had been dreaming about. There were still lots of little Nazi fish swimming out there, because we had been willing to wait to catch the sharks. Missing out on the little fish was the price a sniper had to pay for a moment like this.

I nodded a "yes" towards Nikolai, and he signaled the others. Our shots rang out, three volleys of two shots each. We made textbook head shots, and all four of the Nazis dropped to the earth, their lives draining out of them. Now with the enemy's sniper dead, it seemed Kulikov's challenge would go unanswered. We had sent our rival six feet under.

Ten or fifteen minutes passed, but no one approached the slain Krauts. We were growing bored, when out of the blue, a massive artillery bombardment rained down on us. We crawled underground, waiting anxiously as shells exploded closer and closer.

When a shell approaches the earth, its scream is so intense that it feels like your head is going to explode. You lie there, feeling like your intestines are being slowly yanked out by a winch. You say to yourself, "that one's got my name on it..." but after the impact, if you can look around, you know you are still alive, and you can see that the shell struck somewhere else.

Then the Luftwaffe arrived, dive-bombers that hit us in flights of nine planes each. You know you must have taken out some serious Nazi brass, for them to call in the air power. One of their bombs hit our trench and we were knocked around by the shockwave. Vasilchenko and I were momentarily deafened, while

Kulikov and Morozov got off with just a scare.

For over two hours, bombers, artillery and mortar fire relentlessly pounded our position. When things at last had grown quiet again, an irritated Lieutenant Fedosov showed up.

"What the hell did you guys do to get those Krauts so riled up, huh?"

The Kraut bombardment had also damaged the enemy's artillery emplacements near the railroad tunnel. The wooden panels that had camouflaged their big guns had been torn away, and now the emplacement sat fully exposed. Their gun crews were swarming over the artillery pieces like rats. This was going to be a field day for us snipers!

We steadied our rifles on the embankment. Kulikov and I began by taking out their officers. Because of the torrents of noise that masked the report of our rifles, and because we were so thoroughly camouflaged, the enemy had no idea where our shots were coming from. As their officers fell, the enlisted men nearby froze in confusion. The hot-tempered Dvoyashkin and Shaikin saw what we were doing, and they also brought down many Nazis, face-first in the dirt. Only then did the Kraut artillerymen grasp what was happening. The few survivors dove for cover.

After an attack like this, they weren't going to show their faces in daylight anytime soon, and their artillery was useless after dark. We had thoroughly neutralized them.

In the evening, the snipers met at the rendezvous point and reviewed the day's events. I posed the question: "Now do you understand why we needed to be patient yesterday?"

"We're ready for your next plan, chief," replied Nikolai Kulikov.

CHAPTER 13.
A SOLDIER S SKY

On the battlefield, a soldier's day is full of worry. He's constantly missing something: one day it's food, the next day it's ammunition, and the next – a place to lie down. But one thing that's never in short supply is danger. With danger, you've got to confront it. Otherwise you're dead. But with other menaces, like foul weather, think of it this way: over your head a hole in the sky has opened up and all the rain, sleet and cold in the world has been directed especially at you, so you'll shiver to bone. You feel like a helpless giant.

However, in my opinion this feeling has another, more useful side effect in war. Without hardships like these, we could never have battle-ready soldiers. When a battle is raging, you think that every bullet, every shell and even every bomb has been aimed directly at you. You talk yourself into believing that you have become the enemy's primary target. But don't be a fool; keep your head out of the crossfire and keep clear of flying shrapnel. You've got a brain, so use it. Be a little trickier with the enemy. Transform yourself from a helpless giant into an invulnerable and barely visible mouse.

Now, this inflated sense of your size, and of your exposure to the enemy, doesn't leave you. After all, if the enemy really has focused their assault on your zone, then it follows that you're fighting for the most important land, and you've got good reason to be anxious. Beneath your feet is the very center of the front, the center of the earth, you could say. Nobody can convince you otherwise.

What kind of soldier are you then? You're a giant – because you're defending the center of the earth; and you're invisible – because neither bullet nor shrapnel has touched you.

~~~

These remarks regarding calm on the battlefield come from my experiences in different theaters of action. When things grow quiet in your zone, it could appear to you that the enemy has pulled back on every front. But in reality, the entirety of Stalingrad was bombed and shelled continually, day in and day out. Attack gave way to counterattack; isolated explosions mushroomed into all-out firefights – near the *Krasny Oktyabr* Factory, surrounding the Barrikady, or in the city center. But since we had grown accustomed to the steady din of engagement, we only paid attention to battles in our own vicinity, on the slopes of Mamayev Hill, and to those battles among our neighbors to the right and left.

This day, calm slowly returned, after the Krauts retaliated against us for taking out their officers. But even this was only a relative calm. The enemy had moved up a new machine gun and it tore through the embankments along our trenches. The shooting down in the ravine never let up, and every now and then a bullet burrowed into the roof of our bunker.

Before sundown it began to rain. The heavens had opened up to relieve us of our thirst. The shallower foxholes filled up with water. We placed our pots, buckets and thermoses out to collect rainfall. Okhrim Vasilchenko prepared a *banya*,[34] although obviously without a sauna. He and the others stretched out a tarp over top of the trench and started washing themselves. In place of a washcloth they used the scrap of a soldier's greatcoat. Of course,

[34] Russian '*banya*' : bathhouse or sauna

there were no birch branches available.[35]

Then they ran naked into the bunker and wrung out their drenched clothes as if they were freshly scrubbed laundry. Our uniforms were still filthy, but they were all we had. None of us had extra clothing, as the Military Council had not issued us any.

~~~

For a soldier, his bunker is his home – it's kitchen, bedroom, and bathroom all rolled into one.

Captain Aksyonov ducked into our little palace. He was the assistant commander to the division commander. Aksyonov was a heavyset fellow with a perpetually red face, and thinning black hair that shined with pomade. He was studying the work of sniper groups along the front lines. Apparently he was impressed with our work.

On a dank and rainy night light this, we could sleep soundly, knowing the Nazis would never launch an attack. But their artillery and mortars periodically bombarded our positions, so that the walls of the bunker were shaking.

"Can any of you guys spare an extra *sukharik*?"[36] Aksyonov asked, gingerly. "I haven't eaten a thing since morning."

Okhrim Vasilchenko was on duty that night as the "steward" for our "crew's quarters," as we seaman called our bunker. He was at a loss. He apologized : "We haven't had anything to eat ourselves, for two days."

Captain Aksyonov moved close to our kerosene lamp. He opened up his notebook and started to record our reports and impressions of the day.

I slipped out to check on Dvoyashkin, the duty sniper. A cold drizzle continued to fall, and it was pitch black outside.

A German flare shot up and arced over the ravine. It floated to earth, suspended by a parachute. Rocking back and forth, the flare was descending so slowly that it looked like it would hang

---

[35] Birch branches, used in Russian bathhouses for flagellating the skin, to improve circulation.
[36] *sukharik*: zwieback

up there until morning.

Two figures across the ravine froze in the flare's harsh illumi-nation. I called out:

"Who's there?"

There was no answer. Dvoyashkin grabbed his submachine gun from inside the dugout and began wading through the water to the other side of the ravine. Okhrim Vasilchenko followed. Meanwhile Captain Aksyonov called me to his side.

A few minutes went by. A match flared up by the entrance of the bunker. The tarp was thrown to one side with a theatrical flourish, and Okhrim Vasilchenko tapped a steel bucket as if it were a gong. He and Dvoyashkin entered, making trumpeting noises, as they accompanied two long-awaited guests – Akhmet Khabibulin, our food and supply man, and the *politruk*, Stepan Kryakhov.

Kryakhov greeted everyone with a handshake, took off his overstuffed backpack and handed it over to Akhmet, saying, "Pass this stuff out."

What a godsend! This time they'd brought us more food than we had expected. There were cans of tinned beef from the "second front," and boxes of kasha. Okhrim Vasilchenko clanged some mess bowls together. Then we stopped talking as we fell into the food. All you could hear were lips smacking and food being gulped down. We were all starved. Even Captain Aksyonov kept repeating, "...kasha, it's a fine thing isn't it?"

We knew that Kryakhov, as always, had brought updates from inside Stalingrad, fresh newspapers, and letters from home.

Vasilchenko had barely collected our bowls when Kryakhov reached into his jacket, pulled out a packet of letters and tossed them underneath the lamp. We had passed all of them out within the blink of an eye; the bunker fell completely silent. Each soldier held his breath and read the news from home.

Only Okhrim Vasilchenko was left wondering what to do with himself, as the rest of us enjoyed this fleeting moment of pleasure. He didn't wait for letters anymore; his family were all in occupied territory, near Poltava.[37] It was difficult to look at him during moments like these – I felt like we should put aside reading the letters until he wasn't around. But how could anyone resist, when they have just received something from home?

Kryakhov wasn't oblivious to what was going on, either. He knew about Okhrim's situation, and all of a sudden he raised an envelope over his head and announced: "I've got a letter here from a girl in Chelyabinsk.[38] She's requested that it be delivered to an exceptionally brave soldier. Who do you think I should give it to?"

Without a moment's hesitation, we all answered,

"To Okhrim!"

"Of course, to Vasilchenko!"

"Give it to him, yes, to him!"

And that's how Okhrim Vasilchenko, after a year and a half of war, finally received his first letter.

He took the letter from Aksyonov's hands, but clearly he was afraid to read it. He was so flustered that he didn't know what to do. Finally he tore open the envelope. I was sitting next to Vasilchenko, and I could read the lines written in a straight, clear feminine handwriting. On the page was written:

"I don't know who will end up reading my letter. I'm seventeen years old. If I'm young enough to be your daughter, than I'll call you father. If you're a little older than me, then let me call you brother. The girls and young women in our plant have collected some gifts for the defenders of Stalingrad. We know things must be difficult and dangerous for you in the trenches. Our hearts go out to you. We work and live only for you... Although I'm far away in the Urals now, I live by the hope that I'll someday return to my native Minsk. Can you hear my mother's weeping?..."

---

[37] Poltava: a city in Ukraine.
[38] Chelyabinsk: Russian city about 900 miles due east of Moscow

Vasilchenko turned the page. I managed to read the closing lines:

> "Destroy the Nazis. Let their country be drowned in grief and may their families cry a river of tears. Fight the enemy with courage, like our ancestors fought them before us!"

I could see the emotions rippling across Okrihm's face. He put aside the letter. He exited our bunker and returned a moment later, carrying his submachine gun and a sack full of grenades. He was clearly planning something dire. I stood up and blocked the exit, my legs spread wide in a sailor's stance. Vasilchenko understood my meaning: "You aren't going anywhere."

He took a step back and sat down. In an attempt to explain himself, he decided to reveal his reckless plan.

It turned out that for several days, Vasilchenko and another sniper, Kostrikov, had been carrying out surveillance of one of complexes of enemy bunkers to our east, on the slopes of Mamayev Hill. These two had figured out every one of the enemy bunker's approaches, and had learned exactly where their sentries were stationed, and at what intervals their sentries were changed. All they needed to execute their plan was for the right moment to come along – a distraction, that is, a heavy rain or snowstorm. And now that moment had arrived. Kostrikov had already quietly slipped out of our bunker.

I hollered to our sentries, "Catch Kostrikov and bring him back here immediately!" This was too much for Vasilchenko. He flung his gun and bag of grenades into the corner and started to scream, calling all of us traitors. He was shouting in rage and frustration.

Captain Aksyonov and *politruk* Kryakhov stood up.

"Stop it!" Askyonov yelled at Vasilchenko. "What's with all this nonsense, soldier?" Thick drops of sweat had broken out on Okhrim's face. His eyes grew dim and his mouth was wrenched out of shape. His body shook. It was only then that we realized that he was having an epileptic seizure. None of us had been aware that he had this condition.

Okhrim collapsed like a tree felled by an axe. His teeth were chattering violently and he was shivering. His head was beating against my chest. When the paroxysm finally passed, he fell sound asleep, snoring loudly.

At this point we listened attentively to Kostrikov.

Kostrikov was a wiry fellow with dark hair. He had been an engineer before he was mobilized, and he we was capable of giving a good summing up of his observations, as if they were a scientific report. His plan of attack was quite good, so that even Captain Aksyonov liked it.

The rain wasn't letting up. We knew the Fritzies would be sound asleep. We couldn't let this opportunity slip past us. Who knew if there would be another rain like this anytime soon?

~~~

Kostrikov's and Vasilchenko's position was now being manned by Afinogenov and Scherbina, two more sailors I had recruited as snipers. They had worked in the same engine room in the Navy, and here in Stalingrad they found themselves together again. Afinogenov had fiery carrot-colored hair and temperament to match. Scherbina was skinny with dark hair, a pale complexion, and a perpetual idiotic grin.

We needed their input. First we woke up Afinogenov. He sprung up as if he had been waiting for someone to touch his shoulder.

"Let's go. I know every path in and out of the Krauts' trenches!" he said.

"Wait a minute," I protested, "let me go over the details first."

"I already heard everything," Afinogenov replied. "In Stalingrad I've learned to sleep and still take in the whole conversation."

We armed ourselves lightly – with submachine guns, grenades and knives. Afinogenov led the way, followed by Scherbina, Stepan Kryakhov and myself. We were only worried about one thing: stumbling into a minefield while en route to the enemy bunker. But that was a fate we managed to escape. Soldier's luck was with us that night.

When we reached the entrance to the bunker, a German lance corporal with a Schmeisser around his neck was sheltering from the rain underneath a lady's parasol.

Afinogenov crawled into the trench. His knife glistened in the darkness. He stabbed the sentry in the heart and muffled the Nazi's groans with his hand. The German lance corporal collapsed without a sound.

Scherbina and Afinogenov remained as lookouts on top while Kryakhov and I silently slipped into the trenches below.

I quickly took in my surroundings. By the door there was a rack of nails pounded into the wall. From each nail hung a sub-machine gun. Beneath the guns were helmets, and by the helmets, flashlights. Everything was very orderly, in typical German style. All up and down the sides of the bunker were cots, with German soldiers snoring peacefully beneath their blankets. Their uniforms hung above their heads. In the center of the room was a small electric lamp, which bathed the bunker in a dim milky light.

Kryakhov and I took a couple of submachine guns from the rack for souvenirs. Kryakhov unscrewed the light bulb from the overhead lamp, and we each clipped a flashlight to our belt. Meanwhile the Germans kept snoring.

Stepan Kryakhov gave a loud and firm command: "For the murders of our mothers and children at the hands of these fascist swine – fire!"

Our Tommy-guns spat out streams of hot lead. The Nazis were rudely jerked awake. They looked like marionettes being yanked on broken strings. They collapsed in their bunks, moaning and screaming until the arcs of flying lead raked over them again and shut them up. Their blankets were thrown in heaps in the confusion.

Stepan Kryakhov and I stood near one wall, moving about as necessary. We riddled the cots with bullets, going back and forth and up and down the room. The Nazis never had a chance to get out of their beds – they never had a chance to resist.

Out of nowhere I saw a live Kraut, huddled at my feet. He was only wearing long underwear, and it didn't have a single bloodstain on it. How he managed to escape our fusillade I'll never know. I pointed my gun at him, but Kryakhov grabbed me by the arm.

"Leave him be!" Stepan Kryakhov yelled. Our ears were ringing from the gunfire and Stepan had to repeat himself to make sure I understood. "We've got to bring back a *yazhik*."[39]

The Kraut spread his arms across the floor as if to say, "Look, I surrender; even though I'm prone, my hands are up!"

This German spoke good Russian, which is what saved him. He understood what Kryakhov had yelled, and when we began shooting, he had instantly thrown himself at my feet. He did exactly as we ordered. He threw on an overcoat, stuck his feet in his boots, and we returned to our lines with a prisoner.

We made our way back quickly. At our bunker we were met by Captain Aksyonov, Kostrikov, Khabibulin, and a well-rested Vasilchenko. They looked over the German from all sides, then questioned us about the details of our mission.

It was a hard story to tell. Something didn't sit right with me about what we had just done, but as we recounted the story I looked into Vasilchenko's eyes. They still burned with grief, as dark and miserable as the gray sky hanging over us. As I concluded I spoke my mind out loud: "We may be doomed, but for now we're still the masters in our own land." [40]

---

[39] *yazhik* : an informer. Literally yazhik : tongue.
[40] In the Russian text Zaitsev uses the phrase: "let the soldier's sky be like a sheepskin." "The sky looks like sheepskin," is a Russian folk saying meaning, "this may be the end of us." Many of the Red Army soldiers in Stalingrad believed they were doomed, and did not expect to survive the battle.

CHAPTER 14.
MY OBLIGATION

The soldier's constant worry is how to survive and defeat the enemy. The dead are only present at the morning roll call – it's the living that fight the battles. My obligation went further: to turn soldiers into snipers. Every living thing fights to prolong its own life. Of course, I also wanted to live a long time – if not physically, then at least in spirit. It was my belief that every sniper I trained would be capable of avenging me, and could protect our comrades from a premature death. Even if I should be killed, my students would be able to act on what I had taught them and help bring the war to a victorious conclusion. For that reason, the sniper's art determined my every thought and action.

On the first day of our operations near the *Krasny Oktyabr* Factory, a new sniper named Gorozhaev caught my attention. He was a blue-eyed fellow of average height. His face was engraved with worry lines, such as you would never see on a young man's face in peacetime. He had a short neck and a heavy chin. He acted sullen and withdrawn.

He had reason for this. Gorozhaev had sat for a long time with his partner at the front, without getting a kill. What's more, that morning a Nazi sniper had nearly put a bullet through his head; fortunately the shot had glanced off his helmet and left him unharmed. However, it was a serious warning to the novice sniper: "Be on guard! Change your tactics before it's too late, or give up being a sniper altogether."

Gorozhaev has already made his report, and was embarrassed by his failures.

I sat down next to him, took out my tobacco pouch, tore off a strip of newspaper and rolled a cigarette. Gorozhaev did the same, and we lit up. It was easier for Gorozhaev to look at me, his teacher, through a cloud of cigarette smoke. His sullen countenance disappeared and he confessed: "I can't get the hang of being a sniper. I look through a periscope all day – until I see stars – but I still can't locate a target. Shooting with a Tommy-gun is much easier. They give the command and you blast away. But as far as being a sniper, everything is more complicated."

"It's not more complicated," I corrected him. "It's about awareness and self-control."

"If you say so, Chief," he conceded, reluctantly.

I calmly explained that from the first glance, the sniper must identify his target, immediately size it up, and then destroy it with a single shot.

Since a rapid assessment of elements in the field was not always possible, the important skills for the sniper to cultivate were patience and the ability to map every detail in his head. Small changes that appeared insignificant, could in reality be targets. The sniper had to be able to react instantaneously when a worthy target exposed itself.

I closed the conversation by saying, "I want you to work with me tomorrow morning."

At four o'clock the following morning, the snipers had finished breakfast and were heading out to their positions. Gorozhaev accompanied me to a new position across from the railyard, where a Nazi sniper had been picking off our soldiers and commanders. But first I led my new partner to the bunker of the deputy battalion commander, Senior Lieutenant Arkhip Sukharev. Sukharev had just been wounded in the zone where this Nazi sniper was working. Sukharev was waiting to be evacuated to the other side of the Volga.

We entered the bunker and found Sukharev lying on the ground beneath a blanket. Nurse Klava Svintsova was preparing to dress his wounds. Dora Shakhnovich was helping her, holding a plasma bottle in her hand. The lieutenant sat up and straightened his legs. His face was pale, and drops of blood had collected at the sides of his mouth. He appeared to be in agony. His gaze fell on me. His eyes expressed a great deal, including an undeserved reproach directed at us, as if to say, "...how is it you snipers didn't get to that Nazi sharp-shooter, before he put a bullet in my back?"

I didn't try to explain or justify myself. I just wanted to make sure that Gorozhaev saw the lieutenant's gaze, and he did. Gorozhaev felt it, and he understood how important a sniper is in the eyes of a commander. Without a word, we left the bunker.

A furious battle was raging in the factory's district. Machine guns were firing in all directions.

"Where has their sniper positioned himself," I asked Gorozhaev, "and how are you going to locate him, with all this noise and distraction? What clues have you got, to tell you where he's hiding?" I was questioning Gorozhaev as a teacher to his pupil.

He shrugged his shoulders. "The devil only knows."

"The devil himself wouldn't know where this Kraut is hiding. To begin with, you need a witness, who can tell you where and how Sukharev was wounded."

We managed to locate a soldier from that company, who recounted the following:

"The *Starshiy* lieutenant and Zikov the medic, were walking from the tool room towards our machine gunners in the boiler room. As he was standing in the doorway, the *Starshiy* lieutenant lurched forward, and blood gushed from his mouth. I wanted to help, so I ran to him. Just as I stooped over, a bullet scorched my left shoulder. We took cover behind the boiler, where Zikov bandaged us up…"

"How many soldiers and officers have been hit in that doorway?" I asked.

"Today, three soldiers, plus the lieutenant," he answered.

It was obvious that an experienced Kraut sniper had zeroed the doorway in his sights. "We've got to take up a position close by," I said to Gorozhaev.

The two of us made our way into the boiler room. I set up my artillery periscope on the sill of a blasted-out window, and Gorozhaev did the same.

Our enemy was cunning. He was working beneath the cover of his submachine gunners. The gunners fired one round past my periscope, and then another. The enemy sniper was camouflaging the sound of his shots among the rounds of machine gun fire. But where was he?

We sat for three hours with no luck. Gorozhaev was already grumbling that there was no sniper out there. I stayed silent. I had to figure out for myself whether I had made a mistake or not.

To our right, Nazi submachine gunners launched an assault on the Meatpacking Plant. The battle was spilling over into our lines, but Gorozhaev and I stayed put. As we watched, directly opposite us, from behind the wheel of a railroad car a Nazi submachine gunner leaped out, then a second, a third … a tenth! They were sliding beneath an embankment and disappearing behind the rubble. Where were they going? Then gunfire crackled only a few yards away. A squad of the enemy soldiers had burst through the doorway, toward the window where we were sitting. Gorozhaev's face grew tense, his eyes widened and he feverishly heaved grenades at them. I sprayed the advancing soldiers with gunfire. Once I'd taken out several of them, the rest turned and fled.

Calm returned. Gorozhaev and I resumed our hunt for the German sniper. The field of battle appeared empty again. The slain German submachine gunners were scattered like cut sunflowers, their heads pointing in various directions. One of those still alive called out to his friends for help, but no one came. No one had any use for these men now. They might have made good bait for us, luring out other Nazis with their cries for help, but I wouldn't think of firing on their medics.

Just then Captain Vassili Rakityanskiy turned up. He was an instructor in the division's political bureau and a seasoned *politrabotnik*.[41] He lay down near a hole in the wall and wedged his megaphone between some bricks. I asked him to hear me out before he began his "broadcast."

The captain approved of my plan and agreed to help us; he agreed to use some German language propaganda to rupture their sniper's concentration, and to cause their sniper to act less cautiously. But we miscalculated. In response to Rakityanksy's voice we received a volley of machine gun fire. They fired furiously at the megaphone. We answered with our rifles. The Kraut machine gunners became careless because they were angry over a little propaganda. We sent six of their machine gunners to the "cross battalion in the sky" in a few minutes, but their sniper still wouldn't reveal his position.

Then a brief bombardment began. Bombs rained down upon the rubble of walls, on the factory's machines and on heaps of broken brick. We took shelter in a shaft beneath the boiler.

"Where *Politrabotnik* Rakityanskiy goes, the bombing follows," joked one of my friends.

"Could it be the other way around? Where the bombs are dropping, I follow?" Rakityanskiy replied.

The Krauts' bombing run ended, and we went back to the positions we had recently vacated. Rakityanskiy had dropped his megaphone during the bombardment. It had fallen in a crevice. He reached out and began to pry it loose from the hole. This was just the moment the enemy sniper had been waiting for. The Kraut's bullet ripped through the captain's forearm, but this sniper had finally revealed his location. I caught sight of him beneath a train car where he had set up a position between its

[41] *Politrabotnik*: political field instructor

wheels.

Now I wanted to let Gorozhaev have an opportunity to make the shot. I told him to take up a position deep within the workshop while I stayed up front next to the megaphone, to draw the sniper's attention. But Gorozhaev was too hasty; his bullet passed through a slot in the train's wheel, struck the rails, and ricocheted into the distance. The Nazi sniper was unharmed, and what's more, Gorozhaev's shot had warned him to be on his guard.

We spent that night in the workshop, and at sunup Lt. Bolshapov lowered himself through the boiler's furnace and delivered us a bucket of water.

"Get washed up, rub your eyes clear and get down to work!" he said.

After we freshened up, we took up positions again. I did surveillance while Gorozhaev stood ready with his rifle. "What do you have to do to make the Nazi show himself?" I asked Gorozhaev, rhetorically.

"I don't know," he answered.

"Then watch."

Captain Rakityanskiy's megaphone lay untouched. I stuck my hands between the bricks, reached for the edge of the megaphone and turned it on. It crackled with electricity. Rakityanskiy had taught me some German obscenities and I shouted one into the megaphone. My distorted voice echoed back and forth between our position and the railway yard. Gorozhaev must have understood some German because he started to laugh.

A shot rang out. The bullet flew just over my ear. Yes, their sniper had taken up his position before us and was waiting for an encounter. Two more shots – one right after the other. The Nazi was shooting fast and straight. He had me trapped against the bricks next to the megaphone. I only had to squirm a little bit, and an explosive bullet would whistle by my head.

One hour went by, then two. The sun was warming my right side. I played dead. I could talk with Gorozhaev, but I didn't dare move my head or my arms. I turned my eyes into the sun and was blinded by its rays. I closed my eyes tightly and hit upon an idea: try to blind their sniper with reflected sunlight! I called Gorozhaev and told him: "Take a mirror and bounce the sunlight into that guy's eyes."

Gorozhaev took his knife and started to pry the mirror from an artillery periscope. Meanwhile another bullet singed the air, a few inches from my nose.

"Hurry up," I told Gorozhaev.

Gorozhaev diddled with the mirror and when he figured he had the Kraut blinded he said, "OK, chief!"

I held my breath. I hoped Gorozhaev knew what he was doing. I darted from the spot where the Kraut had me pinned. No shot rang out. Then I took a dummy I had previously prepared and shoved in into my place.

From what the Nazi could see, nothing had changed. He altered his position to escape the glare from the mirror. Now we could clearly see him through the train wheels.

We had to find another position that would give us a clear view of at least the Nazi's head. I figured he was breathing easy now, thinking that he had killed one of our snipers near the megaphone. Meanwhile Gorozhaev and I were crawling to the side, looking for the perfect spot. We were careful to stay hidden from sight.

About thirty yards east of the boiler room stood a huge vat that had once held tar, and on top of it sat a platform for a hydraulic hoist. A short ladder led up to the platform. We climbed up and then lowered ourselves down into the vat. The dry tar that still lined the walls of the vat was sticky, and its odor was irritating.

We pulled a board off the platform above and placed it beneath our feet. The sides of the vat had several small holes, and we selected the least conspicuous ones for our peepholes. From this location, the railway car where the Kraut sniper had positioned himself was in full view. At that moment, the train wheels obstructed our view of the sniper, but we were willing to wait.

Other then the stench from the tar, we had found the perfect position.

When thirty minutes had passed, the Nazi sniper climbed out from beneath the train car. He threw back his shoulders proudly and slung his rifle over his shoulder. Then he took off walking through the trench. He met a fellow soldier, halted and took the rifle from his shoulder, and held it up to demonstrate how he had just made his shot.

I watched through my binoculars while Gorozhaev followed the actions of the enemy sniper through his telescopic sight.

"Take your time," I said to Gorozhaev, "let him make one last little speech and tell the story of how he finished off the Russian with the megaphone."

"OK, chief," said Gorozhaev. He was leveling his rifle slowly and carefully.

"Now, wait for the moment when he turns his straight towards you," I said.

"I've got him in my crosshairs."

At that moment I saw that the Nazi must have noticed the reflection from Gorozhaev's scope. The Nazi sniper's expression changed from gloating to one of alarm, and suddenly he had raised his rifle and was aiming at us.

"Fire!" I said. The word came out like an exhalation.

Gorozhaev's shot rang out. The bullet leveled the Nazi. As he collapsed, his rifle got wedged in between the trench walls, blocking the path of the second German. I had noticed this second German was wearing an iron cross on his chest. I pulled the trigger, and my bullet punctured the German's medal. It sent him flying backwards, with his arms spread.

We left our position very late, but satisfied. We both had reason to be happy. Gorozhaev had gotten a kill and had avenged his comrades, while I had succeeded in teaching a student, further insuring my own safety and advancing our common initiative.

~~~

We were always on the lookout to take live prisoners. We

needed intelligence specific to our area of the front, and our officers and the *politruki* constantly pressured us take prisoners and return them to our lines, in good enough shape to provide information.

After dinner that night, we had got news that a German captive had been taken, just over the front lines from our sniper positions. This capture had been orchestrated by our battalion's mortar commander, Captain Krasnov.

In his own way, every sniper envied that mortar crew. Okhrim Vasilchenko tried to drown the indignity in vodka and cigarette smoke, but basically we were too ashamed to look each other in the eye. The battalion *Komsomol* deputy came by, and there arose an informal *Komsomol* meeting. I took the floor first, and here's what I said:

"How is it that Krasnov's men caught this Nazi, and not us snipers, when we're the ones out on the front lines day and night, when we know every nook and cranny of the area?"

"How is it," asked Viktor Medvedev, "that we missed seeing Krasnov's men cross into German territory, anyway?"

We hadn't even noticed them. Normally the mortar crew worked a fair distance behind us. None of us could believe that Krasnov's men had waltzed right past, without us noticing them.

I scolded my men for their carelessness. I reminded them that our best source of information was our own fellow soldiers, and that we had to keep channels open to them, rather than acting as if we were lone wolves. The group sat in silence as I continued, "If a sniper doesn't rely first and foremost on his fellow soldiers, if he disengages from them and begins to operate on his own, if he locks himself up like a snail in his shell, then nothing but failure awaits that sniper."

The men started talking. My rebuke had cut them to the quick. The *Komsomolyets,* Kostrikov, said that he had killed twenty-six Nazis in all, while Sidorov had seventy. Kostrikov argued that comparing his count with that of the "champion" Sidorov was futile.

"What are you trying to say? Don't beat around the bush!" the others cried.

"What have I got to hide? Let Sidorov himself tell you. If he gets something wrong, why, I'll just correct him."

Sidorov rose to his feet and calmly cast a glance around the room at all those present. He had an impressive appearance: a sharply chiseled face, a large and hawk-like nose, a jutting chin and wavy, light-brown hair that he brushed straight back. He had a broad chest and powerful shoulders. Before starting to speak, he pulled out his tobacco pouch and began rolling a cigarette.

"What's with the silence? If you've got something to say, then get on with it!" someone hollered.

"What, are you blind? I'm rolling a cigarette and collecting my thoughts. I don't know how to give a speech and roll a cigarette at the same time."

Sidorov lit up, exhaled a puff of smoke, and got in staring battle with Kostrikov. Sidorov shook his head and in a single breath pronounced, "This chicken here says that he doesn't want to compare himself to me. What – have I asked to be compared to you, Kostrikov? I'm tired of you telling stories and giving me orders."

Kostrikov leaped to his feet. I had to rush between them to keep them from coming to blows.

"What's happened between you guys?" I asked them.

"He's the one that started this story," said Kostrikov, "now let me finish it."

The *Komsomol* business was forgotten as everyone's curiosity drove them to discover exactly what had happened between Kostrikov and Sidorov.

Sidorov had put a fire to the short fuse of Kostrikov's Georgian temper.

"Two days ago," said Kostrikov, "the fascists began advancing in small groups up the slope of Mamayev Hill. They were using machine guns for cover to their right and left. Our own soldiers had to expose themselves to their machine gun fire, in order to get at the Krauts before the enemy overran our positions."

Kostrikov was recounting events that all of us were familiar with, whether or not we had been there during the action.

"I got busy taking out the machine gunners," he continued, "as we had been ordered. But Sidorov was taking easy shots on Kraut riflemen, so he could pump up his personal headcount. While he was occupied with boosting his numbers, the enemy machine gunners that he should have been taking out wounded four Soviet soldiers! Whether those four guys will survive or not is anybody's guess. Sidorov considers racking up kills more important than protecting the lives of his comrades."

"There's no such thing as a war without casualties," countered Sidorov. "You can't blame me for what happened!"

Despite his efforts to justify himself, we found Sidorov at fault.

That night I accompanied him to his sector. We camouflaged ourselves near a drainage gully of the Dolgiy ravine, and kept watch over an area surrounding a Kraut pillbox. The pillbox's machine gun kept up a steady drone; its tracer bullets stitched stripes through the air across a wide front.

"Why didn't you mention that there was a night-time gunner out here?" I asked Sidorov.

"His bullets won't reach us," he replied.

"Are you crazy?" I said. "I want you out of here! Tomorrow request a transfer to a different sector."

Later that night, Okhrim Vasilchenko and I carried an anti-tank rifle to this same location and got rid of the Kraut machine gunner. It took only two shots. The first shot hit close enough to distract him and make him fire wildly. His erratic firing allowed us to take our time setting up the second shot, and that one blasted him and his machine gun right out of the pillbox.

~~~

Just before dawn, I was visited by a messenger. "The battalion command wants to see you."

"What for?" I asked.

"You'll know in a minute. The battalion commander had you

summoned. He said, 'Let Zaitsev see just what kind of scatter-brains he's got for snipers.'"

In the battalion command's bunker, the prisoner captured by Captain Krasnov was being interrogated. The captive, a stocky private, was begging the captain not to shoot him, claiming he knew a great deal, and promising that he would reveal everything once we took him to headquarters - but not here. Clearly he believed that once he talked and we had no further use for him, we would execute him. This private had been brainwashed by Nazi propaganda. We took very few prisoners during this stage of the battle, because most of the Germans would fight to last bullet rather then surrendering.

So the interrogation drew to a close. But I did manage to find out the details of how this captive had been taken prisoner.

Two days earlier, Captain Krasnov had learned from our scouts about a Nazi anti-tank emplacement, and he decided to see for himself whether or not their report was accurate. Krasnov planned his expedition thoroughly, down to the last detail. He and two soldiers tossed captured German camouflage cloaks over their uniforms. The captain threw some telephone equipment over his shoulder. He and his men wore Schmeissers around their necks and hung German-issue grenades with long handles from their belts. Captain Krasnov, who enjoyed an adrenaline rush, had decided to tempt fate.

He and his helpers passed unnoticed through our positions and across the front line. They crossed the barbed wire and the minefields of no-man's land, and reached enemy territory.

The captain discovered a telephone cable, and he and his men decided to follow it back to the enemy's command post. Soon they ran into a German soldier repairing the phone line, and this soldier started complaining to them about how all the breaks in the line were running him ragged, how he was hounded day and night, and how his battery commander regarded him as an ass.

"That's OK soldier, we'll give you a hand," said Krasnov, who knew a little bit of German.

The German lineman was alarmed by Krasnov's accent.

"Are you Serb?" the lineman asked.

"We're Serbs," Krasnov answered. He realized that if he were to continue with this deception, he was running the risk of being found out.

Krasnov signaled and his men knocked out the Nazi, stuffed a glove in his mouth and dragged him back to Russian territory.

"But how did you manage to move unnoticed through our own lines?" I asked the captain.

The captain smiled as he considered his reply. "When a fisherman sees his bobber jumping up and down, you could set fire to his pants and he still wouldn't notice it. It's a psychological phenomenon. You should take this into account and not chew out your snipers. But you've got to teach them to be more cautious."

I could say only one word to that: "Thanks!"

In a sniper's work, you cannot discount the psychological factors involved in hunting an important target. If you get too carried away by the heat of dueling with a cunning enemy, you stop noticing what's going on around you. You quit taking the necessary precautions. Captain Krasnov had taught me a valuable lesson.

CHAPTER 15.
TRUST

At dusk we made our way to the artillery emplacement of Ilya Shuklin, one of our division's most distinguished tank destroyers. He had already made a name for himself at the battle of Kastornye. And his crew – every last one of them – was as brave and daring as the commander himself.

One of Shuklin's men hailed us. He held a Tommy-gun in his hands and grenades hung from his belt. He suddenly appeared in front of us and pointed his gun's snout at my chest. "Halt," he commanded, "or I'll drill you."

I calmly pushed aside the gun's barrel and replied, "Feofanov, don't be a fool. We're all on the same side here."

"Just checking," answered the soldier. This was my friend, Vassili Feofanov, who later became one of my students.

Feofanov gave a whistle and another soldier emerged from behind a concrete wall to replace him. We headed for the cellar to see the battery commander. Not far away loomed the famous smokestack with its punctured side. Telephone cables from practically every artillery regiment in the army led up to the structure; it was the central node for all of the Red Army's artillery-spotting activities. The enemy knew this, and despite the hundreds, perhaps thousands, of their shells and bombs sent to destroy it, our observers' work there never stopped. Recently, however, Nazi snipers had showed up on the scene, and they had begun to pick off the Soviet forward artillery observers. As the observers went, so did the precision of our artillery bombardments.

The artillery crews asked their commander, General Pozharskiy, for help, and that is how us snipers ended up as Shuklin's guests.

In spite of my first impression of Ilya Shuklin, he was a kind man with an open heart. When Shuklin wanted to reward a soldier for a job well done, he would take him in his arms and give him a bear hug. And now I was in his clutches.

"Oh, Vassili! How could I have turned you away, back in Krasnoufimsk? Then of course, how could anyone tell just by looking at you? You must admit, you weren't much to look at…Anyway, listen to what's happening now. German snipers are putting heavy pressure on our observers in the smokestack. They won't let our guys get near it. And we haven't got a clue where these Heinies are shooting from. Please, Vasya, help us."

The artillery was thundering above, but here, deep in Shuklin's underground headquarters, no one paid any attention to it. Machine gun fire and the explosion of grenades weren't even within earshot.

Shuklin guided us around the bunker. "This will be your room, comrade snipers. Relax and get your weapons ready for action." He pushed back a tarp that served as a door to a room outfitted with three cots. Morozov, Shaikin and Kulikov stayed there, while Vasilchenko, Gorozhaev, Volovatikh and Driker situated themselves in a neighboring section.

"Chief, let's you and me head to my quarters," offered Shuklin. "An intelligence officer from the army's political division has arrived, and he's interested in hearing how you'll be preparing for a duel with the Nazi snipers. He's one of us, a seasoned vet who comes from the Urals."

We cut across the corridor, turned a corner and entered the commander's room. In place of cots were real bunk beds. A table built from scrap lumber stood in the center of the floor, and on it sat a sliced loaf of rye bread and – remarkably – a plate with a heap of fried, homemade *blini*.[42] The smell was intoxicating.

At the other end of the table, next to a lamp, a fair-haired man was sitting, buried in his notebook. He wore the emblems of a captain or senior *Politruk*. I recalled having seen him on the day I arrived in Stalingrad, when we were crossing the Volga. He had been leading the sailors away from the moorings....

However at this moment my attention was focused more on the soft, pan-fried *blini* than on anything else. They were indeed a luxury, and I couldn't help but groan with anticipation.

"You're living quite well, Comrade Senior Lieutenant," I remarked to Shuklin, "maybe you've got some real *pel'menyi* [43] in your kitchen too?"

"We may, we may," said Shuklin, "but let's work on these first. If we wait, my crew will finish them off."

Shuklin sat me down next to him at the table, and we dove into the *blini*. The fair-haired man with the emblems in his button-holes was too slow; without lifting his eyes from his notebook he reached over to the plate, but it was already empty. He raised his head in surprise and came face to face with my smile.

"I see you've received some reinforcements, Comrade Shuklin. From the commander's reserves, is he?"

"Yes," I answered for Shuklin, "from the reserves. From up on Mamayev Hill, that is!"

Apparently missing the irony of my response, he smiled and offered me his hand. "Ivan Grigoriev."

"Vassili Zaitsev," I responded, and we shook.

"So tell me, what happened to you snipers up on the hill?" he asked, as if trying to clarify why we had shown up here, at the *Krasny Oktyabr* Factory.

His question perplexed me.

"We're here on the commander's orders," I said.

[42] *blini*: Russian rolled pancaked with filling
[43] *pel'menyi:* dumplings or raviolis, typically stuffed with beef or onions.

"Of course, of course," he replied, "but I'm interested in something else…"

"What's he driving at?" I wondered, and began to get irritated. I instinctively raised my voice and said, "In the first place, the fighting at Mamayev is every bit as intense as it is here, and secondly…" I sucked in my breath to continue my tirade, but Grigoriev cut me off.

"Don't get upset." After a brief pause he addressed me by my Christian name: "Vassili, you haven't understood me correctly. I'm talking about your morale. I'm not knocking your achievements. In fact, I've been writing about your exploits in my reports for a month now. Mamayev Hill is a key position in our defense; I'm interested in how you and the other snipers are performing there…."

Suddenly it hit me. This Captain Grigoriev was a journalist. I was willing to talk to him now. He produced some cigarettes. I began to recount all that I'd endured and thought about when we were stuck on the slopes of Mamayev.

"…So we're creeping up the hill, near the water towers. Most of us were wounded and some lay dead, but I was unhurt. Lucky, they say. They send the wounded to the field hospital, but I, the so-called "lucky" one, continue with life, crawling through the slime in the trenches. And then I get called down to the banks of the Volga," and here I stuck it to Grigoriev: "..I was ordered to come here, away from that danger zone, but people seem to think I'm guilty of something, for not getting killed back on Mamayev Hill."

"No, I understand, and I believe you," interrupted Grigoriev. "Only, don't be so morbid. Quit harping about dying."

"Fair enough," I said.

"Just don't pay attention to people when they talk like that," said Grigoriev. "They're jealous. They envy all the praise you've received. You were sent here because you're needed here. Let those loudmouths see how a "deserter" like you operates."

Grigoriev was exaggerating my significance, but I appreciated his words. It is important it is to have someone understand and trust you.

Faith and trust – how powerful they can be! When no one believes in you, your soul dries up, your strength is exhausted and you are transformed into a bird with crippled wings. But when people put their faith in you, then even things you would never dream about become possible. Trust is the source of a soldier's inspiration. And faith is the mother of friendship and of a soldier's courage. For the commander, faith and trust are the two keys to a soldier's heart, to that hidden cache of energy that the soldier himself may not understand he has inside of him.

I can say, based on my own experiences, that if my comrades had not believed in me, if they had ever doubted the results of my solitary sniper missions, then probably I would not have taken the risks that I did. What's more, to maintain others' confidence in my results, I never recorded a shot as a "kill" unless I was completely sure that my target was dead.

~~~

Therefore there were occasional discrepancies between the kill figures reported in dispatches and those in my own personal record book. Observers would sometimes inflate my kills, because they would simply count how many shots I had fired. To them, three shots meant to write a '3' for kills. Of course, those observers could not see my targets as well as I could, so they never knew any better. But whether or not my bullets actually penetrated their intended targets – only I knew this.

This sort of "score-keeping" saddled the snipers with a tremendous responsibility. It was the law of mutual trust coming into effect. We had faith in the monitors' numbers; and they took us at our word when we said we had hit a target.

We didn't want our troops walking around with their heads up, as long as there was any possibility of enemy sniper fire in our zone. So I had signs posted that said, "Caution! This zone is under the watch of Nazi snipers."

I hung these signs in areas where I happened to be leading a hunt; and I never took the signs down, until after I was positive that I'd done away with the enemy sniper.

I spoke to Grigoriev about all of this. I told him about the sniper's honor, about my comrades, and about the new things I had discovered as I looked into the tactics of a sniper group. Later this all became the object of a discussion in one department of the General Staff; Grigoriev managed to record my ramblings and somehow passed them on to the high command in the form of an article.

After Grigoriev left, I knew I had to return quickly to the battle with the enemy marksmen who were picking off our artillery spotters.

Within the span of that night, I managed to interview a number of soldiers who had witnessed the deaths of the spotters. Ilya Shuklin helped us draw several maps that allowed my snipers to see from what points, and from what angles, the spotters on the smokestack had been fired upon. We figured out the probable trajectory of the incoming bullets, and therefore, the distance from the enemy snipers' gun barrels to the top of the smokestack. Our calculations, sketches and even a detailed analysis of the bullet-riddled housing of the periscope used by our artillery observers, suggested to us a plan of action for the following morning.

Here in this new location, in contrast with our position on Mamayev Hill, the view of the horizon was obstructed in every direction by debris from the bombed-out factory. Everywhere you looked you saw warped steel reinforcements, upturned metal structures, collapsed roofs, and twisted walls. In order to get a clear shot at our fellows on top of the smokestack, an enemy sniper would have to back up a good distance from the obstructions, or find an opening amid the rubble that afforded an unobstructed path for his bullet. There was no other choice for them. So we began hunting for every such opening and tracing them back to their sources. Our scopes allowed us to literally see the whites of the Nazi soldiers' eyes; but we knew we had to take our time. We restricted our shots to enemy snipers and to the most dangerous of their machine gun posts.

~~~

By midday I had used up an entire clip, as had my partner, Nikolai Kulikov. Morozov and Shaikin had gone through two clips apiece, and Gorozhaev and Vasilchenko were also doing OK. That evening, in order to make sure we'd been successful, I asked Shuklin to post a mannequin up on the smokestack. But the foolhardy Ilya Shuklin decided to climb to the top himself. He was an officer, and obviously I couldn't stop him, but as he crept up the smokestack, my heart was pounding furiously.

He yelled into his telephone: "Artillery! Give me one round on reference point one and fire!"

A minute passed, and I heard the peal of the battery.

"Good shooting. Now, give me two rounds on reference point two…fire!"

That was how Ilya Shuklin rang in the night, with an artillery salute.

The next morning our artillery spotters were able to resume their work. As our emplacements on the far side of the Volga began to fire, I noticed how exhausted I had become. My head was throbbing and my eyes ached like someone had rubbed broken glass into them. I was dying to sleep – if only for an hour - and I lay down in the first cellar I came to. I fell asleep, not suspecting that the resumption of work by our spotters was going to incite a frenzied response from the enemy.

I was dozing when something hit me hard in the shoulder. I leaped up and grabbed my rifle. There was a buzzing noise all around me; bricks were falling from the ceiling and the walls were engulfed by huge tongues of flame. I finally spotted a way out, dashed out of the cellar and pressed myself close to the ground. Bombs were exploding to the right and left – one, two, three…and they were close, only thirty or forty yards away. The force of shock waves rolled me over several times, so that I ended up in the bottom of a ditch. I glanced up at the sky and saw rows of dive-bombers hurtling straight towards the ground, then pulling up at the last possible second, and showering the earth with plumes of fire.

When the air raid finished, Nazi foot soldiers leaped to the attack. Under the cover of the bombardment, their men had assembled near the walls of the factory, and now they were pouring in through the openings in the walls and rushing along the passages between workshops. I could hear their shouts and the guttural barking of their officers.

As if they'd been waiting for that moment, our machine guns opened fire. Grenades started going off, and by the sound of their explosions, I was able to sort out our men from the enemy. I ran to the aid of my comrades. My location was excellent, and I was able to fire accurately on the Nazis who had managed to penetrate our lines. I shot down to my last bullet.

It wasn't until evening that the battle began to subside. I needed to check on my snipers. Our rendezvous point was the smoke-stack, as it was an ideal landmark visible from all sides. En route to it, I passed through remnants of the 39th and 45th divisions. There I found everything turned upside down. Despite our resistance, the enemy had managed to capture the northern portion of the *Krasny Oktyabr* Factory. This had allowed them to move right up next to the banks of the Volga.

In response to this crisis, General Chuikhov was calling reserves, including a large number of fighters from the Bogunskiy and Taraschanskiy Regiments of the 45th, Schor's Division. Their assignment was to wipe out the Nazis who'd just broken through to the Volga.

At dusk I reached the smokestack. In the clearing, just east of where we had arranged to meet, I found the snipers Kulikov, Gorozhaev, Shaikin and Morozov. Vasilchenko, Volovatikh and Driker failed to show up.

After we had cleaned up each other's cuts and bruises, we took off to search of the three who were missing. It took us until morning to locate them, at a medical station by the banks of the Volga.

Driker, Volovatikh and Vasilchenko had not come there of their own volition. Volovatikh and Vasilchenko were shell-shocked and unable to stand on their feet, while Driker had a fever and was vomiting. Their faces were all swollen and their eyes were red. They lay on the stones by the shore, without any bedding. This day had brought in so many wounded that the medics still had not managed to look at them. At this time the crossing wasn't operating - not a single boat was headed over the Volga.

I collected my snipers and took them up along the Banniy Ravine to the position of our own 284th division's command. We were assigned lodgings in two bunkers with some weapons foremen.

The first to visit us was Nikolai Logvinenko. He had received a new field commission, so now he was chief of staff of the second battalion, and he came to regimental staff by the orders of Captain Piterskiy. Then we were visited by Brigade Commissar Konstantin Terentievich Zubkov. The nurses Lyuda Yablonskaya and Zhenya Kosova were tending to the wounded.

Commissar Zubkov noticed that our uniforms were in shreds, and he ordered that we be issued fresh clothes.

Chief of Supplies Mikhail Babaev brought us uniforms. After we washed, visited the barber, and were freshly shaven, we started to look like new recruits – only in mismatched clothes. Everything fit me several sizes too large. My shirt hung over me like a sack, and my boots were huge – they flopped everywhere I walked.

Zubkov brought the division commander, Colonel Nikolai Filipovich Batyuk to see us. To be honest, I was expecting a good dressing-down – for what, I could have only guessed. It's impossible to anticipate what a commander will get upset about.

Batyuk was an intimidating officer. He always looked dissatisfied with something. He couldn't tolerate frivolous reports, so most of his staff did their best to remain silent around him.

As the senior sniper, I started to report our achievements and losses. The division commander looked us over, stared straight at me and burst out laughing. His laugh was contagious, and the bunker started to feel a little warmer and more relaxed.

"Who dressed you up like this?" Batyuk inquired, looking our new clothes.

"Nurse Yablonskaya."

"What does she want to make you look like?"

"'Krauts," joked Kulikov.

"Don't worry," said Batyuk, "you still have a long time until your wedding.[44] Zaitsev, you look like a scarecrow," he continued. "Head over to the brigade commissar's bunker and get changed into something your own size."

I hesitated and Batyuk regarded me with a raised eyebrow.

"Well, what are you waiting for?" he asked.

I exited, then immediately got lost trying to find the entrance among the various adjoining bunkers. In front of one of them, a short, academic-looking type was smoking a pipe filled with *Zoloetoe Runo* tobacco.

"Tell me, professor," I said to him, "is this the commissar's bunker?"

He looked me square in the eyes and responded, "I've been waiting for you, scarecrow. Come in."

As soon as I entered, a very attractive young woman approached me. She was wearing a soldier's blouse that had been tailored to fit extremely tight, and she had a wide officer's belt that held a small holster for a revolver. She offered me her hand.

"Lydia," she said simply.

"Vasilli Zaitsev," I replied.

She began showering me with questions: "Is it true what they write in the papers about you, using a mirror in a duel with that Nazi sniper? Where'd you get the mirror? How did I hear about this, you ask? Our brigade commissar collects clippings from the papers about your exploits. Here's Alyosha Afanasiev himself; he's the one who writes those articles." She tilted her chin toward the "professor."

---

[44] "You have a long time before your wedding" – a Russian saying, a more precise translation would be "it'll heal before your wedding comes."

"I apologize," Afanasiev said, "I didn't recognize your face and thought you were some kind of propagandist here for a meeting with the commissar. He's having a conference today. Are you really Zaitsev?"

I pulled out my Komsomol ID and handed it to Afanasiev.

"Wonderful!" he said. "This will make a great story: 'Vassili Zaitsev comes to visit Brigade Commissar Zubkov'."

Zubkov entered the room. He smiled and said, "Afanasiev, there'll be no such article. Instead you can write, 'Sniper of the 284th rifle division in talks with Lieutenant General Chuikov of the 62nd Army'."

Zubkov walked over to the corner, picked up a leather brief-case, pulled out a notebook, and sat down. He said, "Sit a little closer and let's talk. Our time is short. Speak."

"About what, Comrade Commissar?" I asked.

"Well, give me your life story." He had his pen ready to take notes.

"Zaitsev, Vassili Grigorievich, born in 1915, in the woods, in the Urals…"

The commissar interrupted me.

"Wait a minute, Vassili. How am I to understand that, 'born in the woods..'? You mean, in a country village? The way you've put it, it sounds like you were born in some primeval forest, under a tree!"

"No, Comrade Commissar, I was born in the bathhouse of a woodsman, at Easter time. When I was two days old, my mother saw two teeth in my mouth. Some old villagers said this was a bad omen that foretold that wild animals were going to tear me to pieces...."

"...My father fought in the Imperialist War[45] as a soldier in the 8th Guards Army of Brusilov. He was invalided with a wound and returned home in 1917…"

"…When I was little I was given the nickname 'Basurman.'[46]

[45] Imperialist War – the way Soviets referred to World War 1
[46] 'Basurman': 'foreigner' or someone of a different faith – particularly Muslim

"...There were no schools around. My grandfather taught me to track and hunt. I was a good shot and knew how to set traps along rabbit trails, trap *kosachei* with snares, and I could lasso the horns of a wild goat from a tree..."

I got carried away with reminiscing. Then, in the doorway, appeared Lieutenant Colonel Vassili Zakharovich Tkachenko. Tkachenko was the head of political operations for the 62nd Army. The brigade commissar clapped his notebook shut.

"Fine, Vassili. We'll continue this next time. But now, go get changed."

Afanasiev and Lydia were waiting for me in the neighboring room. A pressed and laundered uniform, complete with a new field cap, was lying there on the bed. There was even a handkerchief! Next to the bed there was a pair of leather boots – a bit worn, but very well made.

As Lydia exited, she said "After you've changed, please join us for dinner."

I was surprised by the uniform and the boots. Everything fit as if it was tailor-made, except for the belt, which needed a few more holes. The uniform turned out to have previously belonged to Brigade Commissar Zubkov. I have never looked so sharp. I had been transformed from a ragged front-line soldier into what Lydia called a "fop."

At three o'clock that morning the snipers in our regiments gathered in the division commander's bunker. We all had sticking plasters and bandages on our faces.

Vassili Ivanovich Chuikov arrived, accompanied by the journalist Captain Grigoriev. General Chuikov went around the room shaking hands. He greeted each of us individually. Then, smiling, he said, "It's good to see you fellows all patched up. Looks like the enemy gave you quite a licking, eh?"

"Comrade Commander," I answered for everyone, "these bandages can't stop us from fighting the enemy. Just give us your orders."

Chuikov regarded us. His gaze was so intense you felt like his eyes could burn holes through you. General Chuikov was always preoccupied with the big picture, and he wanted to explain things to us so that we would grasp his primary concerns.

"You fellows are fighting brilliantly," he said, "and making short work of the fascists. But for every enemy soldier you kill, two more of the scum sprout up. Now we've got a crisis in another sector: the enemy has succeeded in seizing the northwest portion of the *Krasny Oktyabr* Factory. I won't bullshit you, it's a tough fight. That's where we can really use your snipers' talents. I'm aware that three of your comrades lie wounded.."

Chuikov glanced at Grigoriev. Then he continued. "But that happened for a simple reason. You got so caught up in the heat of battle that you forgot your assignment. You turned into Tommy-gunners, into normal infantryman. A screw-up like that demands severe criticism, especially for you, Zaitsev. It's your job to watch out for every sniper in the group."

Chuikov glanced at his watch; he was in a hurry. He stood up and handed the notes he had been using for my interview to Grigoriev.

"I'm not going to waste any more of your time. You have a specific mission: kill the enemy, but remember: you have to pick your targets carefully. We pay for every mistake in blood, so let each one of you give this mission some thought. Try to see this struggle from a broader perspective. Then it will be clear to you how you must act. I wish you success."

With that, General Chuikov exited the bunker.

I remained behind, alone with my thoughts. The fighting at Stalingrad had taught me a great deal. I had matured and become stronger. I knew that I was a different soldier than the one I had been just a month before.

CHAPTER 16.
WRONGED

The situation was becoming desperate. Despite our ferocious resistance, our all-out counterattacks, and the daring missions of our storm groups, the Germans had somehow managed to seize a part of the *Krasny Oktyabr* Factory, and with it a direct approach to the banks of the Volga. What's more, the Soviet regiments around the *Barrikady* factory had been cut off from our main forces.

We understood that a success like this had the power to inspire the Germans with hopes of an easy victory. If the Germans believed that they had the imminent possibility of capturing the left bank of the Volga, they would trumpet to the world that the Bolshevik stronghold at Stalingrad had fallen, and now all that remained was to finish off the last elements of the Red Army....

Given our situation, each of us had to ask himself, have I done everything in my power to repel the fascists; have I fulfilled the hope of the people expressed in the letter to Comrade Stalin: "...the enemy will be stopped and defeated at the walls of Stalingrad."[47]

Yes, the conscience advised – no, not advised but commanded

---

[47] A letter was written to Stalin in November, 1942 by the soldiers, commanders and political instructors on the Stalingrad front, pledging to hold the city.

– that one forget his wounds, ignore his exhaustion, and push all individual concerns out of his mind. Each of us had to mobilize his will and every ounce of strength towards stripping the enemy of any hope of victory at Stalingrad. The conscience ordered us to enter battle and to scorn death. This situation demanded that we not wait for instructions, but rather that we seize the initiative and act, so that the enemy would know who was in charge!

In those heated days at Stalingrad, I wasn't as aware of this as I am today. More likely I was driven by intuition, without thinking about things so deeply. Anyway, during the battle there was no time to think, only to act.

I knew that everyone assembled in the bunker with commander Chuikov at that moment - my snipers and all the commanders and *politraboniki* – understood the gravity of the situation. Everyone, that is, with the exception of Captain Piterskiy.

Maybe, as soldiers are prone to doing, I judged him too harshly. But even now, after so much time has passed, I still can't see things any differently....

~~~

Immediately after the meeting with Chuikov was over, my snipers and I rushed to our positions in the *Krasny Oktyabr* Factory. We ran straight for our destination, through trenches and over foxholes, without stopping to rest. I knew that we had to reach our new positions before the sun came up. We had to assume positions on the flank of the Germans who had made the break through to the Volga. From there, we could pick off the Nazi officers and noncoms.

Daybreak found us at a fork in the Banniy ravine, on the right branch leading to the factory's housing quarters. This was an ideal spot for us to move about almost unseen, and to fire on the enemy flank.

But the Germans weren't sleeping either. Their scouts had already picked up on our movements. Barely five minutes had passed before they began shelling the ravine. Columns of earth and smoke shot into the air. We were trapped in a barrage, and the sky around us grew dark with dust and smoke. Everything was seething with explosions that rocked the nearby banks of the ravine. Half an hour passed with no relief. Then the Nazis split their fire, re-directing part of it to the north, while continuing to pound the area around us. But it was no easier for us, because with the reduction of artillery fire, the enemy cranked up the level of machine gun fire they had targeted against us.

It became difficult to breathe from all the smoke and dust. We were paralyzed. We lay on the bottom of the trench, our hands over our heads, unable to move. We could do nothing except wait for their shelling to end and for the launch of the enemy infantry's next attack. Our Tommy-guns and grenades were at the ready.

Finally the artillery barrage halted, but the attack we were expecting didn't materialize. Instead, like an apparition, a soot-covered man with a pipe stuck between his teeth came strolling along the bottom of the ravine. We recognized him by his droopy moustache – it was Logvinenko. He had noticed us taking cover in this trench and had come to meet with us. En route he had been covered with soot and dust and from various nearby shell explosions, but he was unhurt.

"Still alive in there?" he asked. "This ravine's mighty ploughed up, eh? The Krauts must have thought we had some big numbers down here; turns out it was just me. They sure laid it on me though, didn't they?"

I was trying to figure out what Logvinenko was doing here He hadn't shown up only to draw fire on himself. He lay down against the embankment, borrowed my periscope and then my rifle. Meanwhile the other snipers set about their work. The Germans showed themselves rarely, but whenever they did, none of them escaped a barrage of lead. Nikolai Logvinenko even took a shot at one. I watched through the periscope as his bullet jerked his target's head, and sent the German's helmet flying.

"Well, what do you say, chief – was it a kill?" he inquired, as if whether or not he had hit his target depended on my opinion. Meanwhile, the German was twitching in his death throes.

"Looks like you nailed him," I replied.

Logvinenko paused for a moment, and then, in an altogether different tone, asked "Do you see their observation point, beneath that slab?"

"Yes."

"And that artillery periscope there, do you see it?"

"Yes, the scope too."

"Good, then listen. Three days ago you made it safe for our forward artillery observers to go back to work. Now I want you to do the opposite to the enemy. Blind them. I want you to neutralize their spotters, is that clear? If so, then get to work."

With that, Logvinenko departed, trudging back through the blackened trenches.

This assignment had the highest priority. The enemy's observers and surveillance posts were essential for them to pinpoint their artillery fire. Their shelling was severely hampering our ability to retaliate against the enemy detachment that had broken through to the Volga. Time was of the essence.

Thanks to Logvinenko, we knew where the enemy's main observation point was situated. In no time we spotted the slits through which their observers were keeping watch. These slits were just beneath a giant concrete slab that covered their bunker. The Krauts were sitting there, looking through the polished lenses of their scopes. It was infuriating to think of our enemies, invaders so alien to our land, observing us through their high-powered optics. I thought to myself: "We'll blow holes through those scopes now, you vermin..."

They had a huge post. There were six observation slits. I assigned one to each of my comrades, and I took the last. We agreed to synchronize our shots. Crack! – a volley of six rifles thundered through the ravine. We let three minutes pass. Crack! Another volley. The second volley had been for insurance: "don't even think about raising new scopes to those slits, you swine.

"...We'll take out the next set, too!"

A few minutes after our second set, German bombers began buzzing the factory. Demolition bombs shook the earth with a mighty force and the sky grew thick with stratified clouds of red brick dust, pulverized concrete fragments, black smoke and red tongues of fire. But what could we do? Against aircraft, a sniper's rifle was useless....

Then, without orders, as if jolted by some mysterious force, we charged through the rubble towards the enemy's positions by the factory gates.

A small shell fragment struck Vasilchenko in the cheek, but there was no time for us to stop. Okhrim yanked the fragment from his skin and pressed a piece of cloth against it, to staunch the bleeding.

We jumped into a trench near the factory gates.

"How bad are you hit?" I asked him.

"My head is spinning."

German aircraft continued to circle like vultures. Their machine gun rounds beat down on the brick gates above our heads. One bullet grazed my helmet, then exploded and stung my elbow and shoulder with fine shards of shrapnel.

Instinctively I sprang up. It was a stupid move, but there are some things that can make a soldier lose control over his actions and take off running, not knowing where or why. And to make matters worse, the longer you operate around the explosions of bombs, mortars and artillery shells, the longer you live with machine gun fire, the more comfortable you become with them, and the less you sense their danger. Something like this was affecting me. I was half-crazed, standing straight up, completely exposed to enemy fire.... Fortunately Vasilchenko managed to catch up to me, grab me, and yank me behind a heap of steel reinforcements.

"Chief!" he shouted. "What happened?"

I caught my breath and regained my composure. As I looked around I saw our soldiers huddled in ditches to the right and left.

The enemy's strafing didn't allow them to lift their heads. Meanwhile, the Nazis were strolling along their own front line, with their heads held high. Their soldiers had grown cocky, thanks to their air power. When we saw them acting this way we were insulted. It was hard to choke down our rage. They must have thought we were totally incompetent, and unable to strike at them anymore.

"It's time to teach them a lesson," said Vasilchenko, raising his rifle to his shoulder. I followed his lead. Directly in front of us, four Nazis were ambling along at a leisurely pace, crates of ammo on their shoulders. They were laughing and joking. Without exchanging a word, Okhrim shot the first one and I the second. We ventilated the other two with our next volley. Unfortunately, after his second shot, Okhrim's rifle jammed.

Overhead, the thrum of the Luftwaffe's bombers grew louder. I dragged Okhrim with me, and we ran for cover by the foot of the factory walls. The exploding bombs were chipping away at the walls, and we seemed to be losing more and more of our cover every second.

Okhrim Vasilchenko hung his head, depressed. What good was he without his rifle? But just then I managed to pop the jammed shell out of his weapon, and his sour expression changed to a smile.

At this hour, given how close the enemy had approached, what we needed were submachine gunners, not snipers – this despite the admonition we had just received from General Chuikov. So Vasilchenko and I were once again transformed into Tommy-gunners, leading counter assaults and showering the enemy with grenades.

Viktor Medvedev joined us, and during the frenzy of one counter assault, a group of Krauts ambushed him from behind and knocked him over the head. They immediately gagged him and dragged him off.

How my voice found so much strength I'll never know, but I hollered "Follow me!" and my voice rang over the battlefield like a church bell. We darted through the wasteland of upended railway cars and followed the path the Krauts were using to lead Viktor away. We raced in front of them and cut them off. The Krauts scurried around trying to find cover amid some flattened wooden houses, but we had caught them in a place that had been completely leveled. We were able to free Viktor, and also managed to take one Nazi alive, a big, ginger-haired fellow wearing a woman's fur coat.

This is where my troubles began. The ordeal with Captain Piterskiy that followed all started on account of this captive. The crux of the matter was that we lost our prisoner on the way back. We came under heavy machine gun fire, and unfortunately, the first rounds struck our captive and practically blew his head off. We were trapped by the enemy's fire, and we spent a long day cowering in the bottom of a bomb crater. Meanwhile Viktor Medvedev lay unconscious, his scalp swimming in blood.

It was not until sunset that we managed to reach the bunker of Yevgeniy Shetilov, commander of the third battalion's subma-chine gunner company. That was when we found out that Captain Piterskiy had been searching for me since early morning. He had sent out messengers to locate me, but no matter where they searched, nobody, not even the experienced scouts, had been able to track down a single sniper from our group. Captain Piterskiy was very angry. It was his opinion that the snipers in our group had become arrogant after the meeting with General Chuikov. Captain Piterskiy managed to convince all the regimental com-manders to regard us with suspicion, as if we had been AWOL and shirking our duties. So this was why Yevgeniy Shetilov, who had known me since my first days in battle at Stalingrad, addressed me sternly and suspiciously:

"Where have you been?" Shetilov had thinning hair that he slicked back with pomade and his shoulders were always slumped. He leaned forward and peered at me.

"Well?"

Was he really about to accuse me of cowardice? A cold wave

ran up and down my spine. I couldn't find any words to reply.

"Vasya – I don't believe you've done anything wrong, but you must explain to me, where you were."

Signalman Alexander Blinov had called the regimental staff and reported that the snipers had all returned to the company. Captain Piterskiy, who was our chief of staff, was on the telephone, demanding to speak with me.

"Well sailors, I guess our chief's fallen into a trap, and now he's really going to catch it," said someone behind me.

Blinov whispered to me, "Vasya, keep your cool! Don't let them scare you!"

Blinov was right to warn me. Captain Piterskiy gave me a serious tongue lashing, and any time I tried to say something in response, he cut me off with, "Silence!"

I finally managed to get in a word edgewise: "I request that Captain Rakityanskiy be sent here to sort out the documents of our captive.."

Without allowing me to finish, Piterskiy hollered, "Where is the captive?"

I didn't fully understand the chief of staff's question and replied, "He was killed...." That set Piterskiy off, and if I thought he had been angry before, now he was in a truly rug-chewing rage.

"The firing squad would be letting you off too easy!" he screamed. "We lose some of our best men trying to capture live Nazi prisoners, while you take it upon yourself to shoot one! I command you to report to me this instant and deliver a full accounting of your actions. You are hereby stripped of command of the snipers!"

I passed the telephone to the signalman and walked out of the bunker. The other snipers followed: Kulikov, Dvoyashkin, Kostrikov, Shaikin, Morozov, Gorozhaev, and Abzalov. Viktor Medvedev, who had been really knocked for a loop and could barely struggle to his feet, remained behind.

I explained what Captain Piterskiy had just told me.

There were groans all around.

"Thank God," I thought to myself, "my men still have some respect for me."

I was thinking of what a martinet Piterskiy was, one of those officers every soldier runs into sooner or later – an officer who can only justify his existence by making the lives of his underlings miserable.

"Nikolai Kulikov, you're the next most senior after me, you'll be taking over."

"Why not Viktor Medvedev?" Kulikov objected.

"We've got to get Viktor to the regimental med station," I said. "We can take him now, while it's still dark; we'll go together."

Viktor Medvedev emerged from the bunker, holding on to the shoulders of Blinov, the signalman. "I'm already feeling better," Viktor coughed, "take me with you."

To tell the truth, Viktor looked like death warmed over. The muscles in his face had gone slack, as if he had aged 20 years.

"Viktor," I told him, "we would never consider leaving you behind."

We had been taking cover beneath a train car. From there, we had to cross three hundred yards of open space that traversed the railroad embankment. Along this embankment, even in the middle of the night, enemy machine gun fire criss-crossed the open air. We were going to have to test our luck, in a game of blind man's bluff with death.

"Maybe these are going to be my last steps," I thought to myself, darkly. Then they would post a notice in the newspaper about me, as they did about every casualty, "...died fulfilling his duties on the front...."

A flare soared high above the Banniy ravine, leaving a long, fiery trail in its wake. It exploded with a muffled pop and hung listlessly, like an electric lamp. We dropped to the ground and crawled for cover.

There was an ominous silence – it hindered us from attempting to cross the open territory. We knew the enemy was nearby, listening for the slightest sound. I had to create a diversion, so I stood up. Abzalov got up behind me and we begin walking along the embankment, stamping loudly with our boots. But the enemy remained silent. They were waiting for something more, so I gave it to them. I flung a grenade across the railroad tracks. That was enough of a provocation to make the German machine gunners open fire. Lines of tracers hissed through the air above our heads.

Abzalov and I returned fire, while the rest of the group cut across the danger zone, two of them supporting Viktor Medvedev. The Kraut machine guns kept Abzalov and me pinned under their streams of bullets. We crouched in a gutter, unable to lift our heads or move our legs. Their fire wasn't letting up for a minute.

There was a drainage pipe by our feet. Neither of us had any idea where it would lead. But anything was better than staying stuck crouched in a ball, while so much hot lead was zooming past our faces. Abzalov and I both slid into the drainage pipe and began crawling.

We could hear shells, mortar fire and grenades exploding; every detonation resonated through the pipe, echoing as if it was right on top of us. If the enemy caught us down here, we'd be toast. All they'd have to do was to shoot through the pipe; there was no way they could miss us. We had to get out of there fast! Finally we glimpsed some light ahead.

The pipe led us to another drainage canal, this one lined with concrete. A flare lit up the sky again, and we pressed ourselves close to the canal wall. Nearby, we could hear the racket of a firefight; the dull bang of grenades, the crackle of Tommy-guns and the steady drone of heavy machine gun fire.

"Where are we?" Abzalov asked. "Are we in Kraut territory?"

"No," I said to Abzalov, "I think we're among friends here. We'd know if these were Germans firing nearby; they use explosive bullets, while we use standard ones."

We lay there in silence. The muffled sounds of voices

approached. I couldn't understand what was being said, but it was definitely Russian they were speaking. The soldiers were walking through the dark, stumbling over things and cursing. Another rocket flared up overhead, and in its light we spotted them - two Tommy-gunners - Russians! Now we could make out their conversation clearly:

"They ought to be right here; I'm sure I saw them fall here."

"Well then, smart-ass" asked the second soldier," "where are they?"

"Right here!" I hissed.

The gunners dropped to the ground. Then, realizing we were Russian, they spoke.

"We're looking for a couple of Krauts!"

Abzalov's famous temper showed itself. "While you're at it," he sneered, "make a side trip and take us back to your headquarters!"

On the way back to HQ, we heard, much to our relief, that our fellow snipers had all safely reached the medical station on the Volga.

~~~

At daybreak I arrived at Captain Piterskiy's to deliver my report. I had been more or less paralyzed with anticipation about the meeting with him, but there was no way to avoid it, no matter how unpleasant the task was going to be. I delivered a full account of events leading up to the death of the prisoner, in accordance with procedure. I even clicked my heels.

Piterskiy was a tall, vain man with waxed moustachios, in the fashion of the Czarist era. He glared at me, as if he'd seen something peculiar in me. Then he asked, "Well, what should I do with you? Send you off to a penal company, or up to Mamayev?"

"Sir, if you please, send me where the danger is the greatest!"

"Fine. Medvedev will assume your command. The group will stay around the shooting range, and work the northern edge of the *Krasny Oktyabr* Factory. But as for you, leave at once for Mamayev Hill." He must have assumed this was a death sentence. Apparently he had forgotten that I had previously been stationed on Mamayev Hill and had survived.

"To the hill, yes sir!" I replied, with obvious irony. I turned to walk out.

"As you were!" Piterskiy commanded.

I whirled around to face the captain, repeated his orders, and in an even more pronounced movement, turned back towards the door.

"As you were!" I heard the captain shout, but I had already exited the bunker and was making my way in the direction of Mamayev Hill.

CHAPTER 17.
TYURIN AND KHABIBULIN

I arrived at the third battalion alone. Sergeant Abzalov had stayed behind at staff headquarters. The stubborn and hot-tempered Bashkir couldn't come to terms with Captain Piterskiy's decision. The insult was weighing on me as well.

But, as they say, every cloud has a silver lining. I was sitting next to the submachine gunner company commander's bunker, disassembling and cleaning my rifle, when Lieutenant Shetilov approached.

Shetilov knew about my recent ordeal, and he stood in silence for a moment, then matter-of-factly said, "Hey Vasya, why don't we go take a look up the hill. It seems a Kraut sniper has built himself a nest there."

Yevgeniy Shetilov knew just how to set me right again.

"Take me to the spot!" I replied.

To the south of the water tower lay some sort of depression – what looked to be a bomb crater. A collection of dry branches hung over the right side of the depression. The branches didn't provide much cover, but they did hinder my getting a good view. To the left of the crater was a bush, and next to it, on the rim of the crater, lay the shaft of a mortar shell with its edges blown-out and twisted, like the curled horn of a mountain goat.

"So, what's your opinion, is there a sniper up there?" asked Shetilov.

"The spot's a good one," I said. "He'd have an excellent view, and he would be well concealed."

Sitting in the trench next to Lt. Shetilov was the cool and wiry Stepan Kryazh. He was Shetilov's signalman, known to all by his name and patronymic, Stepan Ivanovich. The other soldiers respected him for his courage, but they feared him as well for his hot temper. When he'd smoked his cigarette down to the butt, Stepan spoke up:

"If I were a sniper, I'd pick a spot right over there…" Stepan Ivanovich stretched out his arm to point. But before he'd finished his sentence, an explosive bullet struck him in the wrist!

Obviously, no one is happy when his comrade is wounded. And although I wasn't happy when Stepan Ivanovich was shot, suddenly my bad mood, and my feelings of bitterness towards Captain Piterskiy, evaporated. Now there was no longer any need for distractions or idle conversation to keep my mind off the ordeal with Piterskiy. Fate had thrown me into a contest with a sharp-eyed enemy sniper, and I could not allow myself to be distracted by my own minor concerns.

To begin, I set up a couple decoy positions to draw my enemy out. Hopefully by this method I could gain a better view of him.

"You've got to provide me with a helper," I told Shetilov, after we'd taken Stepan Ivanovich to see the medic.

"Vasya, as you know," said Shetilov, "we're short men here."

"I only need one guy," I protested. "I need to set up two or three firing posts. There's too much digging, I can't manage it all by myself."

Shetilov hummed a tune to himself as he pondered whether or not to grant this request.

"Alright," he said. Shetilov had decided in my favor. "I'll send someone up soon. Be patient, Vasya."

I returned to my position. While I waited for the helper, I had to keep working.

I estimated the height from which the opposing sniper must have shot, and then scratched a mark in the wall of the trench. Then I began digging armrests into the wall of the trench.

After an hour, I had succeeded in building three potential sniper positions. This was merely to be cautious. If I was going to get into an all-out duel, I wanted to have several possible back-up positions ready and waiting.

As bait, I left a helmet atop the embankment at the third position. It was a crude tactic, but for the moment it would have to do. If the helmet didn't draw my opponent's fire, I would make a dummy later.

I had scarcely backed away from the helmet when there was a tremendous clang, and the helmet was knocked to the bottom of the trench! By the shape of the dent, I was pretty sure that my opposing sniper had shot from the same position he had used to fire on Stepan Ivanovich. "Got you!" I thought, "If you're so anxious, I'll just have to pacify you before the day's out..."

I went back to surveilling the enemy positions with the artillery periscope. At midday I spotted an armored shield. It was the type of shield our heavy machine gunners had fixed in front of their Maxim guns. The shield was lying upright on the ground, at a distance of six hundred yards, camouflaged behind a bush and some dried grass. Between the branches I could see a black spy hole – the space that had formerly accommodated the Maxim gun's barrel. From time to time the tip of a sniper's rifle muzzle would gleam through the shield's opening.

Sending a bullet through that hole wouldn't accomplish anything. My round would merely ricochet off the sniper's barrel and do nothing more than scare him.

I was stuck. I would have to wait until my opponent stood up, or at least raised his head.

Fortunately on this occasion, I didn't have long to wait. Another German delivered the sniper's lunch. Two helmets surfaced above the shield. But which of these belonged to the sniper? Just then something flashed in the sunlight – a cup from a thermos. Aha, I said to myself, they've brought the sniper hot coffee. Now who's going to take a drink? Not the fellow who had just made the delivery. The coffee had to be intended for the thirsty sniper.

One of the two threw back his head. He was drinking down the last drop.

Ever so gently, I squeezed my rifle's trigger. The sniper's head lurched backward. A shiny little cup dropped in front of the shield.

I moved to one of the nearby vantage points, in case my shot had given away my position. But this time I didn't have to worry. At this long distance, with all the other noise on the battlefield, no one in the German trenches had been able to pick out the report of my single rifle. And as it was early afternoon, there was too much light for anyone to have spotted my muzzle flash.

A few minutes passed. A Russian soldier approached. The soldier was about forty years old, with broad shoulders, thick beetle brows, and a fixed grim expression. His head bounced on his neck like a turtle's. He managed to creep up next to me.

"Tyurin!" I thought to myself, "what a surprise!" This turtle-necked fellow was a neighbor from my village.

I was very glad to see someone from home. However, for a prank, I decided to remain silent, as I wanted to wait and see if Tyurin would recognize me.

He introduced himself: "They call me Pyotr - Pyotr Ivanovich Tyurin."

"Greetings, Pyotr Ivanovich," I replied. "What can I do for you?"

"The company commander sent me over here," he said. He was shifting his weight from one foot to the other and glancing uncomfortably around himself, as if he expected to take a Kraut bullet at any second.

"The commander said to come out here and find my country-man from the Urals. I guess the commander must have meant you."

"So then," I said, "you're going to be my helper."

He immediately became insulted.

"Who the hell are you to be ordering me around?"

"Your *tovarich* from the Urals, that's who," I answered, barely able to keep from laughing.

Pyotr Tyurin, nicknamed *Poryadchikov*,[48] still hadn't recognized me!

"Tell me plainly what you want from me," he said.

Tyurin was irritated and appeared to be ready to march away.

On the hillside, to our right, lay an abandoned trench. I nodded towards it.

"Is there any way that trench can accommodate a sniper's position?"

"Swamps can accommodate horses," Tyurin replied, getting more testy by the second. He thought I was playing games with him. "But the horses lose their hooves. We've lost three machine gun crews in that trench. Our company has named it the "trench of blood." The enemy's got it zeroed in. See for yourself, if you're fool enough. But go out there and you're a dead man."

I couldn't believe Tyurin hadn't recognized me yet, and I had to suppress a laugh. My *tovarich* from the Urals was offended that I saw something humorous his description of the "trench of blood." He narrowed his eyes, furrowed his brow and sunk his head into his shoulders, looking like a turtle as its head recedes into its shell.

"What's so damn funny about it?" Tyurin was so angry he was spraying spittle when he talked. "I'll turn around and leave you by yourself. I've come out here to help you, in this stupid position you've chosen, and all you do is poke fun at me...."

Tyurin clumsily rose to his feet and turned his back to me.

"Oh no," I thought, "he's really going to leave." I remembered how stubborn he was.

"*Poryadchikov*," I blurted out, "wait!"

Tyurin spun around. His beetle brows raised and his eyes

---

[48] *Poryadchikov* : someone who follows the rules, a dependable person

opened wide. He thrust his head forward and stared at me, perplexed. "Vassili, is that you?! Grigoriy Zaitsev's son?"

Machine gun rounds cut short our conversation. Explosive bullets ripped into the embankment above, showering us with sand and debris.

Tyurin was shaking. He closed his eyes and pressed tight against the trench wall, hollering: "We've been targeted, now we won't even be able to poke our heads up!"

"Relax," I assured him, "all we have to do is to set a trap for their gunner."

Tyurin pointed. "He's six hundred yards away. You can't trap anybody at that distance!"

I explained to Tyurin a sniper's methods of hunting his prey. I wanted to calm Tyurin down. I took a stick and drew a diagram on the trench wall, showing him the angles from which I could get the enemy gunners in my sights.

"All we have to do is get one of them," I explained, "that'll scare the rest of them away."

"Vasya," protested Tyurin, " don't you know the Krauts have got their own sniper in this zone?" He spoke in a voice barely above a whisper, as if the Germans might be in the next trench, eavesdropping on us.

"*Poryadchikov*," I said, " don't worry. I already plugged up his ears with lead."

My *tovarich* suddenly livened up. He looked to one side, then the other, and then set about digging furiously with his shovel.

"Wait a minute, Tyurin…"

"Call me Pyotr Ivanovich."

"Fine, Pyotr Ivanovich," I said, "But please, let's wait until it gets dark to do the digging. For now, bring me a periscope, a sheet of plywood and some nails."

"Whatever you say, Vasya. But wait – what are you going to do? What about their sniper?"

"He's dead," I reminded him, "dead and gone." I pointed my fingers to my head like a pistol, and pulled the trigger. "*Kaput*."

It was getting cold. Tyurin rubbed his hands together and blew on them. "Vassili, remember to be careful." He turned and crawled away through the trenches, his head sunk below his shoulders, exactly like a turtle's.

For the next two hours I worked on camouflaging my primary position, just off to the side of our main trench. When I finished, I sensed how tired I'd become and how desperately I needed to sleep. Tyurin came to mind, and I started to feel sorry for him. I shouldn't have sent the old guy for plywood. We could have taken care of the construction later.

I leaned back against the trench wall and quickly fell asleep.

Two hours had gone by when through a haze I heard the voice of Pyotr Ivanovich. He was marching up and down the trench, searching for me. I fell back into sleep. As Tyurin walked he mumbled to himself, getting more and more agitated, until finally, as if we were back in the village, he bellowed, "Vasya!"

This time it jolted me awake. But I kept quiet, to see what he'd do next.

"Vasya, come out! Supper's getting cold!"

I emerged from my position. I had been a few inches away from him and he had not been able to see me.

"What do you think of my blind, Pyotr Ivanovich? Pretty decent job of camouflage, huh?"

He ignored my question. Clearly he was offended about my having remained hidden while he was searching for me.

"Lunch is very good today," he said to me. "Barley kasha with meat gravy."

"I asked you about my camouflage skills, and you talk to me about kasha."

"Vasya, I'm not interested in such things right now. It's time to get some food in you."

We sat down to lunch. We took turns drawing spoonfuls from the pot. I saw that Pyotr Ivanovich was taking only kasha, while crowding the meat and the wonderful thick gravy over towards my side of the bowl.

"Pyotr Ivanovich," I protested, "why don't you take any meat?"

"Vasya, today I'm not feeling well…" He did a poor job of explaining himself. "But to change the subject," he said in a soothing tone, "drink some tea and then get a little shut-eye, alright? An hour, at least. You look all disheveled. Your eyes are red and swollen. While you take a rest, I'll get the nails and plywood you need."

The meal made me feel content. A blissful tranquility came over my body. My back was resting against a heap of cool sand on the bottom of the trench, and I fell asleep immediately. I woke up sometime later that night and couldn't believe what I found. Pyotr Ivanovich had wrapped me up in his own greatcoat, put a knapsack under my head, and bundled my feet in a sweater. It occurred to me that you probably couldn't have found a softer, warmer bed in all of Stalingrad.

Tyurin was a few feet away, digging furiously, heaving shovelfulls of dirt over his shoulder.

"Pyotr Ivanovich," I said to him, "you'll freeze without your coat! Why did you…"

"Vasya," he told me, "don't worry, I'm not cold. My work is keeping me warm." It turned out that while I had been sleeping, Pyotr Ivanovich had cleared out a new path from our trench.

As dawn broke the Nazis decided to greet us with an air strike. On this occasion, their aircraft only dropped light explosives, but at least three dozen must have fallen directly into our trench: smoke, dust, and the musty smell of explosives permeated everything. The black clouds of this attack hadn't settled, when the first heavy-caliber artillery began slamming into our trench's embankments. We managed to get out by Tyurin's newly cleared path, seconds before two beams came crashing down from overhead. The blasts of the heavy shells made our bunker rock like a cradle.

"*Mandavoshka!*"[49] Tyurin shouted, then: "*Styervo!*"[50]

[49] *Mandavoshka*: crab louse
[50] *Styervo*: swine

"Pyotr Ivanovich," I asked, surprised to hear my friend using such language, "who are you cursing over there?"

"You know well who...we'll have to *dat'pizdy.*"[51] He was cut off in mid-sentence by an explosion just outside the bunker. It was either a bomb or a mortar shell, which I couldn't tell, but it caused our bunker's entrance to cave in. Only a tiny shaft of light peeked through the debris. Tyurin and I had been knocked to the ground and buried under the dirt.

I ran my fingers over my body. I didn't feel any broken bones and was able to raise my head, but the dirt had clogged my nose and covered my hair. I could hear Tyurin by my side, reciting every curse he ever knew, so I figured he must be OK.

"Well, Pyotr Ivanovich," I said, "get up. Let's start digging our way out of here."

There was no response. I moved around in front of him - he had been deafened by the blast, but when I motioned with my hands, he understood my gestures.

After the shelling the Nazis began an infantry assault. This was what we expected. Their habit was to move up their ground forces after they had "softened us up" with their artillery. We could hear their charge, but exactly where they were rushing, we couldn't see. We were still buried in the "trench of blood." The two of us worked furiously, but we were careful to be quiet, because I could hear the tread of stampeding soldiers up above. We had no clue as to whether the heavy boots pacing above were the enemy's, or our guys.

Tyurin raked away sand with his big, paw-like hands. He scraped and scraped until his fingers were bleeding, as if it were hot coals and not sand that he was digging. Finally he broke through to the surface.

Now we had a narrow space through which we could have a look at what was happening in front of our trench. It was about six inches high and a foot wide – big enough to see out of, but not yet big enough to squeeze through.

[51] *Dat'pizdy*: to kick ass, kick someone's ass

My eyes fell on the broad back of a Kraut in SS uniform. I could have practically reached out and tapped him on the shoulder. At first I thought he was an officer, but then I saw that he was a private first-class. He had a Schmeisser machine pistol. His shoulders shook as he squeezed off a few rounds. When he turned a bit I saw that he was standing next to an MG34,[52] set up on its own stand. The Krauts had to have just moved it up, setting it up literally on top of us! Where the MG34 crew had gone off to, who knows?

I grabbed my Tommy-gun, poked it through the opening, and squeezed the trigger, but nothing happened. The breech of my Tommy was jammed with sand. I was so furious I could have torn the gun apart with my bare hands. Meanwhile the German private's shoulders shook again as he blasted away at our troops. Tyurin was poking me and trying to see what was going on, but there was only room for one of us, so I elbowed Tyurin aside. Then I pulled the pin from a grenade and deposited it by the private's toes. I ducked back into our hole a fraction of a second before shards of hot metal sprayed over our heads.

Tyurin pressed his shoulder to a support beam, but he couldn't muster enough force to shake it lose, so he reversed his position and used both feet to push open a way out for us.

I bent over the slain private and grabbed his machine pistol. There was another dead Kraut submachine gunner lying nearby. I must have gotten both of them with the same grenade. So now I had firepower, but where to shoot? The air was a thick haze of dust and smoke. By the sounds of battle, I could tell the fighting had penetrated deep into our lines. I would have to attack the enemy from behind!

I tinkered with the Schmeisser in my hands but couldn't figure out how to fire it; I had never used this German weapon before. Then I heard a blast of rapid Schmeisser fire from behind me. My heart skipped a beat. I turned around, expecting to get drilled, when I saw Tyurin firing away with the other dead Nazi's

[52] MG34: a German heavy machine gun.

weapon. Tyurin may not have been the cleverest fellow, but he had more experience with the German sub-machineguns than I did.

Then I spotted a German "Pioneer" captain about fifty feet away. His back was to me. He was holding up a pistol and gesturing to his men, who were obscured by the haze of dust and smoke.

I tossed aside the Schmeisser, picked up my rifle, and shot. The captain sank into the dirt. Then I searched for another target, but with all the smoke, I couldn't distinguish anything.

Tyurin meanwhile, had exhausted the clip in his Schmeisser. He dropped it, crawled over to the MG34, and turned it to the right and left. He tested his footing, took aim, pulled back the release, and squeezed the trigger. It was a very well-designed weapon. It kicked in like clockwork.

The advancing Nazis ended up trapped between two fronts. They rushed about in confusion, scattering everywhere. Now the "trench of blood" was sowing death in *their* ranks.

Tyurin kept firing. Every now and then he'd adjust his grip and bellow, "Aha, you *svolochi*![53] Caught 'ya now!"

The enemy mortar crews finally figured out that we had taken the MG34 and were using it against their men. They showered us with a savage volley. I was knocked temporarily deaf, and seemed to be swallowed up by the earth....

I don't know how much time passed, but when I opened my eyes, I saw Tyurin and a couple of Tommy-gunners from Shetilov's company. Someone said that we had beaten back the enemy's attack and had re-established our positions.

There was a buzzing inside my head and a lot of talking going on around me. Colored circles were swimming before my eyes. The trench was spinning and the recently bombed earth was radiating warmth like an oven.

Tyurin was unfastening the buttons on the top of my shirt so I could breathe.

His hands were trembling and his left eye was watering. To top

[53] *Svolochi*: bastards.

off everything, the soles of his shoes had somehow been torn off, although it was only now that he noticed it. Someone jokingly remarked,

"Say, uncle, it's a good thing you're head's still screwed on tight!"

Tyurin later relieved a dead Nazi of a pair of round-toed German boots. They were of excellent manufacture and fit Tyurin perfectly.

That night we converted the "trench of blood" into an acceptable living space. We plugged up the embrasures with sandbags and hung a tarp over the doorway to keep in the warm air. We made the inside into a soldier's delight; the outside, however, we left just as we'd found it. Let the enemy think it was still abandoned – it was well known that two bombs never fell in the same crater!

Breakfast was delivered early the next morning by Atai Khabibulin, a modest and hard-working man. His job was to deliver food to the front lines. Khabibulin was a square shouldered man in his fifties, with a wispy gray goatee and narrow Asiatic eyes. After setting down a thermos of stew in front of me, he gave me a cheerful embrace and then slapped me on the back a couple times, saying "OK, comrade now we eat big, big – and then tea…."

At that moment, Tyurin awoke, jerking up as if he had been scalded with boiling water. His expression was angry. Tyurin was jealous that someone else was taking over his position. He looked ready to pounce on Khabibulin, so I made quick to introduce my old acquaintance.

"This is my old friend from the front lines," I began, "Khabibulin."

"From the front lines, eh?" Tyurin mimicked, "..a hamster..*nachprovodskiy homyak, frontovoj!*[54] A hamster from the front!"

"What you say 'hamster'? Not true!" retorted Khabibulin, taking

---

[54] "...*nachprovodskiy homyak, frontovoj!*" literally, "an eagle on the go wears out his feet." It's spoken of someone who's very busy or energetic

offense.

Then he began telling Tyurin the story, already familiar to me, of how he'd come to fight in the war. Russian was his second language and his speech was sometimes halting.

A Bashkir[55] from the village of Chishma, Khabibulin had ended up in the army purely by accident. He was seeing his son, Sakaika, off to the front. They had arrived at the train station on the back of Khabibulin's chestnut horse. Off to the side of the station stood a string of horse carts; the horses stood unharnessed, tied to the carts, lazily chewing their hay.

"My chestnut – she run all night. Road very, very much long. She tired…" Khabibulin explained.

Khabibulin tied up his chestnut with the rest of the horses – they were part of an army wagon train - so it could munch on hay while he went off to search for his son. He walked up and down the echelon, poking his head in the door of every railway car, - or, "green box" as he called them – yelling to his son. But Sakaika didn't respond.

When Khabibulin returned to the spot where he'd left his horse, his chestnut was gone. The horses and carts had been loaded onto the train.

"A soldier steal my chestnut!" Khabibulin exclaimed.

The trail left by the familiar three-cornered markings of his chestnut's horseshoes led him immediately to one of the "green boxes." He wasn't allowed into the car, so he started calling his horse by puckering his lips and whistling through his palms. His chestnut heard its master and stamped its hooves in response, but the train had already begun to slowly creep forward. Khabibulin managed to leap onto the running board. He had been with the army ever since, his chestnut by his side, working as a horse-keeper for the supplies platoon.

Just before entering battle at Stalingrad, Khabibulin located his son, Sakaika. The father and son decided to fight alongside

[55] Bashkiria is an autonomous republic within Russia. It is located east of Moscow, between 50 and 60 degrees longitude, 50 and 60 degrees latitude. Its capital is the city of Ufa. Bashkiria borders Kazakhstan.

one another in the same regiment, and their chestnut was officially awarded an allotment of the regiment's fodder rations.

"Baba Fyedya is good person," Khabibulin said. 'Baba Fyedya' was the name Khabibulin gave to the supply platoon commander, Master Sergeant Fyodor Babkin. Babkin had set aside one additional horse and a two-horse wagon for Khabibulin.

Their regiment entered into fighting at Stalingrad, and in those first days they took extremely heavy losses. Khabibulin found his son lying bleeding among the wounded. He carted Sakaika off in his wagon to the army hospital, then left the horses and wagon behind in the rear of the division. He then returned to the battle to fight in place of his son. I remembered that day – I had seen Khabibulin with tears in his eyes.

"My Sakaika hurt very bad. Bomb kill my horse. I carry bullets for soldiers, but you call me names…" Khabibulin grew silent.

Tyurin softened. "Forgive me," he said.

From that moment on, the two men seemed to understand each other better, although on occasion Tyurin was still ready to pounce on Khabibulin for one reason or another. Khabibulin began to visit our bunker more and more often. He would bring meals as well as crates of bullets and grenades. He was like a pack-horse, never going anywhere without something on his back. If he brought bullets in one direction, he'd carry a wounded soldier on the way back. He couldn't speak the best Russian, but he knew what our soldiers in the trenches needed most.

Abzalov, the "midget" sniper, was also a Bashkir, and he and Khabibulin would speak to each other in their native language. Khabibulin called Abzalov "my Sakai." In return, Abzalov paid Khabibulin special attention, and addressed him as "ata," meaning "father."

During the course of the battle, Khabibulin was awarded the medal "For Honorable Service." I think he was more thrilled by this recognition, than I had been when I received my "Order of the Red Flag." After two months of battle, Khabibulin was an experienced and brave soldier.

~~~

One day Khabibulin made a single mistake that would cost him dearly. We had just taken a shelling and one of the hits had been near enough to leave me shaking like a man who was palsied. For a few hours I couldn't even close my hands to grip my rifle. Then we heard the chatter of a German machine gun and Khabibulin stumbled into our bunker, his lips blue. He was unsteady on his feet, and he collapsed face forward. It was then that we noticed the two dark spots on his back and blood coming from one arm.

Tyurin tore off Khabibulin's greatcoat and shirt and, applied coagulant to Khabibulin's wounds, bandaging up Khabibulin's shattered elbow. Khabibulin, for his part, didn't groan or even make a sound. I put a flask to his lips, but Khabibulin only smiled and shook his head from side to side.

"Your drink me no take."

"Please," I said, "at least take a sip. You'll feel better."

"Just a drop at least," Tyurin urged. "After all, you delivered it to us with your own hands."

"Fine for you, Ural-man, but for me to swallow fire water is bad. Sinful."

It was only then did we discovered that he didn't drink, and that he couldn't stand alcohol.

"The pain will give him an awful rough time if he doesn't take a drink," said Tyurin. "He needs to get to a hospital."

Then Khabibulin groaned. "Me no go. My Sakaika die there."

This was the first any of us had heard that his son had died of his wounds. We all knew that Sakaika had been wounded and hospitalized, but Khabibulin had kept his son's death to himself.

I wanted to take revenge on the machine gunner who had shot Khabibulin. Abzalov sensed what I was thinking without me having to say a word.

Abzalov gathered up his equipment and crawled out of the bunker. Within a few minutes we heard the loud crack of his weapon, and the enemy machine gun was abruptly silenced. Abzalov clambered back, his face flushed. He looked at me and nodded his head. Yes, revenge had been exacted.

After sunset it was safer to evacuate Khabibulin. Tyurin managed to get Khabibulin on his feet. The two of them, their arms around each other's shoulders, made their way to the entrance of our bunker. On their way they ran into the division's political bureau chief, Vassili Zakharovich Tkachenko, who had come in with a group of my snipers. These snipers and our bureau chief were not in the habit of making way to let either of the "porters" pass.

"Move aside," said Tyurin to the snipers, "How about some respect here? The Urals and Bashkiria are coming through – Tyurin and Khabibulin!"

CHAPTER 18.
DUEL

That night our scouts captured a German soldier and dragged him back with a potato sack over his head. During his interrogation he admitted that the Wehrmacht command was seriously concerned about the damage being inflicted by our snipers, and that a Major Konings, the head of the Wehrmacht's sniper school near Berlin, had been flown in for the express purpose of taking out, as the captive put it, the Russian's "main rabbit."[56]

Our division commander, Colonel Batyuk was in a cheerful mood.

"For our boys, a major is child's play," he joked. "They should have flown in the Fuhrer himself. Hunting that bird would have been a lot more interesting, eh Zaitsev?"

"That's right, Comrade Colonel," I replied.

But in truth I was apprehensive. I was worn down, tired to the bone, and fatigue is the sniper's worst enemy. The sniper who is fatigued becomes hasty and loses his accuracy. Or when a shot comes up, he vacillates. His confidence in himself has been eroded.

---

[56] "Main rabbit/hare," or "head rabbit/hare" is a literal translation. Zaitsev may mean to imply that the Nazis knew his name (which means rabbit) and were punning on it, or if the captive's use of "head rabbit" was just like you or I might say "head honcho" or "big cheese."

Also, I was calculating my odds, and the probability of my continued survival. Every day, on average, I was killing 4 or 5 Germans. This had gone on since my arrival in Stalingrad. And every day I watched my fellow Russian soldiers being killed or wounded. As day after day passed without my being hit, I kept thinking this was like having a run of luck at cards. I knew it couldn't last forever.

When I had first arrived in Stalingrad, the average life expectancy for one of our soldiers on the Stalingrad front was 24 hours. Since then our army had greatly improved on this figure. This was in part due to the success of our snipers, and I was proud of this. But the press I was getting had attracted the enemy's attention, and now a German major had been assigned to wipe me off the map. When I spoke to Colonel Batyuk I had agreed that the German major would be easy meat for me. But even as I spoke those words I was thinking that Major Konings must be one crafty fox. The Germans were no pushovers, and what was more, to be the director of their sniper school, Herr Konings had to have competed successfully against the best marksman in the Wehrmacht. I was turning these things over in my mind when I heard the division commander say:

"So now you've got to eliminate this super-sniper. But be careful and use your head."

~~~

I had already learned how to quickly read the trademarks of different Nazi snipers, by the characteristics of their shooting, as well as by their camouflage techniques. I was able to pick out the more experienced shooters from the beginners; and the cowards from the patient and determined. But for a long time the characteristics of this new super-sniper remained difficult for me to identify. Our daily observations provided us nothing useful, and we could not pinpoint what sector he was in. He must have been changing his position frequently, and searching me out as carefully as I was searching for him.

I tried to analyze my own experiences and those of my comrades, to come up with a prudent plan of action. If I couldn't enlist the help of soldiers from fellow units – ordinary riflemen, machine gunners, field engineers and signalmen – my chances for success were slim. I had to develop sources of information from Soviet units in different parts of the city.

Typically, after I had located an enemy sniper and ascertained his precise location, I would call over, for example, one of our machine gunners. I would give him an artillery periscope, and then would direct his view to the most noticeable landmark I could find. From there, I would guide the machine gunner's periscope along from one reference point to another. And then, when he had spotted the Nazi sniper, when he'd witnessed how craftily the sniper was camouflaged, this machine gunner would become my learned assistant.

A demonstration like that took an hour, sometimes two. Some of our snipers reproached me: "Soldiers have no need for a show like that. If you need an assistant, the company commander can get you one. All he has to do is say the word, and then there's not a soldier who won't run to you."

That was all true. But I preferred to speak to the ordinary soldier in the trenches – to his awareness of the events around him. When we came to understand each other, then a harmony of the minds resulted, and I would obtain the results I was looking for.

Furthermore, in the process of setting up decoy positions and positioning dummies, I got a chance to watch my fellow snipers. Some were brave and energetic, but made for lousy assistants. They were too hot under the collar. Their energy came and it went.

In a protracted battle against another sniper, you could never depend on a soldier like this for help. After the very first brush with danger, he would be likely to make up an excuse to leave you. He would suddenly remember more important business somewhere else. In reality though, this person had simply expended his reserve of courage. You frequently see characteristics like these among beginning snipers.

Analyzing your own fellow soldiers was one thing, but deciphering the characteristics of the enemy's snipers was much more difficult. For me, only one thing stood out about them – they were all very persistent. However, I had found a way to deal with this. First you prepare a good dummy and discretely put it into position. Then you move it from time to time. A dummy, if it's to look like a person, must change its poses now and then. Next to the dummy, you set up your actual position, making sure it is superbly camouflaged. The enemy sniper shoots at the dummy, but it remains "alive;" and that's where the Nazi's persistence begins to work against him. He'll shoot a second time, and try for a third, but by that time, you've got him in your sights.

Experienced Nazi snipers moved out to their positions under cover of machine gun fire, in the company of two or three assistants. Thereafter, they worked alone. When facing such a lone wolf, I would usually pretend to be a beginner, or even an ordinary infantryman. I would dull my opponent's vigilance, or simply play around with him a bit. I would set up a decoy to draw his fire. The Nazi would soon become accustomed to such a target and would stop noticing it. And as soon as something else distracted him, I would instantly take up the position of my decoy. For this I needed only a couple of seconds. I'd kick aside the decoy and catch the sniper's head in my crosshairs.

I divided the process of locating an enemy sniper into two stages. The first stage began with studying the enemy's defenses. Next I would find out where, when and under what circumstances our soldiers had been killed or wounded. Our medics helped me a great deal with this, by telling me where the victim had been picked up. I would go there and locate witnesses, and find out from them all the details of the incident. With this information in hand, I would then put together a diagram showing the enemy sniper's probable location. All of this activity I lumped together as the first stage – the determination of where to search for my target.

The second stage is what I called the actual search. In order to avoid being trapped in my enemy's sights, I always did my scouting and surveillance with a trench periscope. Neither the sight on my sniper's rifle nor a pair of binoculars was as well suited for this work. Experience also told me, that locations which had once been bristling with activity, but which later became dead silent, probably hid a cunning sniper. This is why I told my fellow snipers: if you haven't studied your surroundings, if you haven't spoken with your men on the ground in the area, then don't go asking for trouble. For a sniper, that old saying, "measure seven times, cut once," is very apt advice. Only through hard work, a little inventiveness, careful study of your enemy's characteristics and strengths, and a feeling out of his weak points, can a sniper truly become ready to eliminate his enemy with a single shot.

You can only find what you are looking for by practicing surveillance techniques on the battlefield. Acquiring the right techniques is not that simple. Every time a sniper heads out to his position he must keep himself 100% camouflaged at all times. And a sniper who doesn't know how to carry out surveillance while camouflaged, is no sniper at all. He's nothing but a sitting duck, waiting for the enemy to pluck him.

When you go out to the front lines, conceal yourself from view completely. Lie there like a stone and merely observe. Study the area, and put together a little map of the prominent landmarks. Remember: if you make a careless movement and give yourself away, if you show yourself for just one instant too long, you're the one who will pay, and with a bullet to the head. Such is the life of a sniper. Therefore, when training my snipers, the skills I emphasized most were keeping a low profile and camouflaging their positions.

Each sniper has his own tactics and techniques, his own ideas and powers of ingenuity. But every sniper – whether beginner or experienced – must always remember that across from him lies a mature, enterprising, sharp-witted and accurate shooter. You must outsmart him, draw him into an intricate battle, and, in this way, tether him to a single spot. How do you accomplish this?

You must create distractions, scatter his attention, change your tracks, exasperate him with diversionary movements, and exhaust his ability to concentrate.

My opinion is that setting up a base sniper camp – even during a long defensive operation like Stalingrad – is a bad idea. A sniper is a nomad, and his job is to pop up where his enemy least expects him. He has to be able to battle to gain the upper hand over his opponent. Simply having the clues to the puzzle of your enemy will get you nowhere, if you don't also have the confidence to finish off your opponent with one quick and decisive shot.

Once, near the Icehouse in a sector defended by the 6th Company, snipers Nikolai Kulikov and Galifan Abzalov more or less disappeared for an entire day. They were sitting in a trench next to a railroad track. They spent the day observing all the enemy activity around them, but they never fired a shot, nor did they do anything else to give away their position. After sunset, when the night was at its blackest, they tied some tin cans to a cord and carried them out into no-man's land. They kept one end of the cord in the trench with them.

At sunrise, they tugged on the cord and rattled the cans right under the Germans' noses. The Nazis began looking around; one head poked up, then a second, and Kulikov and Abzalov picked them both off. After a half hour they repeated the trick and killed another couple of soldiers. In this way, Kulikov and Abzalov did away with an entire squad of Nazis by nightfall.

During another period of relative calm I ran into two other snipers, Afinogenov and Scherbina, on the front lines. They were casually ambling my way. Afinogenov had taken off his helmet. His red hair stood out against the leaden colors of the trenches.

We greeted each other, stepped off the path, sat down on some rocks, and lit up cigarettes.

I asked them where they were headed, and they told me they were going back to the company. "The Nazis have gone under-ground," said Scherbina. He had his usual idiotic grin pasted on his face. "They're nowhere to be found," he continued, "so we're

"...going to take a break."

I was irritated by this.

"You're foolish to leave now," I told them. "This is precisely the time to fire some test shots and correct your aim."

The two agreed to follow me, and I led them back out to the district of our shooting range. En route, I discovered that neither Afinogenov nor Scherbina had done any test shooting for potential targets. They considered this unnecessary. They had simply walked amid the rubble, up and down the entire front line, and opened fire on any enemy soldier they saw. They missed fairly often; but how could they expect any different outcome? You can't immediately determine the distance to your target, you've haven't collected any information beforehand that could help you, and the target only shows itself for a couple of seconds at most – so no wonder you can't hit your target! You have to prepare a couple of positions ahead of time, study the area in front of you, select several landmarks and make an exact determination of their distance from you. Then even during slow periods, you'll have success.

We came to a factory's housing quarters and entered one of the bombed-out buildings that I was using for a rendezvous. I showed my comrades the location of enemy pillboxes, machine gun nests, observation posts and networks of defense. I said, "As you can see, if a sniper has kept good notes, he doesn't have to remember that much about his enemy's defenses. When he gets into position, he simply flips to the appropriate diagram in his notebook, checks for any changes in his surroundings, then waits for the right moment. If you're a well-prepared sniper, the target only has to show himself for a fraction of a second. That's when you must catch him in your sights, take aim, and fire."

It was around one in the afternoon. "The Germans will be eating lunch now," I said to my comrades. "They're extremely punctual."

I pulled a piece of plywood from the wall of the little trench. A shooting diagram had been drawn on it. A few figures had been worn off over time. I took out a pencil stub and retraced the fading numbers. I took into account the distance and wind, got ready to shoot, and began waiting. My comrades watched the enemy's movements through periscopes. We all sat quietly and followed the enemy's activities for an hour. My young comrades' excitement and interest in the hunt began to waver; they were bored doing the same thing for so long. They must have felt like moving to a new position so they could hang out with their buddies, and they started whispering back and forth.

"Button up!" I scolded them. "No talking during an ambush."

My friends fell silent. A few more minutes passed and then a head appeared in the German trench. I shot immediately. The Nazi's helmet flew out on to the embankment. Everything fell quiet again. The helmet lay on the very top of the embankment. From within the trench a shovel began popping up every few seconds; the remaining Nazi left in the trench was digging himself in deeper.

~~~

As a sniper, I've killed more than a few Nazis. On some occasions, I had even run across old acquaintances while looking through my scope. I have a passion for observing enemy behavior. You watch a Nazi officer come out of a bunker, acting all high and mighty, ordering his soldiers every which way, and putting on an air of authority. His henchmen would follow his will, his wishes and his caprices, to the letter. The officer hasn't got the slightest idea that he only has seconds to live.

I would see his fine lips, his even teeth, his wide, prominent chin and fleshy nose. I sometimes got the feeling I had caught a snake by the head; it wriggled, but my hand squeezed more tightly – my shot rang out. Before I removed my finger from the trigger, the snake would be thrashing in its death throes.

~~~

The snipers in our division established a ritual of meeting every evening in a single dugout, talking over the day's results, offering our suggestions, and announcing any observed changes in the enemy's tactics.

Once we did several calculations; a sniper needed only ten seconds to aim and fire accurately. Therefore in one minute, a sniper had the possibility of getting off at least five good shots. It took twenty to thirty seconds to reload. As you can calculate, in the span of a minute, ten snipers were capable of killing up to fifty enemy soldiers.

One of our number, a newcomer to Stalingrad named Sasha Kolentiev, was the most talented sniper among us. We treated him with the utmost respect, as we knew he was a graduate of the Moscow Sniper School and that he had a deep understanding of the rules of shooting with a sniper's rifle and scope. Once he opened up his knapsack, tossed out bullets, a grenade, and a dirty rag, and pulled forth a tiny folder in a leather cover. He opened up the folder and read aloud a passage, which I immediately copied down into my notebook:

"The way to the well-aimed shot is a narrow path that beetles along the precipitous edge of a bottomless pit. Every time he enters into a duel, a sniper feels as if he is standing with one leg on top of a sharp rock. In order to hold out and not fall into the abyss below, there are several things, which are absolutely essential: courage, training, and unshakeable poise. The victor of a duel will be the one who is first able to conquer himself."

And so, going back over and making sense of our experiences, my comrades and I sought the path to a decisive battle with the Berlin super-sniper, who so far had outsmarted us. But his talent began taking its toll on us. In a single day he shattered the scope of Morozov's rifle and wounded Shaikin. Both Morozov and Shaikin were experienced snipers who had come out on top in numerous complex and arduous duels; the fact that they had been outsmarted convinced me their opponent could only have been Konings, the professor from Berlin.

At dawn I took Nikolai Kulikov and went out to the same positions where Morozov and Shaikin had been stationed the day before. Before us lay the same, old, long-studied front line of the enemy. We noticed nothing new. The day drew to a close. All of the sudden a helmet rose into view and moved slowly along the trench. Shoot? No. It was a trap; the bobbing of the helmet was clearly unnatural. It was being carried along by the sniper's assistant, while the sniper himself waited for me to fire and betray myself. So Kulikov and I sat still until nightfall.

"Where can that blasted cur be hiding?" asked Kulikov, as we left our position under the cover of darkness.

"That's the rub," I said. "We don't have a clue."

"And what if he's not here?" asked Kulikov. "Maybe he left a long time ago."

Something told me that a sniper as skillful and as patient as Konings could have sat opposite us for an entire week, if he had to, without moving a muscle. It was necessary for us to be especially vigilant.

A second day passed. Whose nerve would break first? Who would outsmart whom?

Nikolai Kulikov, my trusty friend from the front, had become like me, obsessed with this duel. He no longer doubted that our target lay in front of us, and now he also had his heart set on winning this face-off.

That evening, in our bunker, a letter was waiting for me. It had been sent from Vladivostok. My fellow sailors had written me: "We've heard of your heroic exploits on the banks of the Volga. We take great pride in your accomplishments…"

The letter made me feel awkward. I wanted to break our tradition on the front lines and read the letter in private. My buddies had written me about my "heroic exploits," but I knew that for many days had I been chasing uselessly after this same lone sniper with no success. But Kulikov and Medvedev started grumbling, "From the Pacific fleet?! Read it out loud!" So I had no choice.

What resulted was more than a letter. It was as if a Pacific wave had crashed through the room, carrying with it all sorts of fond memories. Viktor Medvedev spoke up afterwards, "We've got to write them back, immediately. Write them, Vasya, and tell them we won't let them down! Tell them we'll uphold the sailor's honor…"

On our third day of surveillance, *politruk* Danilov accompanied Kulikov and me to our position. The morning began as usual: the darkness was dissipating, and with every passing minute, the enemy's emplacements grew more distinct. Fighting started up nearby. Shells hissed through the air, but we stayed glued to our scopes, following the movements directly opposite our position.

"There he is! I can point him out to you…" the *politruk* cried suddenly. And for a half-second Danilov raised himself up over the trench's rim. But that turned out to be enough time for our opponent, and he fired one shot. Luckily, the sniper's bullet only wounded Danilov.

Only a top sniper could have made that shot, could have fired with such quickness and precision. I peered into my scope for hour after hour, but still couldn't locate him. This German was truly a master of the art of camouflage. Over the course of several days I had studied the enemy's front line, and made detailed notes and diagrams. I noticed every new crater and buildup of earth. But I saw nothing suspicious. Our opponent seemed to have vanished from the face of the earth. Nevertheless, by the quickness of the shot, I concluded that the Berlin super-sniper had to be somewhere in front of us.

Kulikov and I continued the surveillance. To the left – a bombed out tank. To the right – a pillbox. Was he in the tank? No. An experienced sniper would never position himself there. In the pillbox? No, he wouldn't hide there, either. The embrasures had been sealed shut.

In between the tank and the pillbox, on a flat clearing just in front of the Nazi line, lay a sheet of iron, next to a small pile of broken bricks. It had been there since we first arrived at this position, and I had been ignoring it. I put myself in the shoes of my enemy: "What would be the ideal sniper's roost? What about digging out a little hole beneath that sheet of iron? I could sneak out to it during the night…" Yes, I realized he was probably right there, under the sheet of iron, lying out in no-man's land.

I decided to check my hunch. I pulled a mitten over a small plank and raised it up. He shot! The Nazi took my bait! Aha – excellent. I carefully lowered the board down into the trench, holding its face in the same direction in which I had raised it. I inspected the hole – it was perfectly flat and round, with a 90-degree angle of entry. The bullet had entered the board head-on.

"There's our serpent…" I hear Nikolai Kulikov whisper.

Now we had to lure him out – if only the tip of his head. It was useless to hope for that immediately. But we could be pretty sure he wasn't going anywhere; knowing his tactics, it was unlikely he would leave such a valuable position.

It was a frigid night. As the sounds of battle subsided and men sought shelter from the cold, the wind howled between the ruined buildings.

The Nazis were firing chaotically. They had got a few mortars close enough to shower our Volga crossings with mortar fire. Our artillery struck back, silencing the German mortars, but the enemy replied with their bombers, Stukas, Me-109s, Heinkels, the whole parade of Luftwaffe might. We kept our heads down and waited for dawn.

When the sun came up, Kulikov fired a blind shot to arouse our opponent's interest. We had decided to stay inactive for the first half of the day. The reflections from our scopes would have given us away.

But after lunch, our guns were completely in the shade, while the direct rays of the sun fell upon our rival's position. Something glimmered beneath the edge of the iron plate – was it a random fragment of glass, or a rifle's scope?

Kulikov took off his helmet and slowly raised it, a feint that only an experienced sniper can pull off credibly. The enemy fired. Kulikov raised himself up, cried out loudly and collapsed.

"At last, the Soviet sniper, their 'main rabbit' that I've hunted these four long days, is dead!" the German probably thought to himself, and he stuck his head up behind the sheet of iron.

I pulled the trigger and the Nazi's head sunk. The scope of his rifle lay unmoving, still flashing in the light of the sun.

The tension of the hunt was broken. Kulikov rolled on his back and broke into hysterical laughter.

"Run!" I yelled to him.

Kulikov snapped to his senses. We took off running as fast as we could to our backup position. Seconds later the Nazis obliterated our stakeout with artillery fire.

As soon as it grew dark, our men attacked the German lines, and at the height of the fighting Kulikov and I dragged the dead German major from beneath the sheet of iron, snatched his rifle and his documents, and delivered them to the division commander, Colonel Batyuk.

"I knew you boys would catch that bird from Berlin," said Colonel Batyuk. "But you, Comrade Zaitsev, have a new task ahead of you. Tomorrow, in a different sector, we're expecting a Nazi assault. General Chuikov has ordered a group of the best snipers to be rounded up and used to foil the fascists' attack. How many remain in your group?"

"Thirteen."

"Bulletproof" Batyuk thought for a moment and then asked, "Well, that makes it thirteen against hundreds. Can you do it?"

"Those are acceptable odds," I replied.

CHAPTER 19
I SERVE THE SOVIET UNION

Bandages covered my eyes and my head was wrapped in a virtual crown of gauze. I couldn't see a thing. It was hard for me to say how many days and nights had passed since I fell into this darkness. A man who can see meets each new day with the breaking of the dawn, and he bids it farewell with the sunset. But with me – it was complete and unending darkness. Just try to count without the help of your daily routine how many days and nights you've been lying in a hospital bed – flying is more like it. Flying into a bottomless abyss…

Thankfully I still had my hearing and sense of smell, which helped me to take in my surroundings and reckon the passing of days, hours, even minutes. This ability does not come immediately, but only after you've had some time to get accustomed to your blindness. It's no wonder the blind develop such an acute sense of hearing that they can measure distance by sound: "seeing ears" they call it. I experienced this myself.

By about my third or fourth week in the hospital, in true sniper fashion, I was able to listen to the echoes, and pinpoint the distance to a dog barking on the edge of the village. I even thought to myself that I could aim and fire just by the line of sound. A funny thought of course, but it showed that during this time I couldn't come to terms with the fact that my blindness might have snatched my rifle from my hands forever.

Various sensations helped me guess who was approaching my bed, be it a doctor or a friend from a neighboring room. The robes of the medical staff gave off the aroma of having been freshly washed, while a soldier's clothing reeked of a poorly ventilated railroad car.

Blackness – the symbol of opposition to knowledge, of oppression and violence; the color of the swastika. They say that Hitler's mustache was actually reddish in color, but it is always depicted as jet black, an alteration that Hitler, the vermin, actually preferred. Blackness on his flags, blackness on his face. The most malicious creatures always rely on the darkness.

This is how I thought about the black mist that had overtaken me. This darkness had robbed me of the greatest contribution I had to offer my country – the ability to see the enemy and destroy him. But I didn't want to acknowledge – and I refused to acknowledge – its power. I could remember everything that happened before my eyes, right up to the moment the shrapnel struck me in the face.

Our commander, Nikolai Filipovich Batyuk, had ordered us to foil the enemy's assault on our regiment's right flank. Our sniper group employed a tactic that took the Nazis by surprise. Since we knew ahead of time what direction the enemy's attack would be coming from, we decided to sight in on the enemy's command and observation posts. We were thirteen rifles, thirteen pairs of eyes, peering through scopes from a multitude of vantage points, high and low. We were able to control the enemy's best reconnaissance points, located deep inside their battle formation.

Ours was a group hunt, and our goal was to behead, if you will, the enemy's companies and battalions, before they began their assault. The plan was simple: when the German officers emerged for their final look at the zone they planned to attack, we would greet each of them with the recommended apportionment of lead.

If some brave soul should try and step forward to assume their place, we would shoot him down, too! If the enemy made an advance somewhere, we would turn all thirteen sniper rifles in that direction, and first cut down the officers. Then whomever you have to teach not to step across that line, go ahead and teach them well, so they would know that only death was waiting for them here.

In short, our "assault of concentrated sniper fire," as we called it, blinded the enemy command points. From the start, we whittled down the chances for their attack.

Our plan was successful in every respect. At dawn, just before their attack commenced, the lenses of high-powered binoculars glittered in the sun atop the Nazi's command posts. Some of the German officers wore "jager" hats, with cockades – we could even make out the colors of the feathers in their hats. These officers were peering in our direction, but they did not realize that against the background of dispersing gloom, they were perfectly profiled. Before the Germans were able to begin their attack I went through two full clips; Nikolai Kulikov also emptied two; Viktor Medvedev, three; and our remaining snipers weren't napping either.

But the German attack began, nevertheless. A fascist officer in a far-off command post that our bullets couldn't reach was driving the enemy soldiers to their doom. Our machine gunners, riflemen, and artillery crews had already zeroed in on all the enemy's paths of advance and retreat, and we were mowing them down. The enemy soldiers were like beasts being led to slaughter. We were pounding them mercilessly.

At this point the Nazis were just waiting for the right moment to throw up their hands. And goaded by some foolish heroic impulse, I tried to capture some prisoners. I guess this impulse came from that same hellish fever of battle that sometimes eclipses clear thinking...

I leaped from my concealment and shot off a yellow flare to signal to our artillery to hold their fire in our sector. Then I ran to the spot where it looked like some German soldiers wanted to give themselves up. I ran up to them, waving my hands, gesturing, "come out with your hands in the air." Several Germans actually got up with their hands raised, and started to leave their positions. At that moment a "donkey" - the Nazi six-barrel mortar – thundered off in the distance. The Kraut command was firing fragmentation shells at their own men! One of the shells was hurtling straight for me; I could see how it turned end over end through the air. Who would have thought that German mortar crews would fire on their own infantry! I didn't want to give the enemy the satisfaction of seeing me drop for cover. The shell landed about thirty meters away from me, bounced once – and boom!

Hot air laced with fiery shrapnel lashed my face, and a thick, swampy darkness immediately enshrouded my eyes. With the blackness came a stinging pain that bore into my corneas, a fire that scorched my scalp; and an unrelenting nausea.

~~~

A week before, after the pains in the back of my head had gone away, my doctors removed the bandages from my eyes. But it was all for nothing. The darkness was as impenetrable as before. What a shame this was! My doctors had the best of intentions.

Meanwhile, the battle had ended with our victory. Thousands, even tens of thousands of captured Germans were dragging themselves along the streets outside the hospital. Here was the result of the battle of Stalingrad! Laughter and tears overtook me. I was crying because I couldn't escape the utter darkness, and laughing at the astonishing array of sounds that reached my ears from both ends of the street, from other rooms in the hospital and from the windows.

"Look, look, on his feet – boots made of straw…"

"What's that one got on his head?! Ha, ha! Riding breeches!"

"Some warriors, eh?…"

But the funniest to me of all the sounds that I heard, was a rooster somewhere outside the hospital walls. He seemed to be sitting on a gate and meeting each new column of enemy prisoners with a slow, drawn-out "koo-koo-re-kooooo!". Then he'd flap his wings as if he were saluting, and finally let out an almost human-sounding laugh. The morning was long over, but he wouldn't quiet down – crowing and laughing, crowing and laughing. You'd never see such a thing, even in a circus!

So I refused to surrender to my blindness. Even a simple barnyard animal had been able to help me see how the battle of Stalingrad had ended.

Another week passed. On the tenth of February, 1943, just before dusk, my doctors decided once again to try removing the bandages from my eyes. A nurse slowly unwound the dressing, coil after coil, until the patches of cotton over each eye fell away. I kept my eyelids closed, afraid that the same thing that happened before would repeat itself..

I raised my arms over my head as the doctor instructed me. I felt heavy drops of perspiration as they rolled down my back. I was sweating from fear; I had become a coward, too timid to face my fate...

"Well, come on now, Vasya. Open your eyes!" the doctor commanded.

I followed his order...and I couldn't believe what happened next. Ahead of me, in front of the window, I could make out the silhouette of a person! My sense of relief was overwhelming; my sight was coming back!

But it had not yet completely returned. In fact, I had a long way to go.

"You're going to need intensive treatment," my doctor told me.

Two days later I was transported to an army medical unit stationed near the Akhtuba River, southeast of Stalingrad. They referred me on to Moscow, to see the army's chief eye specialist. On this same day, I stopped into the headquarters of my division, where I learned that by order of the commander of the 62nd army, V.I. Chuikov, I had been awarded the officer's rank of junior lieutenant.

~~~

...I walked without a guide, but I frequently stumbled over things; I had to lift my legs high as I walked, doing my best to step carefully. When your vision is poor, every path is full of hazards.

I was desperate to get to Moscow quickly, to be treated.

Just before my departure I was invited to the army's political bureau. The bureau's *Komsomol* director, Major Leonid Nikolaev, had learned that I still couldn't see well. He volunteered to be my escort, as far as Saratov.

One of the enemy's captured Mercedes hauled us along the torn up, snow-covered road towards Saratov. The engine wheezed and howled, but the unforgiving Russian road proved too much of a challenge for it. We presented the Mercedes to a collective farm and took a sleigh the rest of the way. Leonid Nikolaev, the 62nd army's unshakable *Komsomol* leader, chased away my gloomy thoughts with his hilarious renditions of the old favorite, "It spins and whirls, the big blue earth."

Leonid threw together a couple of different variants of his own, making up ditties about Hitler, another about Goebbels, etc. He would sing them with ironic sympathy one minute, with biting mockery the next, and then with a side-splitting humor so contagious that it was impossible not to laugh and sing along.

When we reached Saratov, Nikolaev found me a place in the officer's car of a Moscow-bound train. He led me to my seat and then he had to leave me.

Suddenly I felt very alone. Because of my blindness I was isolated. There was no one I knew nearby. I wondered if I was an object of pity to the other occupants of the car.

On the far side of the window, towns, villages, and station houses flitted by. But to my eyes all the details were lost in a dull, gray blur. I could overhear the other passengers – all military men – talking over the significance of the battle at Stalingrad, and expressing their views on the likely path of events to come, but only one thought was gnawing at me: could my eyesight really be gone forever?

In Moscow I was taken to the People's Commissariat

Polyclinic, where for a good while I was led about from room to room. In the end, the chief surgeon pronounced his uplifting verdict: "After you've undergone a bit more treatment, your eyesight will return."

I can't tell you how happy I was to hear this. Day by day my vision was improving – and in a short while, my vision did in fact return to normal.

On the eve of the holiday, Red Army Day, I was discharged from the clinic. I was wearing my same tattered greatcoat, and had my knapsack over my shoulders. I walked into the hotel of the Central Hall of the Red Army. My documents bearing the sweeping signature of General V.I. Chuikov helped me to secure a bed in the officer's dormitory.

The next morning, sitting around the dormitory, we turned on the radio to listen to the latest news. The announcer started reading a decree of the Presidium of the Supreme Soviet, listing recipients of the award of Hero of the Soviet Union. I heard my last name flash by but paid it no mind. I thought to myself: "there's a million Zaitsevs."

Someone in the room joked, "I hope that decree doesn't concern anyone in this room. Otherwise we'd have to empty our pockets buying him drinks!"

My pockets were completely empty, as it was. You could have turned them inside out, but the only thing you would have found in them was my officer's certificate. I couldn't receive any money on that certificate until I completed filling out the financial paperwork for my position. I myself didn't even know what my position was.

I was extremely annoyed, at the clerk, and at the division head of finances. How could they have sent me to Moscow with no money and incomplete documents? As an accountant, it struck me as very unprofessional behavior. I was so fed up that the next day I planned to request a transfer back to my unit.

I wanted to pay a visit to the *Komsomol* bureau of the Central

Political Directorate and meet with Ivan Maksimovich Vidyukov. Major Nikolaev had instructed me to see Vidyukov, before Nikolaev and I had parted company at the railway station.

I arrived at the admissions desk of the Directorate. I was just barely able to squeeze my way through to the clerk on duty and show him my clearance, I asked for a pass to the *Komsomol* bureau.

"Wait over there; you'll be called shortly," the clerk replied.

About twenty minutes passed. A sergeant stuck his head out of the window at the admissions counter. He scanned the room slowly, with a peculiar sort of curiosity. He looked over all the captains, majors and lieutenant colonels standing before him. At last, unable to find the man he was looking for, he called out:

"Is Junior Lieutenant Vassili Grigorievich Zaitsev in the room?"

I didn't hear what he said after that, but the room fell quiet and everyone turned in my direction. At that moment a flushed and excited young woman from the *Komsomol* bureau rushed into the room and shouted, "Vassili Grigorievich! I've just come from Vidyukov's. My name is Nonna…I came to congratulate you!"

I was dumfounded. "What for?" I asked. I didn't like having everyone stare at me, as I was embarrassed by my appearance. I was still wearing my ragged clothes from the front.

"You mean you really haven't heard? Today you were awarded the title of Hero of the Soviet Union! Oh, how wonderful! I get to be the first to congratulate you!" She embraced and kissed me and then whispered into my ear, "Remember, my fortunate one, no bullet will touch you now, no shrapnel will ever wound you again."

Brigade Commissar Ivan Maksimovich Vidyukov, who had been with me during the fighting at Stalingrad, greeted me like a brother.

"Well, hold tight, Vassili! Now you're going to have to withstand attacks of a different kind – first, from the *Komsomol* staff and later from the newspaper reporters!"

~~~

The commissar was right. I probably would have been dragged off to numerous gatherings and conferences if the call from General Schadenko hadn't come in first: Junior Lieutenant Zaitsev was "..to prepare a report of his experiences with group sniper tactics at Stalingrad." Where I would present this report, and to whom, no one could tell me.

When I returned to my room, before I'd had a chance to think over what I'd say or even to open up my notebook, a very smartly dressed young women entered. I wasn't accustomed to seeing such fashion plates.

"Are you Zaitsev?" she asked.

It seemed to me that this "Zaitsev" that everyone was so excited about wasn't me at all.

I replied : "I suppose you've come to invite me to so some sort of dinner party?"

"No," she said, "not quite. You have been invited by Professor Mintz to the Institute for the study of experiences of the Great Patriotic War."[57]

At first I thought, "So this is why General Schadenko called – I'm to deliver my report to Professor Mintz." But what kind of useful report could I possibly present to a professor? And as we approached the Institute together, I asked the young woman, "Are you sure this professor hasn't made a mistake? I mean, I'm nothing but an enlisted man."

"Former enlisted man," she corrected me, and then after a moment she reminded me, "what's more, a hero of Stalingrad…"

We entered the Institute director's office, and I stood at attention and announced in accordance with military protocol: "By your summons, Comrade Professor, Junior Lieutenant Vassili Grigorievich Zaitsev reporting!"

But in the office sat not one man, but two. One was frail, wearing a pince-nez, and the other was stouter, with a dark complexion. How was I supposed to know which one was Professor Mintz? After all, it wasn't written on his forehead.

[57] "Great Patriotic War" - the way Russians refer to WWII.

These two were sitting at an end table, drinking tea, and when they saw me they stood up. I continued standing at attention before them, stock-still and too bewildered to speak. The man in the pince-nez, calling me by my name and patronymic, invited me to the table.

"We're having tea, Moscow style."

A saucer with three cubes of sugar sat next to my teacup. My throat was bone dry, and without waiting for an invitation, I started swallowing gulp after gulp of tea, as I was afraid I wouldn't be able to moisten my throat before they asked me to begin my report. But as soon as I finished one cup, they immediately poured me another. I was beginning to see that these men weren't in a hurry. I drank a second cup, holding a sugar cube in my mouth. Almost as an aside, the conversation began. The tea had eased my tension. I answered their questions and told them about my comrades, without once opening the notebook where I had diligently written down point after point, which were to be discussed during my report.

An hour went by, then two, and I began to wonder why they were taking so long to ask me to give my report. Finally, these two academic types announced that my statements held "scientific value" and that they "warranted further study." I practically gasped with astonishment. What kind of "scientific value" could my ramblings have held? I hadn't given them a single point from my report!

As if understanding my confusion, one of them, Pyotr Nikolaevich Pospelov, the editor of the newspaper *Pravda*, said to me, "This has been very interesting. This won't be the last time you'll have to give these statements, so please, relax…"

~~~

That evening I was told I had been enrolled in *Vystrel*,[58] and granted various other officer's allowances.

---

[58] *Vystrel* means "shot;" here it appears to be a semi-acronym for the phrase "Officer's Advanced Riflery Training" which in Russian is, *"Vyschie Strelkovie Kursi Komandnovo Sostava."*

My financial woes were taken care of the very next day when I received two months of officer's pay. Now I could hit the town in style, as they say – freshen up with a little eau de cologne; take a jaunt to the theater perhaps. But the words of Pospelov continued to hound me: "This won't be the last time you'll have to give these statements…"

And soon enough, I found myself in the General Staff's office. There I met for the first time with renowned snipers Vladimir Pchelintsev, Lyudmila Pavlyuchinko, and Grigoriy Gorelik. General Schadenko admitted us, and straight away we began trading stories of our experiences. We became so engrossed in conversation that we didn't notice night falling; it was nearly three in the morning by the time Lieutenant General Morozov, whom Schadenko called "the Russian army's first sniper," attempted to draw some general conclusions and wrap things up. General Morozov was impressed by my experiences with group sniper operations, but he believed my suggestions needed to be thought through some more. Therefore it was decided to continue the discussion the following day.

It seemed strange to me that General Schadenko, whose time was extremely scarce, would bother to spend another half day with some snipers from the trenches.

The next day as he went over our conclusions, Schadenko said that we had helped him to craft a more precise formulation of section 39, part one, of the infantry field manual, and that our comments had caught the interest of the Supreme Soviet.

"Now go relax for the time being," he said, "only – I wouldn't stray too far away."

In the General Staff dining hall, Ivan Maksimovich Vidyukov came up to me.

"I've got an assignment for you, Vassili," he announced, smiling, "Get down to the supply store this instant; they're going to suit you up in a new uniform. Don't you leave that tailor until they've outfitted you down to the very last stitch!"

The chief army tailor was waiting for me, and within two hours

I could no longer recognize myself. Everything on me was brand spanking new – jacket, pants, box-calf boots and great coat.

"We've got you outfitted like a general!" cried the tailor as he looked me over in front of the mirror. My pants in fact did have general's stripes on them, which we were forced to rip off.

The next morning a magnificent ZIS-101 limousine rolled up to the entrance of our hotel. Pchelintsev, Gorelik and I motored off towards the Kremlin. We passed through the checkpoint at the Savior Gate Tower[59] and in a few minutes found ourselves inside a spacious office. Generals were seated along the walls on both sides of the room, and a long, bare table stood at the center.

We halted at the end of this table, and Kliment Yefremovich Voroshilov[60] approached. He welcomed each of us with a hand-shake, directed us to some nearby armchairs, and took a seat at one end of the table.

"Let's begin, comrades," he said, glancing at General Schadenko. The general nodded at Pchelintsev, as if to say, "You start us off."

The sniper Volodya Pchelintsev, not a timid man, began expressing his ideas, efficiently and eloquently. Voroshilov jotted down notes as he listened, since his comments would be the final revisions to a document to be delivered to Comrade Stalin, containing our statements to the General Staff.

Gorelik rose after Pchelintsev, and then it was my turn to speak. My presentation lasted, it seemed, about three minutes. In reality I spoke for much longer. The fortunate in life never notice the hours, much less the minutes. I was one of the fortunate, for my observations on the role of snipers in warfare would not go unnoticed, and the transcript would be delivered to Comrade Stalin himself. I was proud of the fact that a simple soldier and

---

[59] the Big Ben-looking clock tower at a corner of the Kremlin on Red Square
[60] Voroshilov, Kliment Yefremovich, 1881-1969, Soviet military leader. A Bolshevik from 1903, and an outstanding Red Army commander during the Civil War (1918-20). As commissar for military and naval affairs, and later for defense (1925-40), Voroshilov helped organize the Red Army. In World War II he was the commander of the Northwestern front. Voroshilov was a member of the Supreme Soviet from 1937.

his supreme commander were able to understand one another.

After I finished, Mikhail Ivanovich Kalinin[61] placed the gold star of the Hero of the Soviet Union in my palm.

"Comrade Zaitsev," he said, "I congratulate you!"

"I serve the Soviet Union!" I replied.

One of my comrades helped me fasten the star and the Order of Lenin to my chest. For the next few minutes I was afraid to even breathe. My ears were buzzing from all the excitement. The sound was like an echo of the fighting at Stalingrad, the great battle where we had had to fight to the bitter end, and where for a time we had to forget that beyond the Volga there was still land.

I didn't catch everything word for word that Mikhail Ivanovich said, but I will remember his parting wishes for as long as I live:

"Love your country with the heart of a true patriot, and serve it fearlessly in battle."

---

[61] Kalinin : Old Bolshevik. Elected to the Central Committee in 1912, and co-founder of the newspaper *Pravda*. After the Bolshevik Revolution in 1917, he became mayor of Petrograd. Kalinin was elected to the Politburo in 1919. He was the first chairman of the central executive committee of the USSR, or titular head of state (1919-46). He retained his high government office until he tendered his resignation to the Supreme Soviet on March 19, 1946, shortly before his death.

A   P   P   E   N   D   I   X

Editor's note: This version of Zaitsev's experiences in Stalingrad was published in 1943. It is from an account Zaitsev gave to Red Army reporters in 1942, shortly before he was wounded.
Translated by Elena Leonidovna Yakovleva.
Copyright © Neil Okrent 1996, 1999.

Death to German occupiers
Heroes of the Great Patriotic War
By Hero of the Soviet Union
V. G. Zaitsev

SNIPER'S STORY

Military Publishers
of the People's Commissariat of Defence
1943
Price 10 kopecks

I was born in the Urals, spent my childhood in the forest, therefore I love the woods very much and will never get lost there, even if a forest is unknown to me. In the forest I learnt to shoot well, and hunted hares, squirrels, foxes, wolves and wild goats. My father was a forester. We used to go out hunting with all our family – father, mother, both brothers and our sister with us. Nowadays my mother, although an elderly woman who wears glasses, if she has noticed a black grouse sitting down on a birch-tree, she will go out and be sure to bang it down, and then she will pluck it and cook it.

We have only one younger sister, and my brother and me decided together to make a squirrel fur-coat for her. I was then about twelve, and brother was even smaller. It was my grandfather who taught us to shoot squirrels. This is an art; a squirrel should only be hit with one pellet; if shooting it with a full load, one can beat up the squirrel badly and spoil its fur. We shot about two hundred squirrels and made a fur-coat for our little sister.

When I was over fourteen – it was in 1929 – my parents joined a collective farm, and we moved to the settlement Eleninsky of the Agapovsky district of the Chelyabinsk region. There I went to school in the winter, with the group of over-agers, and in the summer I tended grazing cattle.

I wanted to study very much. While I was tending cattle, I would tether the horse with a long rope and lie in the bushes and read my school books. Another winter came and I went to study at a technical institute. Then I did not choose where to study – if only I could have chosen for myself. I wanted to become a pilot very much, but instead I entered a construction technical school. That is how it happened. There in the technical school I joined the *Komsomol**. I studied and got excellent marks, and received awards for each course.

During my education we built the first and the second blast furnaces in Magnitogorsk. At first I was an assistant, then a technician. While working on the construction, I came to like the

* *Komsomol – Young Communist League*

accountant's profession, and I entered the accountants' training course. Upon finishing that course I was sent to Kizil town, and I worked there, at Raipotrebsoyuz**, as an accountant for three years. The work was to my liking: calm and independent, requiring quickness of wit, precision, and above all, helping me see life deeply.

In 1936 the Presidium of the District Executive Committee of the Town Council appointed me a Senior Insurance Inspector. I remained in that position until I was called to military service.

As one of the *Komsomol*'s recruits I was sent to serve in the Pacific Navy. I arrived in Vladivostok. This is a peculiar town. At first it left a bad impression on me. I thought it was very different from our Ural towns – Sverdlovsk, Chelyabinsk and even Shchadrinsk. But after I lived in Vladivostok for some time, I grew fond of this town. After the war I will certainly apply to be sent to the Far East. I would be happy to serve there all my life. I like that area. Nature is very interesting there, with lots of forests.

In the Far East I finished the Regional Military Economic School with honors, and served in various naval and economic positions in the Pacific Navy 'till Autumn 1942

When the Germans started approaching the Volga River, a group of sailors–all *Komsomol* members such as myself, submitted a petition to the Naval Council to request that we be transferred to defend Stalingrad. That initiative was taken by the Commissar of the base where I served, the old Bolshevik Nayanov. He had worked when he was young in the Volga region, at the bodies of the People's Commissariat of Fishing Industry, and he always remembered the Volga like I remembered the Urals. The petition of our group of *Komsomol* members was received favorably. We quickly got organized and set out to the West. On the 6th of September we arrived at town N. – it is at the Urals, almost at my home. There, on the same day, we were enrolled in the Infantry Division of Major-General Batyuk, and

**Raipotrebsoyuz – District Consumers' Union*

on the next day we got transferred from one troop train to another and went to Stalingrad. So, we bypassed the Urals.

We studied on the road. I remember learning the machine-gun so: putting it on the upper bed, I got a machine-gunner to sit next to me and show it to me.

On the troop train I was offered to be a commander of an economic platoon. I had just came from economic work and was being sent to do economic work again! I thought: people are fighting. I also wanted to fight, really fight, and I asked to join a rifle company.

We arrived in Stalingrad on 21st September. The whole city was on fire. There were air battles from the morning till late at night. Airplanes, one after another, caught on fire and fell. From the Volga River bank we saw tongues of flame rising in different places, and then all of them merging into one enormous ball of fire. We saw wounded soldiers walking and crawling – they were being transferred across the Volga. All this left on us, those who arrived from deep in the rear, an overwhelming impression. We cleaned our weapons, fastened bayonets and waited for an order, as we were 100% ready for action.

On 22nd September we took ammunition with us, crept to the Volga and sailed across to the other bank. We carried mortars and machine-guns with ourselves. We took positions on the left bank of the Volga River.

The Germans were in the town at that time. They noticed us and opened up with heavy mortar fire. There were twelve gasoline tanks in our area. All of a sudden sixty enemy airplanes came flying upon us and started bombing. The gasoline tanks exploded and we were splashed all over with gasoline. We plunged into Volga and put out our burning clothes in the water. Many of us were left with only our sailor striped shirts, and some of us – were naked, but it did not matter – we wrapped ourselves in tarps, took our rifles and went over to the attack. We beat the Germans away from the "Metiz" plant and a meat-processing factory, and we held the line. Some time later the Germans advanced again, but we repelled all their attacks.

After the first battles the Battalion Commander made me his aide-de-camp.

It happened once that in the Dolgy Ravine one of our sub-units wavered and started falling back. The battalion commander gave me an order to detain the retreating men and to straighten the front line. I fulfilled that order: the sub-unit attacked, repulsed the Germans and delayed the German advance. After that battle I was put forward for the medal "For courage".

In October one more important event happened in my life: the *Komsomol* passed me to the ranks of the Communist party.

At that time we were in an awfully hard position. The Germans had encircled us, they pressed our backs against the Volga and hit us with shells and bombs. Several hundred airplanes came flying at us every day. In that situation many of us believed that there was no hope that we would survive, but we did not talk about this. We all felt an intense hatred for the Germans. There are no words to describe what foul rascals they are.

One day we saw several young women and children hanging from nooses in a garden. Another day the Germans were dragging a young woman down the street. A little boy was running after her and crying: "Mama, where are they taking you?" The woman was shouting – it was not far from us: "Brothers, help, rescue me!" But we were preparing an ambush and could not allow ourselves to be spotted. It is really hard to remember that...

Each fighting-man could not think of anything else but of killing as many Germans as possible and of doing them as much harm as possible. We did not feel any fatigue, although often we did not eat from the morning 'till late at night, and would not sleep for several days at a time. And we did not want to sleep. Our nerves were always very strained.

When I was handed the award, I said: "For us there is no land beyond the Volga, our land is here and we will defend it". This is what my comrades *Komsomol* members asked me to pass on to Comrade Stalin.

Once, it was on 5th October, we were together with the battalion commander. Captain Kotov came up to a window. We saw a German darting out in the distance… The Captain said: "Kill him!" I shouldered my rifle, shot and the German fell. The German was 600 yards away from us and I killed him with an ordinary rifle. The comrades got interested. We saw another German running towards the one I had killed. The comrades cried to me: "Zaitsev, Zaitsev, another one is coming, kill this one." I shouldered my rifle again, shot and one more German fell. Everybody looked at me with admiration. I also got interested. I stood by the window and looked – a third German was crawling towards to the two I had just killed. So I shot him too.

On the second day after that the Regiment Commander Lieutenant-Colonel Metelev passed to me, via the Battalion Commander Captain Kotov, a sniper rifle with an telescopic sight and my name engraved on the stock. Rifle #2826. Captain Kotov handed it to me and said: "You will make a good sniper. Learn this yourself and then teach the other men".

So I started learning to shoot with the sniper rifle. One of the *Komsomol* members, Senior Lieutenant Bolshapov, helped me to learn the material part of it. He was my comrade in arms. We fought together, and lived in trenches together.

The sniper Kalentiev also taught me. I went around with Kalentiev for three days, closely observing at his actions, and how he worked with a sniper rifle. Then I went out to set up a stakeout myself. At first, naturally I had inaccurate shots: I hurried and worried, although I am a calm person by nature.

To fight in the streets, where sometimes there are 40 to 50 meters to the enemy, is not the same as fighting in the field at great distances. A lot of advice given to a sniper turned out to be unsuitable. However, the Germans soon learned about me.

I killed four to five Germans every day. Then I started selecting my trainees. At first I selected five or six men.

I taught my trainees at the forge of the "Metiz" factory, where we arranged a shooting gallery. They studied the material part of the rifle in the vent tube of the factory, which served as a very good shelter, where we also cleaned our arms and shared impressions of the day.

Soon afterwards I had about thirty trainees. Most of them were *Komsomol* members. I selected them myself, made friends with them and shared with them anything I had – biscuits or tobacco. When people see that you treat them with an open heart, they develop an affection for you and they remember your every word. They knew that I would not abandon them at a dangerous moment, and I hoped that they would not abandon me either.

I was a member of the *Komsomol* Bureau, therefore I had to visit all sub-units: I normally began with *Komsomol* clerical records and finished with the organization of a sniper group.

When I was convinced that men were competent with their rifles, I took them to a stakeout with me. They got used to shooting and studied the battlefield. The sniper must study every bush, how it stands and how the ground lies around this bush, where and how many stones there are, which trench is targetted by the Germans and which is not. After one has studied the defence in this way, his own and the enemy's, one becomes undefeatable by the enemy.

In the evening I gathered my trainees at one place so that they could share their opinions. When snipers converse with each other after having returned from a stakeout, one hour gives them more benefit than a month in a peaceful situation. Here, for example, what *Komsomol* member Lomako said one evening after a hunt: "I have missed three Fritzes today, shooting from the same distance, and did not hit them a single time."

I got interested in this and on the next day I went together with Lomako to the place from which he had been shooting. It was a factory chimney. We were sitting at the height of ten yards. A Fritz was passing beneath, I shot at him, but he continued walking calmly and did not even quicken his step. I did not shoot at that Fritz again. I lowered down my rifle, sitting and thinking: "If I had shot too high, the Fritz would have bent down; if the bullet had flown ahead of him, he would have stopped." This Fritz, however, walked on without any sign of concern. That means, there is a small distance on the backsight leaf and a bullet does not reach the target, instead it gets stuck in the sand. So I moved up the backsight by one more mark. I was sitting with Lomako and waiting for a Fritz. A Fritz appeared, I took a shot – the Fritz fell. Thus we solved that question, and during the next conversation I told all the snipers:

"- Here is a new thing for you: if you sit higher than the enemy – take a smaller backsight. If you sit lower than the enemy, take a bigger backsight."

Maybe in reality it was an old rule, but for us it was new.

Our experience prompted one more important rule to us: one should choose his firing position where the enemy thinks it is impossible. One must also disguise himself skillfully: if you climb a chimney, smear yourself with soot and become like the chimney yourself; and if you are near a wall, make your clothes match the color accordingly.

So, for example, at the section held by our regiment I stole over to a burned house. But there was no house left, only a stove remained, and the chimney. I lay down behind the stove and knocked out an embrasure in the chimney. The Fritzes could not guess, of course, that a Russian sniper would get into a chimney. From that chimney, however, I had a very good view of two entrances to their shelters and an approach to a three-story building. I killed ten Fritzes from that chimney. It is true that I suffered there myself too, but it was my own fault: I got tired of creeping, deciding to shoot from the same place and took about ten shots from there. The Germans spotted me. They shot at me with a mortar, my rifle got broken and I was heaped up with bricks. My legs got stuck in the bricks.

I lay unconscious for two hours. Then, when I recovered, I scattered away the bricks, released my legs, but the boots were left buried in the stove: they were too large for me – size forty-five. I wound foot-bindings around my feet and hung the broken rifle by its sling on my neck. I wanted to run away, but felt bad about leaving the boots. The Battalion Commander Skachkov used to wear these boots before me. They were important to me. I thought: "If they kill me, well, the hell with them, but I will not leave the Commander's boots here. What if some foul Fritz will use them!" I began to throw bricks out of the stove. Finally, I grasped the boots, and with the boots in my hands, and me covered all over with soot, I ran bare-foot along the lane. I came running to my comrades, who laughed and said: "It would be interesting to take a photograph of you now".

Since then my trainees and myself started acting in a different manner: we started shooting from different places. We did not have more than two or three shots from the same firing position, and we tried to make as many fake embrasures as possible.

On Mamayev Hill some German machine-gunners established themselves firmly in an earthen pillbox. They did not give us a possibility to maneuver, to go from one place to another, or to bring food and drag ammunition to our soldiers. The Command gave us the task of pushing them out. The infantry went to attack the machine guns several times, and several times their attacks failed. Two snipers from my group were sent there, but they missed, were wounded and put out of action. Then the Battalion Commander ordered me to go there myself and take two more snipers with me. So we did. We set out to that district, went along the entire defence line and estimated by the bullet-holes that a Fritz was sitting somewhere and keeping everybody under control.

We hid ourselves in a trench. As soon as I showed a helmet from the trench, the Fritz hit it and the helmet fell. I realized that I was dealing with a skilled German sniper. We needed to find out where he was located. It was very difficult to do, because if anyone peeped out, the Fritz would kill him. That means we needed to deceive him, to outwit him, i.e. to find a tactically correct method.

I hunted him for about five hours. Finally I figured out a method: I took a mitten off my hand, put it on a piece of wood and thrust it out of the trench. The German shot at it. I took the piece of wood down and looked where the mitten was pierced. By the position of the bullet-hole I established where the German was shooting from. Once you establish the enemy's location, you should sit in a comfortable place and wait, but the enemy should not know from which spot you are going to shoot at him.

I took the trench periscope and began to watch. I spotted the German sniper! Our infantry was advancing behind the forward positions. They just needed to make another thirty meters before the pillbox. It was that moment when the German sniper raised himself a little to look, and lost touch with his rifle. At the same time I jumped out of the trench, stood up straight and shouldered the rifle. He did not expect such audacity and was taken aback. He reached for his gun but I was the first to fire. I shot him with a sacred Russian bullet. The Fritz dropped his rifle.

I started firing at the pillbox's gun-port so that the German machine-gunners had no possibility to come up to their machine-gun. At that moment our infantry dashed to the pillbox and defeated it, without any losses. This is what is called a tactically correct method: to deceive the enemy and, without bearing losses to, solve the task.

It does not take much time to kill a German. Every one of our men shoots well, but the Germans are not fools. They are fond of disguise and of using trenches. They dig deep in the ground and very seldom show their heads. To deceive a German, to find the means of deceiving him and to spot him is a very complicated task. Only a sniper with a good perseverance and resourcefulness can do it. We even made up a proverb: one needs to deceive a German first, then kill him. One needs to act like this: climb the tallest chimney or any other comfortable place and see where Fritzes go, then select a firing position, and not only one, but several. Paralyze the enemy with fire, and try to make the enemy give up any movement. In the day-time shots are not seen, and you will never know where their shooting is done from, so you must act at night.

On one occasion German snipers established themselves on a hill. The approach to that hill was very difficult. Our infantry-men went there two or three times , but they did not manage to establish where the enemy snipers were sitting, and our guys could not clear the approches to the hill.

I went there together with the Red Army soldiers Kulikov and Dvoyashkin at 5 o`clock in the morning. It was still dark. We took a stick and made a cross-piece on top of that stick, wrapped it with a white cloth and thus obtained a shape of a face. We rolled a long cigarette with *makhorka* (*Makhorka* – a cheap kind of tobacco) and inserted it in the mouth. We put on a helmet and threw on a fur-coat on it, then showed it. A German sniper saw a man smoking a cigarette and fired a shot. When shooting is done in the darkness, one can see flames from the rifle. Thus I managed to spot where the German sniper was. When Kulikov showed a "man" from the trench, the German started shooting at him. The German took a shot – Kulikov lowered the stick, then showed it up again. The German thought that the "man" was not killed yet and shot again. While the Fritzes were hunting for a Russian "sniper", I had time to spot the location of the pillboxes, from which the German snipers were shooting. I did not manage to beat down their fire. I only established where it was and then got connected with our anti-tank artillery: it destroyed the German snipers' nests.

We also had a good co-operation with our assault infantry detachments.

It happened on 17th December. The Command gave us a task to take over a reinforced concrete bridge. We tried to take it over, but without success. Our infantry attacks failed. We hit it many times point-blank, but the bridge would not drop. The concrete was six meters thick. The shells hit, made a dent and that was all. So I, together with four other snipers, stealthily came up to the

Germans from the flank, actually not from the flank, but rather from the rear.

We crept into a destroyed house. When our assault brigades attacked, the Germans began to run out of their shelters and throw grenades at them. Meanwhile, we shot the Fritzes. They noticed us and rolled out a gun against us. We killed the whole gun crew. The four of us killed twenty-eight Germans, and it took less than two hours. Then our assault men managed to occupy that strongly fortified bridge.

Now I will tell you about my most memorable stakeout. I do not remember which date it was. The Germans were bringing up their reinforcements. I was sitting at an observation point together with the Commander. A messenger came running and informed us:

- "The Germans' movement has been noticed in the sector of observation. Fresh forces are coming up to them."

In order to watch for that reinforcement I went out together with my snipers. There were only six of us who went. We lay in our stakeout in the ruins of a little house. The Germans were marching in formation. We allowed them to approach to about 300 meters away from us and then we began to shoot our rifles. There were about one hundred of the Germans. They were taken by surprise and stopped. One man fell, then another, then the third one. It takes two seconds to take a shot, and the SVT rifle has a ten-bullet clip. The moment you press the trigger, it loads itself and throws out a cartridge-case. We killed forty-six Germans there.

This is how important the snipers' role was in the defence of Stalingrad.

In the streets of Stalingrad our propagandists put the situation so: "If you want to live, kill a German;" "Say how many Germans you killed and I will tell you what a patriot you are". The destruction of the German forces became an honorable thing to do; therefore each Red Army soldier started watching for the Germans. The one who killed the most Germans was the most respected man among the other soldiers.

The agitator Captain Rakityansky, a favourite of all fighting men, was sitting himself with a rifle in his hands all day long, both in trenches and on roofs, waiting for a Fritz. Having noticed one, he killed him and then sat down again, waiting for another Fritz. He is a real agitator indeed!

I have killed two hundred and forty-two Germans, including more than ten enemy snipers. I have always been sure that I am more resourceful and stronger than a German and that my rifle hits more precisely than a German one. I am always calm and therefore I am never afraid of Germans.

ORDER #227
BY THE PEOPLE'S COMMISSAR
OF DEFENCE OF THE USSR, J. STALIN
July 28, 1942
Moscow

The enemy delivers more and more resources to the front, and, completely disregarding losses, advances, penetrating deeper into the Soviet Union, capturing new areas, devastating and plundering our cities and our villages, and raping, murdering and robbing the Soviet people. These enemy attacks continue in Voronezh, at the Don, in Southern Russia, and at the gates of the North Caucasus. The German invaders are driving towards Stalingrad, towards the Volga, and they are willing to pay any price to capture Kuban and the Northern Caucasus, with their riches of oil and bread. The enemy has already captured Voroshilovgrad, Starobelsk, Rossosh, Kupyansk, Valuiki, Novocherkassk, Rostov, and half of Voronezh. Some units of our Southern front, who have listened to panic-mongers, have abandoned Rostov and Novocherkassk, without making serious attempts at resistance. They withdrew without orders from Moscow, and covered their banners with shame.

The people of our country, who used to treat the Red Army with love and respect, are now beginning to be disappointed with it, and they are losing faith in the Red Army. Many of them curse the Army for fleeing to the east, and leaving our people trapped under the German yoke.

Some stupid people comfort themselves with the argument that we can continue our retreat to the east, as we have vast territories, much land, a large population, and that we will always have an abundance of bread. By these arguments they try to justify their shameful behavior and their retreat. But all their arguments are fully faked, false, and only work to serve our enemies.

Every commander, every soldier and every political officer

must realize that our resources are not infinite. The territory of the Soviet Union is not a wilderness, but people – workers, peasants, intelligentsia, our fathers and mothers, wives, brothers, children. The territory of USSR which has been occupied by the fascists, and those territories which the fascists are planning to capture, are bread and other resources for our army and our civilians, oil and steel for our industries, factories that provide our military with weapons and ammunition, and also our railways. With the loss of the Ukraine, Belorussia, the Baltics, the Donetsk Basin and other areas, we have lost huge amounts of territory, which means that we have lost many people, bread, metals, and factories. We no longer have superiority over the Nazis in human resources and in materials supply. If we continue to retreat, it will mean to destroy ourselves and also our Motherland. Every piece of territory that we give up to the fascists will strengthen the fascists, and weaken us, our defenses, and our Motherland.

This is why we have to eradicate all conversations which say that we can retreat endlessly, that we still have a vast amount of territory, that our country is rich and great, that we have a big population, and that we always will have enough bread. These conversations are lies and dangerous, as they make us weak, and strengthen the enemy. If we do not stop retreating, we will be without bread, without fuel, without steel, without raw materials, without factories, and without railways.

The conclusion we must draw, is that the time has come to stop our retreat. Not a single step back! From now on this will be our slogan. We need to stubbornly protect every strongpoint, and every meter of Soviet land, until the last drop of blood. We must seize every piece of our land, and defend it as long as possible. Our Motherland is going through hard times. We have to halt, and then throw back and destroy the enemy, whatever the cost may be to us. The Germans are not as strong as the panic-mongers say. The Germans have stretched themselves to the limit. If we can withstand their blow now, it will ensure victory for us in the future.

Do we have the possibility to stand and throw the enemy back to the west? Yes we can, as our plants and factories behind the Urals are functioning perfectly, and every day, these factories supply our military with more and more tanks, planes, and artillery. So what is lacking? We lack discipline and order in our divisions, regiments, and companies, and in tank units, and in our Air Force squadrons. This is our most important problem. We have to introduce the strictest order and a strong discipline in our military, if we are to reverse the situation and rescue the Motherland.

We can no longer tolerate commanders, commissars, and political officers, whose units abandon their defenses. We can no longer tolerate the fact that the commanders, commissars and political officers permit a few known cowards to run the show on the battlefield, and that panic-mongers carry away other soldiers in their stampede to retreat, and open the way to the fascists. Panic-mongers and cowards are to be exterminated at the site.

From now on the iron law of discipline for every officer, soldier, and political officer will be – not a single step back, without order from higher command. Company, battalion, regiment and division commanders, as well as the commissars and political officers who retreat without orders, are traitors. They should be treated as traitors to the Motherland.

The fulfillment of this order means that we can defend our country, save our Motherland, and destroy and overwhelm the hated enemy.

After their winter retreat under the pressure of the Red Army, when morale and discipline fell among the German soldiers, the enemy took strict measures that led to good results. They formed 100 penal companies made up of soldiers who had broken discipline due to cowardice or nerves; they then deployed these men at the most dangerous sectors of the front, and ordered them to redeem their sins by blood. The enemy also formed ten penal battalions, made up of officers who had broken discipline due to cowardice or nerves. The Germans stripped them of their

medals, and ordered them to even more dangerous sections of
the front. These officers were ordered to redeem their sins by
blood. And finally, the enemy created special SS units and
deployed them behind the penal units, with orders to execute
panic-mongers, if they tried to withdraw from their positions
without orders, or if they attempted to surrender. We saw that
these measures have proven effective, because now the German
troops fight better than they fought last winter. The new situation
we face, is that the German troops have acquired good discipline, although they do not have the higher motivation, of the
protection of their homeland.

   They have only have one mission – to conquer our land. Our
troops, who have the defense of the defiled Motherland as their
goal, do not have the same discipline as the Germans, and therefore
our soldiers have suffered defeat after defeat. Shouldn't we learn
this lesson from our enemy, as our ancestors learned from their
enemies, in order to overcome their enemies? It is my belief that
we should.

THE SUPREME COMMAND OF THE RED ARMY ORDERS:

1. The Military Councils of the fronts, and all front commanders
should:
a) Decisively eradicate the attitude of retreat among our troops,
and prevent propaganda that we can and should continue the retreat.
These measures are to be taken with an iron hand.
b) In every circumstance, arrest officers who encourage retreat
without authorization from higher command, and send them to
Stavka for court-martial;
c) Form within each Front from 1 to 3 (depending on circumstances) penal battalions; with commanders and political officers of
all ranks from all services, who have broken discipline due to
cowardice or nerves. These battalions should be put on the more
dangerous sections of the Front, and given the opportunity to

redeem themselves by blood.

2. The Military Councils of armies and army commanders should:

a) In every circumstance, arrest army commanders and commissars, who have allowed their troops to retreat without authorization from higher command, and send them to the Military Councils of the Fronts for court-martial;

b) Form 3 to 5 well-armed guards units, deploy them behind the penal divisions, and order them to execute panic-mongers and cowards in case of a chaotic retreat, giving our faithful soldiers a chance to do their duty before the Motherland;

c) Form 5 to 10 penal companies, with soldiers and NCOs, who have broken discipline due to cowardice or nerves. These units should be deployed at the most difficult sectors of the front, giving their soldiers an opportunity to redeem their crimes against the Motherland by blood.

3. Corps and division commanders and commissars should:

a) In every circumstance, arrest commanders and commissars who allowed their troops to retreat, without authorization from divisional or corps command, strip them of their military decorations, and send them to the Military Councils for court-martial;

b) Provide all possible assistance to the guards units of the army, in their work of strengthening discipline.

This order is to be read aloud to all companies, troops, batteries, squadrons, teams and staffs.

The People's Commissar for Defense
J. STALIN

REGARDING DAVID ROBBINS
AND *WAR OF THE RATS*.

Readers of *War of the Rats* will notice numerous astonishing similarities to Zaitsev's *Notes of a Sniper.*

An example follows:

(From p. 206-207, Bantam paperback edition. *War of the Rat*s, published June 2000.)

> "My name is Hannah. I do not know is reading this letter, but I am sure you are the bravest one if it was given to you. I am seventeen years old. If that makes me your daughter, then I will call you father. If not, I will call you brother. The girls in my plant have gathered presents for the defenders of Stalingrad. We know it is hard for you in the trenches and our hearts are with you. We work and live only for you. Even though I am far behind the Urals, I have hopes of returning to my native Smolensk. I can hear my mother crying in the kitchen. Kill the nazis so we can go home. Let their families wet themselves with tears. I am just a girl, and I stand in a line assembling parts for trucks and tanks. But I feel I am fighting, too, just by staying alive, just by hating the Germans every minute. I do not like to hate; it is not natural for a Russian, don't you think? But we must, until they are gone. Fight hard, my father, my brother, and I will, too."

From Zaitsev's original (p. 148, 1971 edition):

> "I don't know who will end up reading my letter. I'm seventeen years old. If I'm young enough to be your daughter, then I'll call you father. If you're only a little older than I am, then let me call you a brother. The girls and young women in our

plant have collected some gifts for the defenders of Stalingrad. We know things must be difficult and dangerous out there in the trenches. Our hearts are with you. We work and live only for you. Although I'm far away in the Urals now, I live by the hope that I'll someday return to my native Minsk. Can you hear my mother's weeping?"

Vasilchenko turned the page. I managed to read the closing lines:

"Destroy the Nazis. Let their country be drowned in grief and may their families cry a river of tears. Fight the enemy with bravery like our ancestors fought them before us."

Readers of *Notes of a Sniper* are invited to make further comparisons, and to draw their own conclusions.

C O N T R I B U T O R S   T O   T H I S   B O O K

Translator **David Givens** studied at the Kazan State University in Russia. His degrees are in Economics and in Russian from the University of Virginia. He has traveled and worked in a number of former Soviet Republics, including Russia, Georgia, and Uzbekistan. Mr. Givens currently resides in Philadelphia.

Translator **Peter Kornakov** is a university teacher (St. Petersburg, Glasgow, University of Bradford). He is an interpreter, translator, journalist, and photographer.

Translator **Konstantin Kornakov** was born in Moscow in 1983 and raised in Havana, St. Petersburg, Glasgow, Barcelona, and Bradford in the UK. He is a graduate student in Modern European History at the University of Bradford. He is an interpreter, translator, and journalist.

Translator of the short book titled "Sniper Story," **Elena Leonidovna Yakokleva**, lives in St. Petersburg. She studied at St. Petersburg State University.

Illustrators **Anthony Cacioppo** and **Ed Coutts** reside in Hicksville, New York. They can be reached c/o Mr. Cacioppo's web site, kasocomics.com

Max Hardberger, writer of the introduction, is the author of *Freighter Captain,* a highly recommended memoir about tramp freighters in the Caribbean. His books are available online at high-seas.net

Librarian **Jennie Dienes** is a research specialist at the University of Kansas Map Library.

Layout design artist **Sonia Gunawan Fiore** is a graduate of the Otis School of Art and Design. She is a resident of Los Angeles. She can be reached at soniagunawan@hotmail.com.

FORTHCOMING MATERIAL

An Audio Book version of *Notes of a Sniper* will soon be available on CD. To order, please contact the web site notesofasniper.com)

A black and white version of the front cover illustration will be available as a t-shirt. To order, please contact the web site. A color version of the *Notes of A Sniper* logo will also be available on a t-shirt.

For further information, please go to the web site, notesofasniper.com